SUN, SAND AND SINGLE

Sun, Sand and Single

AN AMERICAN WOMAN IN SAUDI ARABIA, 1960-62

NANCY GRAY

Around the World Press
HUNTINGTON BEACH, CALIFORNIA

Copyright © 2017 by Nancy Gray

All rights reserved. No part of this publication may be reproduced, distributed or transmitted in any form or by any means, without prior written permission.

Around the World Press
9151 Atlanta Ave # 8127
Huntington Beach, CA 92615
aroundtheworldpress.com

Publisher's Note: *Sun, Sand and Single* is based on the author's recollections of her life as a single American woman in Saudi Arabia and neighboring Middle Eastern countries more than half a century ago. Fictionalized aspects of the story include all dialogue and the names, physical descriptions, and other identifying characteristics of all persons who appear in her memoir, with the exceptions of Willard and Christina Jones and Federico Vidal, whom she met through family connections during her school days and with whom she had the conversations summarized in this work.

Book Layout by Gatekeeper Press
Cover Design by © Kit Foster Design
Maps and Illustrations by © Tim Barker Studio
Author Photograph Courtesy Heidi Langway

Sun, Sand and Single/ Nancy Gray. -- 1st Ed.

Library of Congress Control Number 2017917350

ISBN 978-0-9986279-0-8
eISBN: 9781619848306

To the refugees and displaced persons in today's world:

May you find welcome, hope, and peace at last.

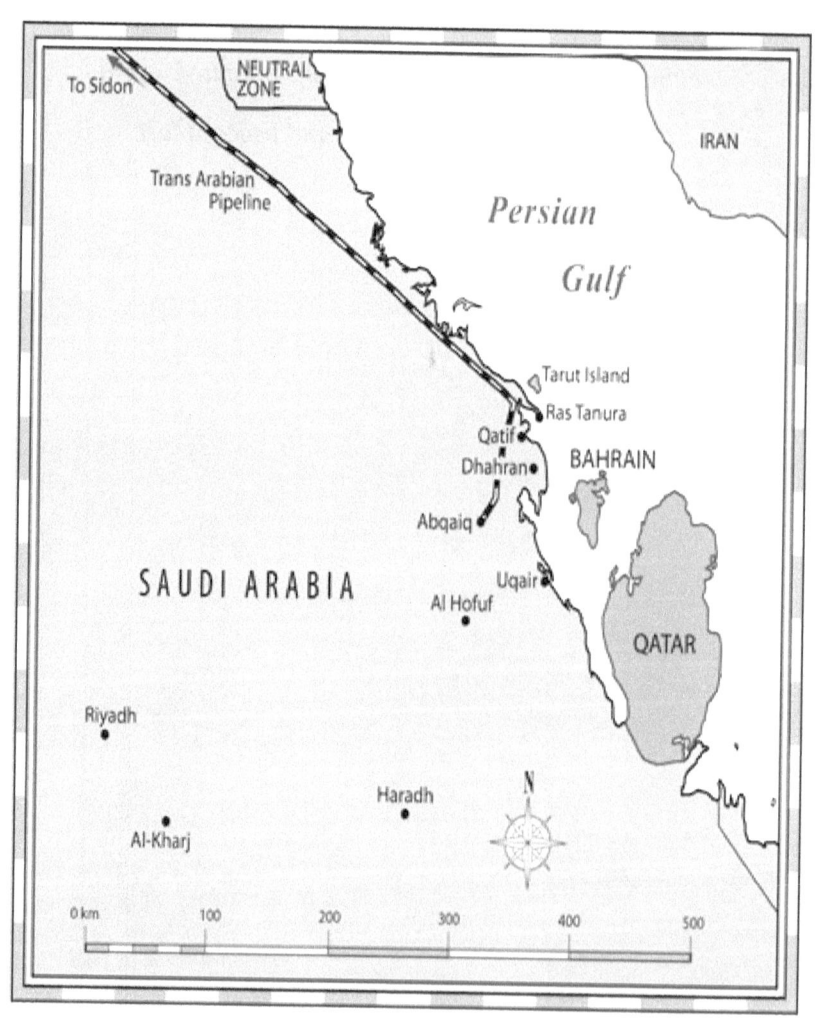

Aramco Field of Operations, 1960-62

CONTENTS

1. PREFACE 1
2. ARRIVAL 5
3. DECIPHERING THE SYSTEM 13
4. BUSINESS MATTERS 19
5. CHECKING OUT MY WORKSITE 23
6. SINGLES' SOCIAL LIFE: MISSING IN ACTION 27
7. SAUDI CULTURE 101 31
8. LIFE BEHIND THE VEIL 39
9. BUNKER GOLF 43
10. ARAB-STYLE SHOPPING 45
11. TARUT AHOY 55
12. ARABIAN MASS COMMUNICATIONS 61
13. MYSTERY SOLVED 67
14. ABQAIQ'S FIRST STILL 73
15. RETHINKING MY SOCIAL STRATEGIES 77
16. AGAINST ALL ODDS 81
17. PSEUDO-ROMANCE AMONG THE DUNES 89
18. AMATEUR "SPIES" IN CAIRO 95
19. A BUSINESS PROPOSITION 99
20. A WELCOME SURPRISE 105
21. LEBANON: PROGRESS, INTRIGUE AND DIVERSITY 109

22. NATALYA (1)	115
23. VISIT TO THE GOLD SUQ	121
24. BACK IN BUSINESS	125
25. PRODUCT-LINE EXPANSION	129
26. THEFT PREVENTION	137
27. SIDETRIP TO DAMASCUS	139
28. DAMASCUS CITY TOUR	147
29. THE CLIMATE'S REVENGE	153
30. JOMO THE BUDDING TYCOON	157
31. A WELCOME CHANGE OF SCENE	159
32. MIRACLE ON THE BOSPHORUS	163
33. KUWAIT AND BACK TO ARABIA	173
34. A DIFFERENT KIND OF DESTINATION	179
35. MODERN AND HISTORICAL IRAN	183
36. THIRD-GRADE THANKSGIVING	195
37. REGINALD REDUX	199
38. NATALYA (2)	205
39. JERUSALEM, DAY 1	209
40. JERUSALEM, DAY 2	215
41. REUNION WITH FAMILY FRIENDS	225
42. CATCHING UP WITH THE JONESES	229
43. RAMALLAH, 1922-1939	233
44. WW2 AND UN RESOLUTION 181	239
45. GUERILLA TACTICS TO FULL-SCALE WAR	243
46. MUCH NEEDED HELP—AT LAST	255
47. JERICHO	261
48. CHRISTMAS EVE IN BETHLEHEM	267
49. BACK TO ARABIA	271

50. THE GREAT DECISION 277
51. FAREWELL TO BEIRUT 283
52. NATALYA (3) 287
53. RIYADH AFTER ALL 291
54. ROUGHING IT BEDOUIN STYLE 297
55. INTO THE FUTURE 303
56. DEPARTURE 309

ACKNOWLEDGEMENTS 317
ABOUT THE AUTHOR 319

CHAPTER ONE

PREFACE

I'D NEVER GIVEN serious thought to writing a book on any subject until my eightieth-birthday party. I probably wouldn't have considered it then had it not been for the dogged persistence of a clutch of my former students from the nineteen sixties and seventies. Their plans for my retirement were more ambitious—and energy-sapping—than mine. I wasn't exactly surprised.

They'd floated the book idea before. To fend off my stock excuse that I didn't remember my youthful adventures in sufficient detail to use them as raw material for a book I wasn't planning to write, my classes gave me a surprise birthday party the year I turned forty. Featured entertainment was a takeoff on *This is Your Life*, a popular television show of the time. Skits based on my memories of growing up on a series of Indian Reservations and living as an expat in four countries during my twenties were the centerpiece of their highly original and meticulously documented magnum opus, *This is Your Life, Nancy Gray*. The tagline for each skit was "You ought to write a book."

I thanked the organizers and attendees for reminding me of selected highlights of my past that had somehow slipped my mind. I added, quite sincerely, that their production was an artistic masterpiece and that I expected to see some of their names among the credits rolling at the ends of future award-winning television shows and films. Through the years, I occasionally have.

The assembled well-wishers responded with their habitual refrain, "You ought to write a book." Not wanting to splash cold water on the convivial spirit of the occasion, I assured them that I would consider their suggestion carefully, but not just then. Between my teaching schedule and my dissertation woes, I was suffering through a crippling spare-time deficit. Taking on another multi-year project was out of the question in the near future. Maybe later.

Fast forward to my eightieth-birthday bash. Dozens of my former students from the sixties, seventies, and early eighties were in attendance, including a trio of the instigators of the *This is Your Life, Nancy Gray* blockbuster. I hadn't laid eyes on any of the three since they went off to college, but their conspiratorial manner led me to suspect that they were on a mission—most likely one involving me. I was right. After a round of the usual pleasantries for such occasions, they took up the "you ought to write a book" conversation exactly where they'd left it forty years before.

They began their campaign with a preemptive strike on my threadbare "I don't have the time" excuse. They reminded me that I was closing my business—a fact of which I was well aware. I was even then sweating through the ordeal of hauling the remnants of my soon-to-be former office to my garage for storage until I could figure out what to do with them. "Now you have the time," they chorused in a noticeable "gotcha" tone.

I parried their thrust with my time-tested failing-memory ploy. "No problem," they assured me. They whipped out their class notes from forty years before and regaled me with their favorite tales of my youthful escapades in what they considered exotic locales. "Just think," one of them insisted, "you could be the Grandma Moses of the memoir set."

Grandma Moses probably hadn't tried to paint anything she hadn't seen for more than half a century. Still, I had to admit—but not to a bunch of zealots bent on making a writer out of me in my declining years—that those anecdotes from the life of a much younger me had had remarkable staying power.

Over the next few weeks, I found myself remembering more and more incidents from my younger days that would fit right into the book I was absolutely not going to write. Why was I devoting all that time and effort to thinking about a hypothetical project I'd already ruled out?

What about those scads of books I hadn't had time to read; the trips I'd wanted to take, but felt I couldn't be away from my business that long; and the invitations I'd declined because they conflicted with client meetings? Valid points all, but an outline for a book about my Arabian years continued to germinate in my age-befuddled brain without conscious encouragement on my part. I developed a cover concept, settled on a list of illustrations, and divided possible content into chapters. My literary fantasy was out of hand.

Could my compulsive book-planning be an octogenarian thing? Yes, I decided, that's exactly what it was, but not in the sense that I'd crash-landed in my dotage when I blew out eighty candles instead of seventy-nine the year before.

It's just that a heightened awareness of personal mortality worms its way into the psyches of the newly eighty. We have no way of knowing how much time we have left, but a few too many trips to the emergency room and a raft of aches and pains remind us that our stay on this planet might draw to a close any day, hour, or minute. So how do we react to that sobering thought? It varies.

Some still frisky octogenarians work down their bucket lists with a dedication that astonishes the rest of us. An afternoon of hang gliding holds little appeal for eighty-year-olds exhausted from a morning of sorting through stacks of medical bills and insurance claims.

Even so, as we approach the final summation of our lives, I suspect all of us are more alike than different. We reflect at least occasionally on how it all began, what we accomplished during the time granted to us, and what legacy of experience we have to leave to those who mean the most to us.

Maybe the "you ought to write a book" crowd was onto something all along. Perhaps I *should* write a book about a time when most of my life lay before me, and I was game to try almost anything at least once. Would I like that twenty-something me or think that what she needed most was a good talking to? Would knowing her better help me to understand some of the choices I made later in life?

I dropped by the Office Depot the next day for a generous supply of file folders to house research notes and chapter drafts. Then I sat down at my computer to rescue half-forgotten memories of my Arabian sojourn from the oblivion to which they were otherwise destined. Four years later, I held in my hands a copy of *Sun, Sand and Single*—a chronicle of my stay in the Middle East during a critical time in my life and its history. Maybe writing this book wasn't such a wacky idea after all.

CHAPTER TWO

ARRIVAL

Two hours into the 6,585-mile flight from New York to Dhahran, I'd already worked three crossword puzzles and exhausted the entertainment potential of thumb twiddling. My relentless search for something—anything—to do had yielded zero results. Magazines? Not even the company rag in sight. My seatmate was holding forth nonstop about the intricacies of refinery operation to a dazed new hire across the aisle. Not a topic to which I had much to add.

In desperation, I fell to concocting an elaborate scenario in which I would star as a latter-day Gertrude Bell, the WW1-era British intelligence agent and friend, colleague, and mentor of T.E. Lawrence of Arab-Revolt fame. I could just picture myself fetchingly attired in pith helmet, khaki culottes, and hiking boots as I set out to retrace the footsteps of my pioneering role model.

Great theater perhaps, but preposterous, and not just because of my failure to tuck a suitable costume for my upcoming Gertrude Bell impersonation into my overstuffed bags. In August 1960, I was a single, still-wet-behind-the-ears twenty-something transferring to the Arabian American Oil Company from its Venezuelan affiliate.

Aramco, which had already invested a princely sum to transport me and my worldly possessions halfway around the globe, was under the impression that I was coming to Saudi Arabia *to work*. And so I was, but my pre-arrival vision of life in Arabia was a tad more colorful than the day-to-day routine in a desert oil camp turned out to be. Enroute, though, my most outlandish fantasies about my next two years among the sand dunes were alive and well. Surely the mysterious East would toss me an exotic adventure or two, if I lasted long enough.

Wardrobe issues weren't the only flaws in my singularly implausible script. Unlike Ms. Bell, I spoke neither Arabic nor Farsi and held no honors degree in Middle Eastern Studies from Oxford—or anywhere else. My senior year in college, I took one upper-division course in Middle Eastern history to fill out my schedule, but the instructor's syllabus ground to a halt at the Ottoman conquest. The information I was counting on to guide me as I made my grand entrance onto the Arabian stage was inadequate, outdated, and irrelevant.

Still, having previously studied in France and Mexico and worked three contracts in Venezuela, I deemed myself a seasoned expat. How could I possibly fail to make a speedy and painless transition to living and working in Saudi Arabia, a country about which I knew considerably less than I thought I did? Here's how, beginning with the moment our plane touched down on the Dhahran airstrip with a bone-rattling jolt.

We had finally taken off after a prolonged ground hold at an obscure terminal at Idlewild Airport, now JFK. Charter flights got no respect at Idlewild, much less any priority. The flight promised to be endless. It came within a hairsbreadth of achieving that goal.

While his captive audience across the aisle made a pit stop, my seatmate informed me that the company had bought a brace of DC-6Bs some years before and retrofitted them to shuttle employees between New York and Dhahran. DC-6Bs, a propeller aircraft, couldn't travel very fast or very high by today's standards. That explained why we were plodding toward our destination at such a leisurely pace.

The military had originally commissioned the super-reliable DC-6 series to fill a wartime need for a short-distance freight carrier. The possibility that the airborne workhorse they were designing would end up transporting human cargo across multiple time zones, rather than spare parts to battlefields, must never have occurred to the engineers in charge of the DC-6 project. Hence the need for four fueling/maintenance stops—at Gander, Amsterdam, Rome, and Beirut—before we caught our first glimpse of the ramshackle thirties-style Dhahran Airport.

Accommodations aloft for most of us were pretty basic, even for 1960. After a few hours in transit, stiff necks spread through the passenger cabin like an infectious disease. Women with small children had access to the few sleeping compartments in the rear. The rest of us had to tough it out as best we could. Had it registered with me how long we'd be in the air, I'd have seriously considered borrowing—or, failing that, renting—a well-behaved child for the duration.

Cabin service was outstanding, at least in the opinion of most of the in-the-know passengers. Bar supplies filled, and occasionally overflowed, every conceivable storage space. The libation queue formed long before the captain turned off the seatbelt sign, and business remained brisk until we began our final descent into Dhahran. Saudi Arabia was dry in more than one sense, so the better-informed bar patrons loaded up with triples when the last-call went out.

I was not among them. Booze, which I didn't care for anyway, was the last thing on my mind after thirty-six hours enroute. I just wanted to set my feet on solid ground, or the nearest thing to it the Arabian Desert had to offer.

Queasiness swept over me as our plane rolled down the runway and onto the taxiway. We were closing fast on the only building in sight: a nondescript, weather-beaten prefab almost certainly devoid of air conditioning—no doubt where we were to collect our belongings and clear Immigration and Customs. How long that would take was anybody's guess.

Had I asked the right questions about staff living conditions in Arabia prior to agreeing to my transfer? My overwrought imagination was working overtime to conjure progressively more distressing images: housing in a Bedouin tent, a daily diet of camel's-milk yogurt, and kerosene lamps for lighting. Well, I would just have to make the best of whatever the Aramco job entailed—for two long years.

A flight attendant readied the door for arrival. As I brushed my matted hair, I could make out tiny beads of perspiration on my forehead despite the comfortable 70-degree temperature in the cabin. The door swung open. The temperature rose to 122°. Dazed by the blast of heat, we passengers trooped down the ramp toward the arrivals shed. It was even hotter inside.

Joan and Ethel from Abqaiq Senior Staff School awaited me. Their driver loaded my eight pieces of luggage onto an accompanying truck. The three of us squeezed into the backseat of an ancient taxi, which proved reluctant to start. The driver spoke sharply to it and attacked the steering wheel with his fists—more for show than as a problem-solving strategy. Just as well that none of us understood what he was saying. Finally, with a sigh of exhaustion, the taxi sputtered to life and eased onto the main highway with a swaying motion that left me wishing for a stiff dose of Dramamine.

Our driver's difficulty keeping the vehicle pointed in a consistent direction was not reassuring. Later, I learned the reason for the taxi's meandering. During the Arabian hot season, driving was akin to navigating through a layer of wet sand, even on main roads. High temperatures softened—or, in extreme cases, melted—paving materials.

We traveled some distance in semi-silence. In the relentless heat, the slight breeze caused by the motion of the car provided no relief. The sound emanating from the radio approximated the cries of a cat someone was swinging by its tail. My new colleagues assured me I would get used to Arab music.

I was too tired and my companions too drowsy from the heat for anything but desultory chitchat. They pointed out the halfway house, a derelict structure amidst a trackless expanse of sand. In a probably unconvincing attempt to make a good first impression by appearing upbeat and interested in my surroundings, I asked the building's purpose. Joan roused herself sufficiently to say she didn't know. The conversation petered out. I drifted off and dreamed I was traveling by camel.

The Dhahran-Abqaiq Road

Half an hour later, I came to, gasping for breath. My escorts were struggling awake for the same reason. Drawing on my limited knowledge of basic chemistry, and detecting the unmistakable stench of rotten eggs, I identified the culprit immediately: hydrogen sulfide gas. In as neutral a tone as I could manage, I asked why that particular odor was assaulting us in the emptiness of the Arabian Desert.

"We're only about four miles from Abqaiq. The smell is coming from the GOSP."

"What's that?"

Ethel let out a jaw-popping yawn. "A gas-oil-separator plant."

I feigned intense but unlikely interest. "I didn't smell anything out of the ordinary as we skirted Dhahran. Why does Abqaiq need a foul-smelling facility like that?"

Ethel looked as if she wanted nothing more than to go back to sleep. "The GOSP removes sulfur compounds from crude oil and vents them into the air to get rid of them. Then workers load the desulfured oil into the pipeline for transport to the refinery at Ras Tanura." Where was the local equivalent of the EPA when we needed it? Discharging concentrated hydrogen sulfide gas into the air almost guaranteed acute respiratory distress—or worse—for anyone within a five-mile radius.

We came within sight of Abqaiq camp. The odor of hydrogen sulfide was overpowering now. Flames shot skyward from a veritable forest of pipe chimneys. Ethel was visibly nodding off. I ached to join her.

I turned to Joan. "What's burning?"

"Natural gas. That's the easiest way to get rid of it."

"Why doesn't the company sell the gas to nearby countries and make some money out of it?" I clapped both hands over an alligator-like yawn in a futile effort to stifle it.

"Gee, I'm not sure." She shook Ethel and shouted, "Wake up. Nancy wants to know about the gas flares."

That could have waited. The hydrogen sulfide must have gone to my head.

Ethel shot Joan a poisonous look. "Natural gas is worthless; it costs too much to ship it to customers." I only hoped she wouldn't remember being roused from slumber to answer one inane question after another.

* * *

Drab, weather-beaten prefabs indistinguishable from one another surrounded us as we drove into camp. My guides pointed out the cash office, where I could write a dollar check and receive its equivalent in *riyals,* the local currency. They also showed me the dining hall, where I should plan to eat until I exchanged money. Two right turns later, we passed the commissary, the only place in camp to buy groceries once I had a supply of *riyals* in hand.

Another right turn, and we arrived at our destination: a dormitory-like structure that housed a dozen single female employees. The hurricane-force frigid air that greeted us as Ethel opened the street-side door confirmed the availability of air conditioning, although I was soon to discover that the cooling equipment offered only two settings: "on" and "off."

The interior of the residence, with its off-white walls and sand-colored woodwork, exuded all the charm of an army barracks. Beige venetian blinds of uncertain age that somehow managed to clash with the woodwork served as window coverings. The premises reeked of pine-oil disinfectant. I listened for the slightest sound of human habitation, but the silence was absolute except for the persistent drone of the air conditioning.

Ethel explained that two residents shared a bath located between their respective rooms. A communal kitchen equipped with a stove, a refrigerator, and a sink occupied the space at the end of the hall. A dog-eared wooden table with four chairs stood against one wall. Neatly stacked crockery with the Aramco logo on each piece and basic pots and pans filled the shelves on either side of the sink. Drawers held cutlery and miscellaneous kitchen implements. Clearly, this setup wouldn't encourage gourmet cookery, but convivial suppers for twelve wouldn't be feasible anyway with only four chairs.

At least my assigned room wasn't the Bedouin tent of my anguished imaginings. I spotted my luggage piled high in one corner, although a single bulb hanging down from the ceiling gave off so little light that I could barely make out the rest of the room's floor plan. On the bed lay a stack of sheets, a pillowcase, towels, and a nondescript woolen blanket.

Ethel announced that they must be going. They handed me the keys to my room and the street entrance, wished me a pleasant night's sleep, and headed for the door. Then, as if they had forgotten something, they turned back. "Welcome to Arabia," they chorused, without a trace of detectable irony.

CHAPTER THREE

DECIPHERING THE SYSTEM

THE NEXT MORNING, I awoke to find myself lying under a sheet and the blanket on the bare mattress. At least I'd managed to put the pillowcase on the pillow. Why had I reached for the blanket in my minimally conscious state? Easy. It offered the only protection against the glacial onslaught of the air conditioning, for which I was nevertheless devoutly grateful.

Still wrapped in the blanket and carrying a towel Aramco had so thoughtfully provided, I ventured into the bathroom. No toiletries on the vanity suggested that the room opposite mine was currently unoccupied. The used toothbrush near the sink had to be mine.

I headed for the shower. No soap? Uh-oh, I must be expected to provide my own. I added that item to my mental list for the commissary. Meanwhile, I scrubbed myself as best I could with several squirts of toothpaste on the moistened corner of the Aramco towel.

Back in my room, I searched my luggage for something to wear that wouldn't look too much as if I'd slept in it. Since I fully expected to swelter outside, I picked a loose-fitting gauze number with a crinkle finish that disguised at least some of the wrinkles.

Once dressed, hair combed, and minimal make-up applied, I wondered what time it was. I lifted a slat of the venetian blind at my room's one window to discover that the sun was already high in the sky, busily desiccating all that lay below.

My stomach reminded me that I'd eaten nothing since deplaning the day before. Without much hope of finding so much as a piece of chewing gum in my carry-on bag, I emptied its contents onto my bed—just in case. Much to my surprise, I found a smallish apple that I'd squirreled away on the plane just before we landed. I demolished my find with a few deft bites, but one apple wasn't going to keep me going for long. I wandered down the hall to the kitchen in search of something more substantial to pacify my by now furiously grumbling stomach.

I still hadn't heard the faintest sound of anyone else since my arrival, so I was surprised to see a woman sitting at the kitchen table finishing her breakfast. Whoever she was, she seemed friendly.

"Are you new here?"

"Yes, my plane landed in Dhahran about three-thirty yesterday. Immigration and Customs were a real hassle. My taxi didn't arrive in Abqaiq until after six."

"Then you haven't had a chance to buy groceries, have you?"

I shook my head no, whereupon she asked if I'd like some cereal. I was ravenous enough to chew on the edge of the table, but I took a deep breath, thanked her, and said I'd love some. She filled a bowl with a generous serving of bran flakes and poured milk over them while I fixed a predatory eye on my breakfast-to-be, lest she change her mind about feeding me.

"Sugar?" I nodded yes. She handed me the bowl along with a cup of wonderfully hot coffee.

I thanked her even more effusively now and took what I hoped would pass for a dainty bite. "My name is Nancy. I'm a teacher."

"I'm Isabel, a nurse. Did you have any trouble sleeping last night?"

"No, I was borderline comatose after the long flight from New York." At least talking slowed me down to a socially acceptable rate of mastication. "By the way, how many women live here besides you and me?"

"At the moment, eight. We're expecting Mona, another new resident, next week. She's my replacement. I'm leaving on September 15 to become Director of Nursing at a California hospital."

"Congratulations. I hope everything works out well for you." I meant that sincerely, but with more than a tinge of disappointment. Isabel seemed to have the makings of a good friend and possible traveling companion—that is, if we ever had the same days off.

Isabel glanced at her watch. "Well, as soon as I clean up these dishes, I must be on my way. I have to iron a uniform if I expect to have one to wear to work today."

"Just leave your dishes; I'll wash them with mine if you'll tell me where to find some soap and a dish towel."

She pointed to a nosebleed-level shelf to the left of the sink. "My bottle of detergent is up there. You'll have to stand on one of these chairs to reach it. Help yourself. We're really supposed to keep our cleaning supplies in our rooms, but no one bothers to climb up there to check, so I've yet to be busted for improper storage practices. As for a dish towel, there's a rack under the sink. Put the dishes in that to drain. They'll be dry in ten minutes, guaranteed.

"Hilda, one of our housemates, has rather eccentric ideas about stacking dishes on shelves. You'll need intensive coaching before you tackle that level of the kitchen protocol. A word to the wise, though: under no circumstances admit that you're the one who left dishes in the rack. Hilda's a secretary. Let's just say she's detail-oriented. Having all of us follow the rules—most of which she's made up—is like a religion to her."

"Thanks for the warning. If you don't mind, I'll warehouse my cleaning products up there with yours when I get them. I'll have worries enough finding a place to store my nonperishable groceries. And thanks again for breakfast. The mere thought of another day on an empty stomach would have sent me running for cover under my Aramco blanket."

* * *

I washed our dishes except for my cup, which I had refilled with the slightly gritty remains in Isabel's coffeemaker. The kitchen tidied, I climbed up to deposit the detergent in its customary hiding place.

Odds were that Isabel's warning about Hilda was well founded.

Dish-stacking and cleaning-product-storage fetishes would be difficult for most people to dream up. Anyway, I saw no point in calling my innate unfitness for residence living to the attention of interested parties, whoever they might be.

Physical evidence also backed up what Isabel said. I'd already noticed that all the handles of the cups on the shelves were positioned at precisely the same angle. Were we expected to use a giant protractor to achieve that effect? Surely not.

As a veteran of boarding schools and rented rooms in other people's houses, my track record for feigning good humor in the face of nitpicking behavior was none too promising. On the other hand, engaging in a long-running feud with Hilda in full view of the expat community would be a serious tactical error. I'd be tagged as a chronic malcontent forever.

What I needed was an effective exit strategy from the residence, and I needed one right away. Isabel's description of Hilda's kitchen tyranny had shattered any illusions I was still harboring that I could cope with close confinement in a postage-stamp-sized room for two weeks—let alone two years. Even before the "rules" issue arose, I knew that dormitory living wasn't going to work for me, not to mention for my bulky shipment of household goods already on the high seas.

I turned my attention back to my last few sips of coffee and my growing commissary list. I had identified the whitish liquid on Isabel's bran flakes at once as KLIM—*i.e.*, powdered whole milk. Despite its nutritional value and shelf-stability, that product had a significant drawback in 1960: adamant insolubility. The delightfully smooth consistency of the liquid on my cereal was nothing short of miraculous. Isabel must have strained the mixture through an unusually fine sieve or invested considerable time and energy beating the stubborn powder into the equally resistant water.

For such technical reasons, not to mention the taste of the liquefied product, I'd never been a great fan of KLIM, but that morning, I'd had to restrain myself from asking for a glass of it to drink with my cereal. I knew this newfound infatuation with potentially lumpy powdered milk wasn't going to last for long; I placed a KLIM substitute at the head of my grocery list.

By then, it was almost noon and well past time for an expedition to exchange money and purchase a minimal supply of items needed to keep body and soul together. I just hoped the cash-office staff didn't all take their lunch breaks at the same time. Otherwise, a trip to the commissary would be a monumental waste of my waning supply of energy, not to mention a grave disappointment to my restive stomach.

My new friend, Isabel, was doubtless catching forty winks before her afternoon shift. Anyway, I could hardly expect her to rescue me from famine again only a couple of hours after the breakfast she had so generously provided. Sponging off my "phantom" housemates, on whom I had yet to clap eyes, seemed improbable. Bottom line: no lunch for me today unless both the currency-exchange and commissary operations panned out.

Hilda, on the other hand, seemed all too likely to burst in at any moment, not to spare me the proverbial crust of bread, but to conduct suitable forensic tests to determine who had violated her rules by leaving dishes in the drying rack. Oops! My dirty coffee cup would doom me to the maximum penalty if I were dragged before Hilda's drumhead tribunal. Covering the offending piece of crockery with my hand as best I could, I tiptoed to the kitchen door and looked up and down the hallway.

The coast was clear. I rushed back to the sink, rinsed my cup out with hot water, and placed it in the rack. I didn't dare climb up to get Isabel's detergent again and risk exposing its hiding place to Hilda, should she stride through the door looking for miscreants like me. The very thought of her interrogating me at length as to any part I might have played in the desecration of "her" kitchen by using the dishrack for its intended purpose galvanized me into action. I snatched my grocery list, fled down the hallway to my room, grabbed my purse, opened the street-side door, and made good my escape into the noonday heat.

CHAPTER FOUR
BUSINESS MATTERS

A T THE CASH office, a new panic seized me. What could I use for identification? I had had to surrender my passport for safekeeping upon arrival. Aside from an expired New Mexico driver's license, I had nothing to prove I'd ever existed.

My fear of starvation for want of local currency proved groundless. I gave my name and presented my check. The clerk counted out my *riyals*.

My neighbor in the cash-office line pointed me toward my next destination. Turn right at the street and go straight for two blocks, then turn right again, he said. The commissary would be on my left. That was good news. The temperature outside seemed poised for an exponential leap. Even in the shade, my skin felt as if I'd spent the morning roasting on a spit.

That wasn't all. The force of gravity seemed to have doubled—or even quadrupled. Picking up one foot after the other as I battled the squishy tarmac took almost more strength than I could muster.

At the commissary, I tugged on the door. Nothing happened. Oppressive heat, lingering fatigue, and absolute cluelessness about how to do the most ordinary things in Arabia had taken their toll. I was almost in tears when the other side of the door opened, apparently without much effort on anyone's part. Out came a shopper followed by a dark-skinned man dressed all in white—probably her houseboy, since he was carrying her groceries.

Inside, the air conditioning was on steroids. My teeth chattered as I collected a shopping cart, but my body rallied enthusiastically and adjusted to the lower temperature almost at once.

The first thing I spotted was a display of cans labeled "whole milk not from evaporated sources" from Foremost Dairies. Despite that disclaimer, I had lingering doubts about the Foremost offering. I'd always associated dairy products in cans with the unappealing taste and smell of evaporated milk, but, suppressing my misgivings for want of an obvious alternative, I gave pride of place in my cart to one of the admittedly pricey items.

I tried to avoid buying anything else in cans that day for another reason. I'd have to lug whatever I bought through the noonday heat to the residence and find some place—heaven knew where—to store the lot until needed.

My limited-can policy proved impossible to stick to. Whatever the texture and taste shortcomings of their contents, cans were always the containers of choice in Arabia to avoid spoilage, breakage, heat damage to packaging, and/or incursions of rodent teeth at sea, on the pier, or in Customs.

Restricting my food purchases to quick- or no-preparation items for two or three days' breakfasts and lunches was easy—as long as I wasn't too picky about what I was willing to eat. For dinners, I'd have to brave the dining hall until I understood the residence system better. How twelve women could prepare their meals simultaneously in a communal kitchen inadequate for a single cook was a mystery to me. Where was the schedule for use of the stove—or a sign-up sheet? Surely Hilda, the domestic despot, would have insisted on one or the other, if not both.

Still no sign of human habitation at the residence. Maybe my housemates took all their meals at the dining hall. Otherwise, mealtime congestion would have been unavoidable. Eating elsewhere would avoid the risk of tripping over other cooks in the minimalist kitchen, not to mention annoyance of complying with Hilda's nonsensical cup-stacking regulations. But where was Hilda herself? Eating a meticulously prepared sandwich at her typewriter?

For my fashionably late lunch, I heated a can of lentil soup and ate a banana. The soup was tasty enough, but the banana left plenty to be desired. I learned later that company planes made weekly runs to Beirut and Asmara for fresh produce for resale in the commissary. On the basis of climate, Asmara must have been the guilty party on the banana front.

After lunch, I traipsed down to my room for the detergent I'd bought at the commissary and a clean Aramco hand towel. I washed and dried my dishes and arranged them on the shelves in a way I hoped would withstand Hilda's inspection. Instead of climbing up to deposit my detergent in Isabel's hiding place, I thought it wiser to store it under the sink in my bathroom for the time being. That would avoid any risk that Hilda or one of her tale-bearing minions would catch me red-handed flouting the house rules.

CHAPTER FIVE

CHECKING OUT MY WORKSITE

After lunch, in a fit of self-justification, I decided I deserved a break before heading to the school. Maybe if I delayed that expedition until later, the heat might have abated. Pretending to believe that fanciful bit of fiction for the moment, I hoisted myself onto the bed, elevated my swollen feet, and worked a crossword puzzle I'd clipped from the *New York Times* prior to my departure for Dhahran.

By two-thirty, I had to admit that I could scarcely put off reporting to the school much longer, even though I would have liked nothing better than to wrap myself in my sheet-and-blanket combination and take a long nap. I broke out my umbrella in lieu of a parasol and drank about a quart of water to stave off dehydration. Then, assuming the mantle of martyrdom, I let myself out the street-side door and set out for the place where I would be working for the next two years.

At the school, several of my coworkers-to-be were engaged in light-hearted conversation in the teachers' lounge. Andy, the principal, came in to join us—and doubtless to check me out. I struggled to be on my best behavior, a tough act to pull off with a fatigue-addled brain.

Brewed coffee was at the ready, and someone had brought homemade cookies. I helped myself to both. I doubted anyone had whipped up those cookies in a kitchen like the one at the residence. Other housing options had to be available.

I broached the subject of lodging by asking the basis for rooming assignments. Seniority was the answer. Not what I'd hoped to hear. Unless I could finesse the system, I'd be stuck in my residence "cell" until I'd served out my full two-year sentence. I trolled for more encouraging news, but cautiously. Two of my new colleagues had mentioned that they lived at the residence.

From what they'd said, they weren't new to Arabia. If they wanted more generous housing, they'd obviously be ahead of me. I cudgeled my brains for a tactful way to find out whether either of them was on an upgrade list, but then decided not to ask. If the answer was yes, and I, a rank newcomer, somehow ended up with more spacious living arrangements than theirs, they'd be bound to think I'd elbowed them out of the way. They'd already lived for at least a year in claustrophobic residence rooms like the one I was so desperate to escape after a mere 48 hours.

My original line of questioning having failed to produce useful results, I maneuvered the conversation onto housing costs—a very large and slightly smelly red herring. To my amazement, that digression eventually yielded exactly the information I was seeking. Ginette, one of the primary teachers, said that moving to a *barasti* had saved her five dollars a month.

*Barasti*s were prefab units put up during the postwar development of the Abqaiq field. By 1960, most of them were nearing the end of their useful lives, but they accommodated only four persons instead of twelve—a decided plus. However, according to Ginette, *barasti* bedrooms were the same size as those at the residence. Kitchen facilities were more limited. The latter scarcely seemed possible. Were they cooking over Bunsen burners? Cheaper rent—not my objective—seemed to be the sole advantage of *barasti* living.

As I was casting about for a way to find out the rent for an apartment and develop a strategy for securing one, Leo, a junior-high-school teacher, came to my rescue. He explained that after three years in Arabia he had qualified for a one-bedroom apartment. The monthly rent was a manageable twenty dollars more than I'd be paying at the residence. Never mind. I'd have sold apples door-to-door at high noon in the August heat for lodging where I could sit somewhere other than on my bed and had a fighting chance to hang my clothes in a real closet.

By then, I'd realized two things. A less public forum would facilitate matters at the next stage of my housing-improvement campaign. I also needed to bring in the big guns by enlisting Andy's aid.

An opportunity for a private discussion about my housing concerns arose the following week. Was he willing—and able—to help me, I asked. He was, and he could. Andy pointed out to the Housing Office that my service in Venezuela with an affiliated company should count toward seniority. I jumped to the head of the upgrade queue and was comfortably settled in a one-bedroom apartment within the month, well before my multi-crate shipment of household goods could possibly arrive from the US.

CHAPTER SIX

SINGLES' SOCIAL LIFE: MISSING IN ACTION

THAT FIRST DAY at school, I'd asked my coworkers about their favorite off-duty activities. They must have found somewhere to unwind after work; I doubted that they just sat on their beds until dinner and later until bedtime. Joan rummaged through the magazine rack for a copy of the weekly bulletin. "Maybe something here will appeal to you. Sponsors of sports competitions and special-interest groups use the bulletin to publicize their activities."

My eyes lit on the opening hours for the swimming pool. I'd taught swimming and lifesaving as a teenager and swum in a water-ballet troupe in college. A few laps after work would be an ideal way to get some much needed exercise, except for one minor detail. The pool was open only during the daylight hours. That ruled me out. Exposure to the Arabian sun at any time would guarantee me a third-degree burn within minutes. The gene that controls the darkening of skin pigment must have been left out of me when I was assembled.

The other bulletin notices weren't any more helpful. My distinctly amateurish skills ruled out duplicate bridge. I would draw the immediate wrath of any bridge aficionado unfortunate enough to be saddled with me as a partner. The camera club wasn't an option: I hadn't owned a camera since my then five-year-old brother hammered nails into my Brownie. A book club met during the daytime, when

I would be teaching. Three cryptic notices advertised the times and locations for Catholic, Church of England, and interdenominational Protestant services, all of them necessarily operating beneath the radar of Saudi law.

Where were the camp-wide gatherings at which expats could meet others who shared their interests? I was soon to discover that such events were rare to the point of nonexistence in Abqaiq. No wonder my social circle remained stuck at fewer than a dozen. Unless I cracked the code of expat social life soon, someone would be loading me onto a departing aircraft in a strait jacket.

Nothing made sense. In 1960, employees on daytime shifts worked from 8:00 to 4:00 Saturday through Wednesday and 8:00 to 12:00 on Thursdays. Even assuming an improbably early bedtime of nine or ten, that left at least five hours each weekday and a day and a half over weekends for leisure activities. If the entire workforce joined all the groups advertised in the bulletin—unlikely, I thought—they'd still have long stretches of free time on their hands.

Desperate for more varied companionship, I struggled to understand how a thousand Western-expat employees could have become invisible. After work, I met very few people on the streets, exchanging money, collecting their mail, shopping in the commissary, or eating in the dining hall. So where were they? Maybe the heat kept them huddled close to their air conditioning units, but they had to eat somehow. Take-out was not a 1960s option.

Employees in family quarters were no doubt doing family things and/or socializing with their similarly housed peers, but, according to the orientation materials we received as new hires, married expats accounted for only about twenty percent of the Senior-Staff workforce in 1960, and substantially less than that at Abqaiq. Most of the rest of us were crammed into quarters that precluded anything of a social nature other than having one or two friends over for a fun-filled evening of recycled gossip. Surely, my fellow single expats didn't just stare at the walls of their *barasti* or residence rooms until bedtime. Or did they?

When Aramco offered me a transfer, I immediately sought

advice from my aunt, who had worked as a secretary in Dhahran from 1947 to 1951. Although she warned me about the climate and the inconveniences of *barasti* living, her social life must have been satisfactory. She didn't mention it as a major drawback of Arabian employment. Thus reassured, I leaped to the unwarranted conclusion that I understood exactly what I was getting myself into, and that didn't include perpetual social isolation. Besides, Aunt Charlotte had managed to travel extensively while remaining extraordinarily gainfully employed. That sounded good enough to me.

With an overdose of misplaced confidence, I never doubted that my adjustment to the Arabian climate would be a snap. I had attended boarding school in Tucson—where similar temperatures are not unknown—before the days of residential air conditioning. My school didn't even have evaporative coolers. Tucson, however, didn't belch hydrogen sulfide gas into the air seven days a week. Nor did it suffer from the supplementary heat generated by around-the-clock gas flares.

Living in an isolated community wouldn't be a problem. All but one of the Indian Reservations where I grew up were miles from, and years behind, "civilization." Bureau of Indian Affairs (BIA) families were subject to frequent transfers "for the good of the service." We took a series of adjustments to unfamiliar languages and tribal customs in stride. Transfer-induced culture shock seldom lasted very long. Mail service only twice a week and making do with the limited offerings of the nearby trading post were manageable once we got used to them.

* * *

Thanks to my childhood experience as a BIA "brat," adapting to the lifestyles of French universities and the jungles of Eastern Venezuela had been a cinch compared with the challenges of adjusting to Abqaiq living. So why did I still feel like a square peg in a round hole nearly two months since my August arrival?

My problem was definitely not work-related. Time spent in my classroom was the highlight of my day. Aramco was delivering exactly what it had promised and what I thought I wanted when I agreed to my transfer. Statements from my US bank confirmed the punctual deposit of my very generous paycheck each month. The Middle East offered a tantalizing array of travel opportunities, although I realized I'd have to wait until I'd accrued the necessary vacation time to avail myself of any of them. I'd originally hoped for meaningful interaction with the local population, but, by late September, I was ready to write off my expectations for multicultural experiences in Arabia as hopelessly naïve. Then the company's good intentions and a stroke of blind luck changed my mind.

CHAPTER SEVEN

SAUDI CULTURE 101

LIKE MOST NEWCOMERS to Arabia in the 1960s, I'd brought along an ample supply of outdated and even ridiculous misconceptions about Saudi life in my intellectual baggage. They added up to a chaotic amalgam of tales of my aunt's experiences in Dhahran, improbably romanticized notions gleaned from a Rudolph Valentino flick, Bob Hope's and Bing Crosby's "discoveries" on the road to unidentifiable exotic destinations, and fantasies perpetuated by *A Thousand and One Nights*. The company must have assumed a similar level of cultural ignorance among most, if not all, of us new hires. To address this problem, management had devised a two-phase plan to replace the fanciful with the factual.

Each of us received a copy of the inch-thick, hard-bound *Aramco Handbook*—a treasure trove of information about regional history, traditional Saudi culture, and the role of the oil industry in the modern Middle East. As a follow-up, the company required all of us newbies to attend a series of lectures in Dhahran focusing on Saudi lifestyles, social customs, and etiquette.

Mandatory training often elicits groans from the intended participants, but not this time. No one groused about the hour-long trek to Dhahran sans air conditioning. We welcomed a few hours' relief from the odor of hydrogen sulfide, from which no escape was possible in Abqaiq, even indoors.

As a bonus, the lectures actually held our interest. Presenters were

Arabic-speaking employees from the Government Relations unit—specialists in key areas of Middle-Eastern studies. Some, although American by nationality, were Middle-Eastern born. The bicultural children of American missionaries in Syria, they had learned both English and Arabic in early childhood.

On the scheduled day, the Abqaiq contingent was seated near the rear of a large auditorium. With nothing more constructive to do between presentations, I perused the names and company positions of the speakers. My eyes lit on an "F. S. Vidal, Head of the Translation Division."

That name rang a bell. When I was still in high school, a Spanish-born doctoral candidate in anthropology from Harvard named Federico Vidal had paid two visits to our home in Arizona to talk with my father, who was then serving as Western Navajo Superintendent. In his twenties, I remembered, that F.S. Vidal had worked as a colonial administrator in Morocco, where he became proficient in both Arabic and Berber. Could this possibly be the same person? If so, what was he doing on the speakers' dais in Dhahran?

I leaned forward in my seat and squinted in a futile effort to bring his features into focus, but the silhouette looked right. At lunch, I flagged down an official from the Aramco Education Office and asked him if this F.S. Vidal had worked in Morocco early in his career. He didn't know, but he would ask. At the end of the afternoon session, the official lay in wait for me. F.S. Vidal had indeed worked in Morocco and was eager to meet me. He showed up almost immediately.

I explained how and where we had met. He was gracious enough to say he recognized me at once, but I doubted that. When he'd seen me before, I was early-teen pudgy, with a thick pelt of out-of-control hair down to my waist. In 1960, I was thinner, and my overly abundant head of hair had made the supreme sacrifice at the hands of an Italian hairdresser in Venezuela a couple years before.

The post-haircut transformation of my appearance must have been remarkable. Even several people who saw me every day didn't recognize me at first. All those years later, Federico Vidal probably didn't either. Nevertheless, he said that he would be in touch with me as soon as he checked his wife's calendar. He wanted me to visit them for a mutually convenient weekend, which we later settled on as the last week of October.

* * *

The first night of my eagerly anticipated visit with the Vidals, I asked Federico how common polygamy was in modern Arabia.

"The Koran sanctions marriage to up to four wives at any one time, but the *practice* of plural marriage has never been a realistic option for the overwhelming majority of Muslims."

"Why not?"

"An Islamic marriage requires a serious financial commitment from the bridegroom."

"Even in the West, husbands are theoretically responsible for the support of their wives and children, although these days, their wives sometimes end up as their families' primary breadwinners."

"Islamic doctrine makes that scenario inconceivable in traditional Muslim countries. At the time of marriage, the prospective husband must pay a sum of money, called the *mahr*, to his bride. Men of modest or no independent means typically work several years to accumulate the funds necessary to undertake even one marriage."

"What is the rationale for the *mahr*?"

"The *mahr* becomes the irrevocable property of the wife. Its original purpose was to ensure her financial security if her husband predeceased her—an all too likely possibility on the intertribal-violence-plagued Arabian Peninsula."

"Does the wife have any financial protection if her husband divorces her?"

"Yes. Islamic law requires a Muslim man who divorces his wife to compensate her with a payment called a *mut'a*. He must also provide a reasonable standard of food, clothing, and shelter for any children he fathered. If his children live with their mother, her ex-husband must support her at the same level as the children."

"Is lack of financial capacity as much of a deterrent to plural marriage in areas near Aramco operations as it is elsewhere in Eastern Arabia?"

"According to the findings of a recent company study of family composition in the Qatif and Al Hasa Oases, the answer to your question is a strong 'probably.' Less than one percent of the adult males at those two locations had taken more than one wife."

"Well, so much for the fantasy—fueled by B movies in the West—that polygamy is rampant in the Islamic world. But why did the company commit staff time to carry out that study?"

"Aramco offers long-term loans to Saudi employees to build houses near their work locations. Family composition and Saudi cultural norms have a direct bearing on construction costs for suitable residences and therefore on the size of the loans the company offers to prospective borrowers."

"I can understand how family size would affect the number of bedrooms needed, but I take it the study didn't investigate fertility rates."

"Family size is only one factor in estimating residential-construction costs for Saudi employees. Floor plans of such houses require separate living areas for men and women. Thus, even the least expensive units must be somewhat larger than houses for comparably sized families in the West. The need for separate sanitary facilities also increases plumbing costs. On the other hand, the study confirmed that space for separate households for multiple wives and their children isn't necessary at either of those locations, except in extremely rare cases."

Another women's issue had puzzled me ever since my arrival. I recalled that when I toured overwhelmingly Muslim French North Africa in the 1950s, many younger urban women of means favored styles direct from the Paris runways or adaptations of mainline fashion houses' wares by local tailors. Most women in major cities who chose to swathe themselves in black and peer at the world over half-veils appeared to be elderly, or at least middle-aged.

As we lingered over our breakfast coffee the next morning, I commented that the range of feminine apparel I'd observed in North

Africa had led me to believe that laissez-faire in women's attire was an emerging trend in the Islamic world. What I had seen during my few weeks in Arabia had changed my mind about that. "Why do Saudi women stick to shapeless, all-black garb and thick black veils that make it impossible to tell one from another? Are they forced to dress that way? If so, by whose authority?"

"That dress code is mandatory for Saudi women and older girls, depending on the latter's stage of physical development. The religious police *(mutawa)* enforce that rule."

"Why the *mutawa*? Does the Koran spell out the details of appropriate feminine garb?"

"No. If it did, standards for women's dress would be uniform throughout the Islamic world. You have seen that that is not the case. The Koran does mandate modest clothing—for both genders—but Muhammad didn't specify acceptable cut or color.

"Perhaps he deemed further comment unnecessary. In seventh-century Arabia, neither gender had much choice as to the fiber or color of their clothing. Local weavers used the hair of the black goats still common in Bedouin herds to fashion the textiles used to make wearing apparel. The alternatives—imported Egyptian cotton and linen—would have been far too costly and too fragile to clothe desert-dwelling populations eking out a precarious living in a barter-only economy.

"We can't be sure, because images of people don't appear in Arab art after the rise of Islam, but the style of clothing required for modern Saudi women may well resemble that in vogue during Muhammad's lifetime, or even earlier. 'Covering up' made perfect sense in the seventh century. Men had to protect their women, without whom there would have been no next generation. A tribe with a seriously declining population was on a short list for extinction. Clothing women from head to toe in black cloth must have made it more difficult for would-be kidnappers—or slave traders—to decide who was worth abducting. Imagine thinking they were getting a fertile young woman, only to find that they'd snatched a toothless old crone."

"But why are Saudi women willing to wear such garments today?

Times have changed since the seventh century. Besides, they must bake in the 'official uniform' during the hot season."

"Although there may once have been separate cultural and religious rationales for 'covering up,' any distinction between the two had disappeared on the Arabian Peninsula by the 18th century. During the religious revival in progress at the time, the style of clothing Saudi women wear today became an integral component of the fundamentalist version of Islam called Wahhabism or Salafism that is still the official state religion of Saudi Arabia."

"But why does Arabia need a state religion at all? Most countries get along perfectly well without one."

"That's true now, but it hasn't always been that way—even in the West. Diversity of religious belief and practice was once considered a threat. Civil authorities burned or hanged religious dissenters as heretics—and potential traitors.

"That changed with the growing secularization of European civilization, but even today [1960], several European countries still have official churches, including England, Scotland, Ireland, Sweden, Portugal, Monaco, Croatia, Slovenia, and Luxembourg. Although the law no longer requires membership in or attendance at the services of the "official" churches of any of these countries, they still receive privileged treatment and, in some cases, tax-funded subsidies from their respective governments. This special treatment honors the historical contributions of religious institutions to education, care of the sick, services for the poor, and national unity and cohesion.

"More recently, Islam played a key nation-building role in the formation of the Kingdom of Saudi Arabia a little more than a generation ago. Shared religious beliefs and practices greatly facilitated the unification of peoples from backgrounds as diverse as those of the desert tribes of central Arabia and the urban societies of the Red Sea coast into a single state. This commonality of belief and practice still serves as glue to bind Saudis of different backgrounds together today, however much they may differ with respect to other matters."

* * *

My weekend with the Vidals was more valuable than a full-fledged graduate program in Middle Eastern studies could possibly have been in preparing me to benefit from, rather than merely suffer through, my time in Arabia. With such limited opportunities to mix with local people, I would have left Arabia knowing little more about Saudi life than I did when I stepped off that New York-Dhahran flight in August.

At the Vidals' urging, I enrolled in the next available Arabic class. I did learn some basic Arabic vocabulary and develop fragmentary insights into the structure of the language, but the curriculum for those classes was in no way geared to the linguistic needs of Aramcon women. Lessons were the same for everyone regardless of gender or job description, so we spent most of our time memorizing the Arabic for such gems as "Hand me the wrench," and my all-time favorite, "Crawl under the truck to see if the jack is in place." Somehow, I just never got an opportunity to show off my oilfield-ready erudition. I learned more useful Arabic from my houseboy, our neighborhood gardener, and the merchants in the *suq* than I ever did in the classroom.

In the name of completeness—or, more probably, to enable him to address his memsahib students appropriately—our instructor *did* present the feminine forms of the language, but he certainly didn't dwell on them. Since Saudi women rarely appeared in public and then only when attired in the required *abayat* (floor-length black cloaks) and nearly opaque veils, words appropriate for conversations with them would never be any more useful for me than the Arabic words for "jack" and "wrench," or so I thought.

CHAPTER EIGHT

LIFE BEHIND THE VEIL

I FOUND OUT THAT I was wrong about that three months before I left Arabia for good. A couple of overseas-Arab nurses, Naida and Munira, ran a health-education center in the nearby *medina* (Arab town) under the auspices of some charitable organization. They taught local women best practices of childcare, nutrition, and basic homemaking. Somehow, they had acquired half a dozen treadle sewing machines and were looking for someone to demonstrate the use of the equipment. Such machines were the norm on the Indian Reservations of my youth, so I agreed to help out if I could get the necessary time off work.

Andy's response was predictable: "You agreed to do *what*?" However, he gave me his blessing, probably because classes weren't in session that month. (Vacation months in Aramco schools were December, April, and August.)

I spent the afternoon modeling the foot rhythm required to operate the treadle at a steady pace, slow it down, and speed it up. Then I showed the "class" how to fill the bobbin and thread the needle; how to follow a design printed on paper or cloth; how to sew two pieces of fabric together; and how to reverse direction and stitch over the original seam to secure it against raveling. The women could barely contain their eagerness to take the amazing contraptions for a test drive.

Munira produced some scraps of cloth for them to practice on. I relayed instructions through her and, when necessary, got down on the floor and worked the treadle with my hands so the women could see the timing without my body's blocking their line of sight. When one of them succeeded in producing a reasonably straight seam with a minimum of jerks and tangled bobbin threads, they giggled like teenagers.

My "teaching" assignment was rewarding enough on its own merits, but a surprising bonus came with it. The end of the session gave me a brief glimpse into the domestic lives of Saudi women and a very limited two-way conversation about their aspirations for themselves and their children. Realizing that this was a one-time opportunity for the multicultural interaction I had hoped for even before I first set foot on Saudi soil, I asked Naida if I might ask the women a few discreet questions. "Sure, but if I suddenly raise my hand slightly, you'll know you've strayed onto dangerous ground." Then she explained to the "class" that I was interested in learning something about their lives. "Would it be all right if the memsahib asked you a few questions?"

"*Na'am* (yes)," they chorused shyly.

Since Arab women always appeared in public in several layers of clothing, I asked if they found that attire uncomfortable in the hot season. Not at all, they said. Their clothes were very loose, which allowed air to circulate under them. They flapped their arms to demonstrate how this worked. Besides, they never went out in the heat of the day. I asked whether their veils got in the way of doing household chores.

"No. We don't wear veils—or *abayat*—at home unless unrelated men are present." Besides, they explained, Arab men stay as far away from housework as humanly possible.

"If you have shopping to do and the *suq* is too far away for you to walk to it, how do you get there?"

"We wouldn't walk to a *suq* regardless of its distance from our homes. Men in our families would do our shopping or drive us to the *suq* and stay with us while we made the rounds of the stalls. Then they would take us back to our homes again." I refrained from asking if the women carried the grocery money and whether their male kinfolk carried their purchases. Questions like those would surely have drawn the dreaded hand signal.

My last questions were more open-ended. I asked them what, if anything, they would like to have changed about their lives. I had seen no raised hand so far and didn't get one then, possibly because the women hadn't understood what I'd asked. I relaxed, trusting Naida to smooth over any unintentional cultural faux pas I committed.

The women talked briefly among themselves. Then Naida said, "They wish they hadn't had so many children at such young ages. Some of them already have seven or eight children, and those mothers aren't yet thirty."

I asked whether the mothers could think of anything that would make it easier for them to manage their large families more efficiently.

Unlike the other questions I'd asked, that one required no group consultation at all. They wished that disposable diapers, which they'd heard about, but never seen, were sold at the *suq*.

Their response astounded me. Paper diapers had yet to make appreciable inroads into the US market. They were unlikely to be available anywhere near Arabia for several years. Then, I hit upon the houseboy network as the most likely source of the women's information. Some family must have stocked up on the paper wonders while on home leave and brought them back to the Arabian field. Their houseboy, upon seeing the new product in action, slid seamlessly into his auxiliary role as town crier. The news spread like wildfire.

While the women were busy practicing their newly acquired sewing skills under Munira's supervision, I asked Naida what the legal age for marriage in Saudi Arabia was. "At this time [1962], the government has never specified a minimum age for the marriage of females, probably because the Koran doesn't address that issue. We see twelve-year-olds who are married and girls barely thirteen who are pregnant. We hope this will change eventually, but there is no sign of that yet."

After everyone had had a fair share of time operating one of the sewing machines, I ended the question-and-answer period by asking the women what they most desired for their children. Again the mothers chatted among themselves. Then one of them announced that education, even for their daughters, was first on their list. I asked why this was so important to them. Still no lifted hand, so I must not have blundered across any lines in the sand. Another woman said something to the general agreement of the other participants.

Naida relayed the message. The women were worried that it might be difficult or even impossible to find suitable husbands for all their daughters. Many Saudi men, including some of the women's own kin, had gone to other countries to study and had come back with educated women they had married abroad. These foreign wives were particularly attractive to men with middle-class aspirations. They could teach their children of both genders to read. This accomplishment put the illiterate Saudi women at a serious disadvantage in the marriage market.

I was burning to ask one last question, but I knew it would surely provoke a startled hand signal. That question was "What would your reaction be if your husband told you he planned to take another wife?"

CHAPTER NINE

BUNKER GOLF

By mid-October, I had to admit that my social-circle-enlargement campaign had been a miserable flop. I was increasingly desperate for interesting leisure-time options—solo ones, if necessary. Just as a stopgap, I assured myself.

Forced to remain indoors for almost three months by heat that refused to recognize that autumn was technically upon us, I had already exhausted the supply of reading material and crossword puzzles I'd brought from New York. But what else would keep me pleasantly occupied during those long off-duty hours? I was fresh out of ideas.

Then, in November, things began to look up; the heat finally began to abate. Surely more people would be out and about now. Even if they weren't, a little outdoor exercise might put me in a more positive frame of mind. I eyed the golf group advertised in the weekly bulletin with some interest. I'd played every day in Venezuela, but my skills were bound to be rusty after four months of heat-enforced sedentary living.

Never mind that; I might at least meet other golfers at the course. If not, I could at least shape up my game. My golf clubs, which were coming by sea, had yet to arrive, so I borrowed a two-wood, a five-iron, a wedge, and a putter from one of the nearby *barasti* dwellers. He neglected to warn me what I was getting myself into.

Early one Thursday morning, I set out for what was described—euphemistically, as it turned out—as the camp golf course. The "fairways" and "greens" were pure sand, although someone had made a partially successful attempt to smooth out and oil the latter. The "rough" was also sand as far as the eye could see. That was irrelevant; I hadn't the faintest idea where the fairways ended and the rough began anyway.

I tried to play a hole, but I couldn't plant a tee solidly enough in the loose sand for the ball to be anything but a moving target. I dispensed with the tee, set the ball directly on the firmest piece of ground I could find, and hit it with the two-wood.

The ball went a respectable distance with no obvious signs of hooking or slicing. Not that either would have mattered. With no flag in the cup, I'd had only the vaguest notion where to aim my shot. As I half expected, I couldn't find my ball once it rolled down what I'd assumed was the "fairway."

Perhaps golf balls in Arabia should have been painted red like Aramco cars so the latter could be seen from the air if their passengers became lost among the dunes. I didn't pursue that line of thought for very long, though. My golfing experiment went steadily downhill—figuratively, anyway. (The course was flat as a pancake.) Only the wedge worked as its developer(s) had intended, but a game limited entirely to shots customarily used to extract balls from bunkers was scarcely worth the effort.

Worse yet, my golfing outing hadn't netted me a single new acquaintance. Even if golfers were legion in camp, I doubted that many of them were enthusiastic about that course.

However, I found out later that some intrepid golfers were more creative than I was at devising solutions to the shortcomings of the Abqaiq landscape as a place to indulge in their favorite sport. They brought squares of carpet with them to create surfaces on the sand solid enough to give them at least some control over where their balls went when they hit them. As for me, I just wrote my golfing morning off as a total loss.

CHAPTER TEN

ARAB-STYLE SHOPPING

O N SECOND THOUGHT, I did learn something useful from my brief brush with desert-style golfing. Hydrogen sulfide gas was nauseating enough indoors. It was absolutely overpowering in what passed for Abqaiq's "fresh" air.

What I needed was a way to get out of Dodge long enough to remind myself what normal breathing felt (and smelled) like. Without much hope of finding anything even mildly helpful, I scrutinized the bulletin for ways to escape Abqaiq temporarily and rehabilitate my lungs. The same ads reappeared week after week, but this time I spied a new notice just below the activities section. Modified schedules for the company buses were to take effect immediately. "So what? Just so much bureaucratic housekeeping," I muttered to myself.

Then I did a double take. The schedule for the Dhahran route included a stop at Al-Khobar—the largest *suq* within commuting distance. In the teachers' lounge the next day, I asked if anyone was interested in a jaunt to Al-Khobar the following Thursday. Ginette said she'd love to go, so we set a time to meet at the bus stop.

The Al-Khobar *suq* exceeded my expectations, for both shopping and people-watching. A few steps from the entrance, a number of men had gathered at a coffee "house," or, more accurately, a coffee tent. Each customer had a *finjan* (a tiny handleless cup), from which he was sipping strong coffee mixed with cardamom-flavored evaporated milk—the traditional welcoming beverage in Bedouin Arabia. Two large Arab-style coffee pots were warming on live embers. A young boy poured refills for those who signaled that they wanted more. Some customers chatted with friends and acquaintances. Others fingered amber worry beads in silence as they listened to their more talkative neighbors.

Bedouin-Style Coffee Pot with Finjan

None of that surprised me, but what I saw next did. Three men in one corner were smoking a *shisha* (hookah—or, as we expats called them, a hubbly-bubbly). As a long-time fan of Baudelaire's poetry, I jumped to the conclusion that the three must be smoking hashish. Shushing me urgently, Ginette disabused me of that notion. The men were only smoking tobacco; the water cooled the smoke they were inhaling. Saudi penalties for the use of narcotics were severe. After that near-fatal brush with foot-in-mouth disease, I suggested that we put as much distance between us and the *shisha* as possible.

* * *

Just beyond the *suq* entrance, a crowd of men were gawking at something and talking excitedly. As we rubbernecked to see what all of the ruckus was about, the men parted to let us memsahibs go through.

There, we beheld the pinnacle of the day's shopping experience, and, given the nature of the merchandise, it didn't involve a stall at all. Before us stood a shiny, silver-colored recreational vehicle—the first either of us had ever seen.

Unashamedly, we asked the merchant to show us the RV's many features, which he did with cheerful good humor, probably winking at the men, who were eagerly following the proceedings. The merchant had to know that we couldn't be potential customers even if we had the full cash price for the vehicle in our oversized tote bags. (Installment sales were not a feature of the Saudi consumer market in 1960.) As women in Saudi Arabia, we'd have had to hire a man to drive our prize back to Abqaiq. Even then, we still couldn't have driven it except for occasional discreet turns within the confines of the camp.

We cheerfully went along with the extended charade. We obligingly marveled at the compact galley; inspected the placement of the bottled gas for cooking; sat briefly at the fold-away dining/work table; checked out the tiny shower that had about two inches of clearance on either side once a human body—*i.e.*, one of ours—was in the stall; and bounced up and down on the cushions in the living area to rate their comfort. We could barely tear ourselves away, but we were getting nervous about taking so much of the merchant's time.

As we headed toward the first stall, the merchant eyed us speculatively, perhaps wondering whether we had male friends or spouses with whom to share the news of the stunning automotive breakthrough then starring at the Al-Khobar *suq*. Or, he may just have considered our show of interest a gold-plated endorsement of the item for sale. It didn't take much imagination to visualize him telling future looky-loos, "Two memsahibs were here last week. They said they had never seen anything like this fine vehicle in all America. They promised to bring their husbands with them next time they come to the *suq* so that I can show the sahibs its remarkable features."

Continuing on our way, we came to a bakery. We watched men

shoveling risen dough into open-flame ovens for a few minutes. Then we plunked down two *qirsh* each (about three cents) for pieces of flatbread to fortify ourselves for strenuous "window" shopping and a very modest level of buying.

To wash the bread down, we bought bottles of tamarind juice from a nearby drink stand. Then, we strolled along the walkway looking for stalls offering merchandise more in line with our personal interests—and financial capabilities.

Ginette had an eye out for red-and-white-checked *gutras* (head cloths worn by Saudi men) to use as coverings for card tables, so she made her purchase while I looked at locally crafted brasses at the next stall. They were very attractive, but I had no intention of toting cumbersome articles like Bedouin coffee pots around for the rest of the afternoon. There would be time enough for that later.

Next, we came to a stall with ceramics for sale—some glazed and some not. The glazed pieces were light beige or medium brown, while the unglazed pieces were a grayish color. The unglazed pots, all of them shaped like very wide-mouthed urns, seemed to be intended as planters—perhaps for herbs. Unfortunately, my Arabic wasn't good enough yet to ask the articles' purpose or even to understand the answer should I manage to cobble together a comprehensible question.

Some glazed pieces had lids; others didn't. I was intrigued by large jars with screw lids that stood about three feet high. When I became a little more fluent, I learned that they were for storing water brought from springs in smaller, more portable containers.

Dozens of glazed pieces about the size and shape of cereal bowls puzzled me. They came with lids, but why? Sensing my unspoken question, the merchant pointed to a swarm of flies buzzing about a paper that had once held food. The lids were to keep flies away, a very useful function in one of the world's most extreme desert climates.

Arabian flies are so desperate for the slightest hint of moisture that they crash-land on human skin—or worse yet, in human or animal eyes—every chance they get. Any expat or servant who let a fly into a house was lucky to escape with nothing worse than ostracism. Once a fly landed on anyone's skin, it resisted even the most determined efforts to dislodge it. Rubbing the fly off was the only workable solution. Some old-timers even carried scraps of burlap for that purpose.

On our way to the next stall, I asked Ginette (who was on her second contract and much more in-the-know about Arabian life than I was) whether the ceramics vendor was the artist who had fashioned the pieces for sale.

"Not a chance. I visited a potter's 'studio' a couple of years ago when I went on a day trip to Uqair. That's the port that served this area for centuries. You really should go to Uqair, if you have a chance; fine examples of Portuguese and Turkish architecture still line the waterfront."

"I'll keep that in mind, but tell me about the potter's 'studio'—and the potter."

"The potter was covered from head to toe with such a thick layer of fine clay particles that he resembled a life-sized unglazed replica of himself. He did his work in a low-ceilinged cave, and apparently rarely left it. We didn't tarry long. The clay particles swirling about reminded me of a really bad *shamal*. I'm not medically qualified, but I bet a lot of potters die young from consumption or acute attacks of asthma."

"What's a *shamal*?"

"A very strong, very hot wind that blows mostly between May and July. The sand in the air is so thick that you're lucky if you can see an arm's length in front of you. If you're caught out in one, it will straighten your hair and scrub the freckles right off your face."

"Well, I wouldn't mind the latter, but I'm partial to my curls."

Next, we came upon two stalls of interest only to men from the general camp, judging from their clientele. They gave me my best insights yet into the lives of "the other expats"—contract laborers—and the kinds of purchases that tempted them to part with their hard-earned cash.

A barber presided at the first stall. A man awaiting service sat cross-legged on the ground on a floral-patterned tablecloth like the ones we'd seen for sale at the entrance to the *suq*. The barber was busily filling a basin with water from a large metal can and setting out supplies for a haircut and shave for his client. As the barber plied his trade, other shoppers with time on their hands stopped to comment on the proceedings, exchange gossip, or tell a joke or two.

At first, the scene reminded me of an illustration for an oriental fairy tale, but, on second thought, I realized that the subject was timeless and universal. Had he been an Arab artist, Norman Rockwell might well have painted that scene. His work would surely have rendered a faithful portrait of the typical goings-on in the male sanctuary of a barbershop—as translated into Arabic, both linguistically and culturally.

At the adjacent stall, half a dozen men stood solemnly waiting their turns in front of a youngish man seated behind a low table, a generous supply of paper, pens, and ink within easy reach. Unlike the customer and the kibitzers at the barbershop, those in line at this stall didn't seem disposed to socialize, and they attracted no attention from passersby.

A bit farther down the path, I inquired in what I hoped was an inaudible whisper, "What was going on there? Why does that stall attract only men from the general camp?"

Ginette replied equally *sotto voce*, "The young man writes letters for illiterate customers." That explained the silent queue: the men must have been composing messages to send to their loved ones. General-camp residents were not from nearby; the company provided shuttle buses for commuters. Some contract laborers even came from the poorer Arabic-speaking countries, where they couldn't find employment that paid a living wage—or any employment at all. Prime recruitment areas for foreign unskilled workers, such as Yemen, the Sudan, the Aden Protectorate, and Somalia, were far away and reachable only by travelers willing to spend several uncomfortable days camping out on the decks of coastal sailboats.

The men awaiting their turns probably had families from whom they were destined to be separated for years on end. Meanwhile, letters dictated to a scribe would be their only link with their loved ones, including, perhaps, children born after their departure.

It must have been difficult to include even a trace of intimacy in letters dictated to an impersonal stranger. Or had the men been away from their families for so many years that intimacy had long since died a natural death? Since the ultraconservative religious establishment in 1960s Arabia considered photographs of people graven images, contract workers from distant countries had no way to send snapshots home. Children too young to remember their fathers would have no idea what they looked like.

The recipients of these letters were undoubtedly illiterate as well. They would have to pay a local scribe to supply the final link in the fragile chain of communication that began with the senders' determined efforts to keep in touch. However poverty-stricken the addressees were, they must have been perennially impatient for news of their faraway sons, husbands, and fathers. To them, the scribe's fees must have seemed well worth the price.

Continuing down the street, we looked at rugs for sale. They were mostly wool, but a few were silk. Ginette explained that the merchant had probably acquired the silk ones from men making the *hadj* (the annual pilgrimage to Mecca). Less well-off pilgrims often brought salable goods from home to defray their travel expenses and raise money for the obligatory fees.

We detoured off the main walkway for our next stop. Ginette wanted me to see the metal workers' fire pit. The craftsmen used bellows to increase the temperature in the forge until the lump of metal in contact with the flames softened sufficiently to work. Then they used gigantic tongs to remove it from the fire pit and position it on the anvil.

After a few minutes, we moved on. We needed to wrap up our shopping to avoid missing the last bus. On our way toward the last few stalls, we happened by the meat market. Flies covered the meat like a shroud. I only hoped that anyone who bought that meat cooked it very, very thoroughly.

We held our noses, figuratively at least, and hastened to the spice dealer's stall, where the fragrance of the merchandise partially offset the ammonia-like stench from the butcher shop. The spices were lined up on the dirt flour in unlabeled ten-gallon metal containers. The merchant spoke little English, so I got down on my hands and knees to survey his inventory.

Spice Merchant's Mortar and Pestle, Al-Khobar Suq

I pried open a container of turmeric, only to find that the spice came with a generous complement of protein supplements. Miniscule worms cavorted on the surface of the contents. My neighbors told me later that passing spices through a clean nylon stocking would remove the extracurricular wildlife. I discovered that actually worked, but the mere thought turned my newbie stomach that afternoon.

We concluded our shopping at a grocery stall, where I bought two tins of cocoa mix that I thought might disguise the telltale taste of KLIM, or worse yet, evaporated milk. That would save the more expensive Foremost milk for my cereal, where flavor mattered most. My other purchase was a large *bacalao* (salt cod), the main ingredient of Portuguese fish stew, a taste I had acquired in Venezuela. The vendor wrapped the *bacalao* in several sheets of paper, but its fishy aroma permeated the bus on the way home, probably much to the discomfort of the other passengers.

On the other hand, the *bacalao* had formidable competition, so maybe its scent was barely noticeable. Only affluent, educated

Saudis—who were seldom, if ever, passengers on the company bus—used deodorant in the 1960s.

* * *

Aside from my sensitivity about the odor of the *bacalao*, the trip back to Abqaiq was quite pleasant—a far cry from my experience the day I arrived in Arabia. It was cooler, and the sun, already low in the sky, no longer produced its blinding glare. The landscape I had once thought so drab took on subtle shades of color. The dust-induced coral pink in the western sky deepened by the minute.

About halfway to Abqaiq, we witnessed a pivotal act of Islamic life in its natural setting: it was *Salat al-Magrib*, (evening prayer time). The driver stopped the bus and got out, followed by all the Muslim passengers. No water was available, so they cleansed themselves with sand. Then the driver led them in prayer. I found this unfamiliar ritual strangely moving, and I silently joined my prayers with theirs. Then they climbed back onto the bus in absolute silence.

The bus roared into action. We continued to our destination, hydrogen sulfide, gas flares, and all.

CHAPTER ELEVEN

TARUT AHOY

Since Ginette's and my recreational tastes had meshed so well on our Al-Khobar trip, I made a point of ferreting out other possibilities for us to get out of camp even for a few hours. Thanks to the only occasionally helpful camp bulletin, I learned of an upcoming excursion sponsored by the Dhahran Outing Group (DOG) to Tarut Island, just offshore from Qatif Oasis. I'd never heard of Tarut, but its location virtually guaranteed a full day of fresh sea air. That alone was reason enough to get up at five o'clock to catch a special Abqaiq-Dhahran-Ras Tanura bus. Two places were still available on the tour, so I called Ginette to ask if she'd like to join me. She jumped at the chance.

I had scant hope that the school encyclopedia would even mention Tarut, but I was pleasantly surprised. True, it didn't tell me much about what we should expect to see on Tarut in 1960, but it did describe the island's location in detail and discuss its economic importance under successive Persian, Parthian, Portuguese, Ottoman, and Saudi rule. The main attraction on the island was a derelict fortress traditionally thought to be of Portuguese construction, although a revisionist view then gaining traction insisted that local people had built the structure as protection *against* the Portuguese.

If the latter explanation was correct, the stronghold failed of its purpose. The Portuguese occupied the island anyway until Ottoman pressure forced them to retreat to their principal outpost on Bahrain several decades later.

The participants' fact sheet told us to bring a lunch that didn't require refrigeration and one or more bottles of juice. No food or drink would be for sale on the island. More ominous still, no restrooms would be available either, which seemed just short of unbelievable; we were scheduled to spend several hours on Tarut. The fact sheet also warned us to wear clothing and shoes that wouldn't be damaged by salt water. Were we going to swim to Tarut? Not exactly.

Crossing the Strait to Tarut Island

Early one Thursday morning, twenty-five of us boarded a bus that normally worked the Abqaiq-Dhahran route. That vehicle was marginally acceptable for the first leg of our journey, but Abqaiq-Dhahran-Ras Tanura and return was pressing the envelope. The ride amounted to more than fifty miles each way.

After taking full advantage of the thoroughly modern and well-maintained restrooms at Ras Tanura, we reboarded the bus and headed a few miles northwest along the Gulf shore to a flat stretch of beach. Today, a causeway provides automobile access to Tarut, but in 1960, crossing the strait was a more memorable experience.

Two-wheeled donkey carts with planks for flooring and stacked two-by-fours for sides awaited us at the shoreline. The tide was out—essential for us to visit Tarut at all.

Tarut's setting reminded me of Mont St.-Michel in France and its virtual clone in Cornwall, St. Michael's Mount. However, riding horseback across the seabed at low tide is reputedly possible at both of those locations, although not recommended. At Tarut, almost half a mile of sea water separated us from our destination. Maybe we *were* going to swim to the island—fully clothed, shoes and all.

Our guide interrupted those unsettling thoughts to inform us that each cart could accommodate two passengers for the crossing. One passenger should position himself/herself on the right edge of the cart and the other on the left.

Arab handlers then took up their posts on the front edges of the carts, reins in hand. They urged the donkeys into action, and we clattered pell-mell across the beach toward the sea.

The donkeys didn't even slow down at the shoreline. When we reached deeper water, the wooden carts floated up. Water slopped over our shoes and pants legs "that wouldn't be damaged by salt water." The donkeys' noses barely cleared the surface of the water. Just when I thought the poor beasts would have to tow us to Tarut, the water became shallower.

The donkeys didn't stop even when all the carts were out of the water. I supposed they'd be eager to snack on whatever vegetation they could find. But no. They knew, even if we didn't, that the discomfort we had endured bouncing along while seated on two inches of wood was not yet at an end.

After a couple hundred yards or so of agony on our part, the carts came to a more or less orderly stop at a large pool in the center of Tarut's main settlement. One by one, the handlers led the donkeys down an ancient stone staircase and washed off the salt water clinging to their coats, massaging them as they worked. The donkeys brayed what I took to be their thanks and readied themselves for the climb out of the pool. When they were all on dry land again, the time was apparently right for donkey refreshment, which they wandered off to find.

I had a horrifying thought. "Ginette, do you suppose that pool is the town's only water supply?"

"Probably, but if they drink that, it must be like gargling with salt water. Besides, can you imagine sharing a bath with a bunch of donkeys?"

* * *

We ate our lunches in the shade of the ruins of the Portuguese fort. When we had finished, the guide launched into a detailed post-lunch lecture about the history of Tarut. An Arabic-speaking Aramco employee provided an English translation.

Tarut had been inhabited since about 5000 BC. During early Christian times, the island was a center for Nestorian Christianity—later declared a heresy, but still favored by some isolated Middle Eastern communities.

Tarut, the guide explained, is part of the Qatif Oasis geological system. The water table is higher and the soil richer on the island than in the Arabian Desert beyond. "Okay, if the water table's so high, where's the fresh water?" I hissed under my breath.

Tarut was once a hub for the pearl trade. In its heyday, the island forged strong commercial ties with communities all along the Gulf coast, Mesopotamian trading centers, and more distant Indian Ocean ports. The now-ruined fortress was built early in the sixteenth century.

When the guide had finished his presentation, we were free to explore the island until low tide, when we would again use the donkey carts to return to the mainland. We wandered about looking at ruins of what had once been prosperous villages and visited the contemporary camps that ringed the main settlement.

However, after a couple of hours, we Abqaiq women were becoming more and more distracted. We were searching with increasing urgency for a secluded spot to use as an emergency *hammam* (restroom), but no such luck. Curious children stuck to us like glue.

At last, the tide was low enough for amphibious donkey transport. We hastened to position ourselves in the donkey carts as previously instructed. The bouncing and bumping of the carts on the beaches on either side of the strait did little to alleviate our acute physical distress.

Fortunately the ride to Ras Tanura was short. We mobbed those lovely restrooms with undisguised appreciation before walking over to the dining hall in search of an evening meal.

While we were eating, I asked Ginette if she had seen Arabs using buckets to scoop up sea water and deposit it in forty-gallon cans secured to the decks of their small boats. She hadn't seen them, but she knew what they were doing. Strong artesian pressure at some points in the Gulf drives fresh water to the surface. The Arabs were "harvesting" the water for reasons neither of us understood.

"Even if that artesian water starts out fresh, contamination by the surrounding sea water must make it brackish by the time it reaches the surface," I protested.

"Beats me. Maybe the interpreter can enlighten us. Look, he's wolfing down his dinner at the second table on the left, so it must be almost time to go. If you want to ask him any questions, you'd better be quick about it. He'll be leaving us at Dhahran."

"I'm on my way. Save me a seat on the bus in case the explanation takes longer than I think it will."

Taking care to walk between the exit and the interpreter's table in order to head him off at the pass, I caught him with no time to spare and asked my question. He replied that the water was indeed brackish, but not nearly as salty as sea water.

"So what do they do with brackish water?"

"Date palms—a major source of income for residents of Tarut and the Qatif Oasis—are able to tolerate irrigation water with concentrations of up to five grams of salt per liter and still thrive." With that, he took off to find our driver.

CHAPTER TWELVE

ARABIAN MASS COMMUNICATIONS

THE NEXT MORNING, I perused the camp bulletin yet again for any singles' social activities that might have escaped my attention. Nothing there but the same tired old ads. Then I remembered seeing a notice several weeks earlier that a departing retiree had a radio and a television set for sale. Tuning into static-prone radio broadcasts or watching any TV programming available in the Arabian boondocks didn't sound very exciting, so I'd ignored the details of the offer.

Now, the more I thought about it, the more convinced I became that I had to have both items—sooner rather than later. Granted, neither would provide an adequate substitute for an active social life. Still, listening to Saudi radio stations might improve my Arabic, which was in dire need of a heavy infusion of vocabulary useful in settings other than oilfield operations. Besides, the Vidals had praised the Aramco TV channel's English-language documentaries about Saudi history and culture highly.

Then I had a depressing thought. What if the owner had already disposed of his cast-off entertainment equipment? Fearing the worst, I contacted him right away and was relieved to learn that the items had not yet sold. Better yet, he offered me a two-for-one special if I bought both the radio and the TV. Could I come by his *barasti* that very day to view the merchandise? Coyly, I asked him to wait while I consulted my nonexistent social calendar. I came back a couple of minutes later to report that I would be free from four to six that afternoon.

The seller turned out to be an older man with snowy white hair and the weather-beaten complexion typical of the oldtimers who had worked outdoors for years under the merciless Arabian sun. Momentarily, I wondered what he had to go back to after so many years abroad. Then I refocused my attention on the matter at hand and got down to business.

Most of his belongings were already packed for shipment, but the TV and radio were sitting forlornly on a company table just waiting for someone to adopt them. I asked for a demonstration that both items worked, and bought the pair of them for a mere pittance.

The seller seemed as pleased with the deal as I was. The date for his departure must have been fast approaching. He even offered to deliver the equipment to my apartment. I'd been wondering how I was going to manhandle that TV set with its backbreaking 1960s-style picture tube into a taxi.

* * *

My new radio gave me access to the company's closed-circuit FM service, which broadcast static-free music 24 hours a day. After several years of straining to hear AM transmissions from technologically challenged stations in underdeveloped countries, that was a relief. I did think it odd that no one ever announced the names of the selections or identified the featured performers. When I inquired about this curious omission, my coworkers informed me that reproduction of the human voice constituted "a graven image" and was therefore *haram* (forbidden) in Arabia.

So informed, I stopped flipping through the dial hoping to find what I eventually realized were nonexistent Saudi stations. I shifted my search to include Arabic-language broadcasts from elsewhere in the Middle East. My first discovery was Radio Cairo, which evidently benefited from an extraordinarily powerful transmitter. I was able to

Sun, Sand and Single

receive its signal loud and clear from over a thousand miles away—even in the daytime.

The station's programming consisted almost entirely of lengthy harangues by President Gamal Abdel Nasser. Given his extensive mass-communication commitments, I could only wonder how he found time to govern Egypt at all.

* * *

Radio Cairo programming was informative after a fashion, but I am still amazed that I devoted so much time and effort to deciphering formulaic speeches about repetitious topics in a language I barely understood. Suitable reading would have provided more varied and balanced coverage of Middle Eastern affairs. Unfortunately, print materials about any subject as sensitive as Middle Eastern history or politics in any language I could read fluently, or even in languages like Arabic that I couldn't read at all, were unobtainable in Abqaiq.

With an eye toward filling the information void, I asked my colleagues if subscribing to American or European magazines would be practical. Don't even consider it, they said. The police swooped in regularly and confiscated any periodical(s) deemed inimical to Wahhabi morality, local social customs, or Saudi religious and political policies. Subscription to Western magazines would be a colossal waste of money.

At first, I pooh-poohed their advice, but when the school's new encyclopedias arrived missing the "I" and "P" volumes—for Israel and Palestine, respectively—I became a true believer. Until I could make a trip to Beirut, where books in English and French were reputedly widely available, my craving for even-handed treatment of Middle Eastern topics—as opposed to a one-sided seminar on Egyptian affairs—was destined to remain unsatisfied.

* * *

I turned my attention to my new-used TV, which one of the bachelors had volunteered to hook up. My expectations for the set as a source of entertainment were modest, but I soon became a regular listener to the company channel for reasons that had probably never occurred to the Saudi censor.

Programming began each day in the late afternoon with the King chanting verses from the Koran. The intent of this unusual television fare must have been to reassure any Muslims able to tune in that carefully controlled television content posed no threat to the cultural or religious orthodoxy of the state.

While I became a regular viewer of the company's well-researched and professionally produced documentaries, the heavily censored American sitcoms—the mainstays of daily transmissions—turned me into an instant company-TV addict. The audio was in Arabic, sometimes with English subtitles, sometimes not. All drinking, gambling, card-playing, swearing and obscene language, kissing, immodest dress, and inappropriate relationships between men and women as viewed from the local perspective were deleted. So were the commercials. That shortened episodes considerably. Challenged by such brevity, we became quite proficient at figuring out what was missing from the original script. My all-time favorite example of the "guess-what-we're-not-seeing" game was an unusually short episode of a western series, as "edited."

The bad guy, attired in a designer cowboy outfit with an authoritative-looking firearm at his hip and commercial quantities of cartridges in his belt, kicked his way through the swinging door of what was obviously a saloon in the original. Inside, the room was overflowing with men in discount-store togs that bore a superficial resemblance to those sported by the bad guy. Scantily clad floozies must once have occupied several otherwise inexplicable spaces created by the censor's ham-handed handiwork.

The men all had standard bar glasses within easy reach, from which they were sipping, or in some cases chug-a-lugging, the contents. The Arabic sound track assured us that the suspiciously clear liquid was orange juice. Some of the men were staring intently at the table tops in front of them for no discernable reason. We ventured a guess that cards, poker chips, and/or dice may once have graced those surfaces.

The bad guy shouldered his way toward the drink stand (bar) with scant attention to the collateral damage he was causing. Slamming his fist down on the counter, he barked, *"Salaam aleikum."* ("Peace be with you.") I somehow doubt the accuracy of that translation; I rather imagine he was demanding a triple. The bartender, cringing visibly, poured him a glass of "orange juice" and murmured, *"Wa aleikum is-Salaam."* ("Peace be with you, also.") I *am* prepared to believe that rejoinder sincere, although overly optimistic. The bad guy stomped out without paying for his drink.

CHAPTER THIRTEEN

MYSTERY SOLVED

One day as I was leaving work, who should be heading for the door at the same time but Hazel and Marjorie, two of my erstwhile housemates? I asked if they were going back to the residence.

"Eventually," Marjorie replied, "but we're making a commissary stop before going on to the dining hall."

"Would it be all right if I joined you? I don't feel like cooking this evening. Besides, I'd really enjoy getting better acquainted with you over dinner. All we talk about in the lounge is school stuff."

Hazel opened the door and waved me through. "Sounds good to me."

As we walked along, I asked how things were going at the residence.

"Pretty much the same as always. A couple of new nurses arrived last month, though."

"Did anyone I might know leave? Someone must have, because when I moved out, all the rooms were occupied."

Hazel thought for a minute. "Well, Janice's stateside boyfriend wrote proposing marriage. She resigned and was out of here like a shot. She definitely didn't want to be late for her own wedding."

"How does Isabel's replacement like Abqaiq? I think her name is Mona. She was my suitemate of record for about a week, but I only saw her once or twice."

Marjorie laughed. "Her? She's long gone. She only stayed about a month. All she ever did was bellyache about having to do shift work. She managed to alienate the entire nursing staff, who wondered out loud if she'd even bothered to go to nursing school."

"Did anyone else I might know leave? We never hear about farewell parties for people in other departments."

"Well, Hilda finally packed it in. She had fifteen years' service, so she was fully vested in the pension fund. One of the nurses told me her father was quite ill. That's probably why she left mid-contract. She must have thought she was the only person qualified to supervise his care."

I suspected the same thing, but I knew better than to utter a word of that out loud. If I did, everyone in camp would know exactly what I'd said within the hour.

When we arrived at the commissary, I made the excuse of not wanting to lug groceries to dinner and then back to my apartment. That way, I could wander about to see if anything new was on offer while Marjorie and Hazel were otherwise occupied.

The canned goods section was heavy with expat staples like peas, green beans, and corn, but just beyond the vegetables and across from the infant formula, I made a startling discovery. An artistically stacked display looked suspiciously like beer cans. I picked one up. A large map of Saudi Arabia covered most of the front of the label. The fine print on the back identified the cans' contents as a product of Carlsberg, the celebrated Copenhagen brewer.

I sidled up to Hazel and Marjorie. "What are those?"

Hazel laughed. "Ersatz beer. It tastes like beer, but it has no alcoholic content."

Marjorie grinned. "Do you like beer? No problem. Beer drinkers here buy this concoction for the taste and spike it with hooch in their quarters."

I thought that by then nothing about Abqaiq living would surprise me. The revelation that people regularly gulped down can after can of beer-flavored carbonated water in what had to be a futile attempt to satisfy their craving for their favorite brew changed my mind.

Sun, Sand and Single

My brain ground on in heat-induced low gear. I tried to grasp the full implications of what Marjorie had just said, but I couldn't quite connect the dots... yet.

I knew that no expat—or anyone else—would dare be seen imbibing beer or anything stronger in public anywhere in Saudi Arabia. Even new hires just off the plane didn't need to be reminded what would happen next: immediate deportation by the company to protect the erring employee from the harsher penalties of Saudi law—*e.g.*, the lash.

So how effective had shutting off legal supplies of alcoholic beverages and threatening clandestine drinkers with what most Westerners would consider "cruel and unusual punishment" actually been? Not very, as I should have suspected from experience in another context. I began my college years in a dry state, and one of the first things new enrollees learned was the phone numbers of bootleggers who delivered orders to designated neutral spots.

Production of an adequate supply of drinkable alcohol and establishment of a foolproof distribution system must have required greater ingenuity and tolerance for risk in Arabia than in dry American counties and/or states. Nevertheless, Aramco employees had risen to both challenges with conspicuous success several years before my arrival in Arabia.

At first, I didn't see any connection between widespread expat consumption of illegal alcohol and Abqaiq singles' nonexistent social life, but something told me there had to be one. Only gradually did it dawn on me that when prohibition forced drinking behind closed *barasti* doors, it must have dragged singles social life inside with it. Alcohol-free, all-camp events couldn't compete with clandestine drinking sessions and soon disappeared from the official social calendar entirely.

* * *

Prohibition had a negligible effect on the drinking and social habits of employees in family housing once a workable method for liquor production was in place. Family housing conformed to US standards, including a reasonable level of privacy. With facilities to host parties and opportunities to attend social functions in other private homes, married couples had little difficulty finding ways to socialize during their off-duty hours—with or without alcohol.

Barasti dwellers had unlimited access to alcoholic drinks in some form by the mid-1950s, but prohibition exacted a crippling social price from the bachelor crowd. With negligible space for entertaining guests in their quarters, two or three visitors to a *barasti* constituted a crowd—in practice, a single-gender crowd.

However, singles' cramped housing and lack of privacy weren't the only obstacles to what most adults would consider a normal social life. The composition of the expat workforce by the 1960s would have ruled out mixed-gender socialization for the overwhelming majority of single male employees even if the alcohol issue had never arisen. At Abqaiq, expat men on single status outnumbered unattached female expats by almost seventy to one. Imagine what a dance would have looked like with those demographics.

In Venezuela, single-expat men outnumbered single women, but only by about three to one. Singles of both genders also had the option of dating non-US expats and local people, so the social scene was similar to what we had experienced in the US.

Not so in Arabia. Had any expat man made the slightest move to establish any sort of relationship with a Saudi woman, he would have ended up with a knife between his ribs before sundown. Saudi law would have sided with his attacker. That left cards, other forms of gambling, and yes, drinking, as the predominant leisure-time activities of male *barasti* dwellers.

Some old-timers seemed able to tolerate a long-term absence of female companionship. Perhaps they had always been loners. Others may have stayed the course through inertia or because they had nothing more promising to go back to.

Newcomers like me made up a third group. A significant percentage of us would leave Arabia at the end of our first contracts. Quite a few didn't make it that long. Those who chose to stay on either had to adapt to the loneliness of typical single evenings and weekends or put forth a heroic effort to find or create satisfying opportunities for socialization. Even though I planned to be a short-timer in Arabia, I was determined to do the latter, but I hadn't the remotest idea where to start.

CHAPTER FOURTEEN

ABQAIQ'S FIRST STILL

ALL AT ONCE, I remembered Aunt Charlotte's description of social life in Dhahran in the late forties and early fifties. It included such intriguing tidbits as whiling away autumn evenings over Napoleon brandies (the real stuff) and expeditions to the commissary to pick up the generous monthly ration of booze (seven bottles per adult). What, exactly, had changed during the nine years between her departure and my arrival?

My coworkers filled me in as best they could, but Hazel had been in Arabia only since 1957 and Marjorie since 1956. They had to rely on camp folklore for the details of the debut of what many long-serving expats regarded as their signal engineering triumph of the decade.

In 1952, they told me, King Abd al-Aziz ibn Saud had revoked the exemption from Saudi liquor laws previously granted to non-Muslim foreigners living apart from the local population. This policy shift so deplored by most expats resulted from an incident at a party at a foreign diplomat's residence. Heavy drinking was in progress. In the course of a violent argument, a youthful Saudi prince fatally wounded his host.

Had all the attendees, including the diplomat and his assailant, been non-Muslim expats, the incident might have escaped official notice altogether. In this case, had the victim survived, he might have been declared *persona non grata* and expelled from the country for serving liquor to any Muslim, let alone to a prince of the blood.

For the Old King, this incident must have been the last straw. He had made every effort to accommodate the cultures of the thousands of non-Muslim employees of foreign companies operating within the Kingdom. Now, they had shown their appreciation by taking advantage of his magnanimity. The King did, however, permit previously exempt persons to consume liquor imported prior to the date of his decree, provided expats did so within the privacy of their employers' camps.

According to Abqaiq old-timers, the supply of pre-decree booze was exhausted by early 1953 except for an outrageous oversupply of Drambuie. Drambuie is not to everyone's taste, so the expat community belatedly took up the challenge of finding a way to make it taste like anything else. Drambuie martinis, anyone?

When the last drop of underappreciated Drambuie disappeared down some ungrateful gullet, Aramco expats finally had to face facts. Some seriously parched throats were in the offing unless they came up with a workable plan to circumvent the Old King's decree. One would think that the operators of one of the largest refineries in the world could have solved the refreshment crisis in record time. Alas, one would be mistaken.

The reputed cause of this delay was the difficulty of constructing an operator-proof still for home use by not particularly gifted amateurs. If successful, the resulting equipment would minimize the risk that the wholly inept or the hopelessly inebriated would blow the roofs off company housing.

Meanwhile, the thirstiest simply couldn't wait. They drank undistilled mash. Obviously these were people who had long since lost all sense of taste—and smell. I asked how long the quest for a potable form of "lubrication" had gone on. Neither Hazel nor Marjorie knew for sure, but they'd heard it had taken several months.

Were my former housemates leading me on? I could ask any of the old-timers for verification, they said, and I would get the same story. Hazel and Marjorie had been right all along. Some of my

Sun, Sand and Single

longest-serving informants confirmed what my colleagues had told me and amplified their accounts with vivid—and probably heavily embroidered—descriptions of the premier public performance of Abqaiq's first operational still.

On that memorable day, they agreed, the whole camp turned out for a demonstration of the revolutionary new household appliance. Families brought picnic baskets; chilled soft drinks were available for purchase. Volunteers organized games for the children, a wise precaution. A forty-gallon still run is a lengthy process during which there isn't much to see.

A winner-take-all betting pool catered to adults willing to wager a *riyal* on the exact moment the first drops of distillate would run down the output tube from the condenser. The air was electric with anticipation. With great ceremony, a member of the design team flipped the toggle switch to turn on the heating element. The long wait began.

To the unrestrained delight of the adult attendees, concentrated alcohol vapor eventually passed through the lyne arm (the horizontal piping of the still) into the condenser. The design team hovered about to monitor the temperature. Moments later, the first drops of the elixir of expat life trickled into the collection vessel, to rousing cheers from the crowd.

Self-identified eye-witnesses to the prototype still's debut differed as to who had the privilege of being the first to sample the new and, after a prolonged liquid diet of undistilled mash, much improved product. The still's developers had been excluded from consideration automatically on the entirely reasonable assumption that they had probably sneaked a nip or two during test runs of the apparatus. The most believable version of camp lore was that the winner of the betting pool was allowed to be the first in a very long line of thirsty consumers.

All those who claimed to have been present on this momentous occasion agreed that, as the first drops of distillate flowed from the condenser, someone began to hum *In the Still of the Night*, and the crowd joined in with unbridled enthusiasm, if less than perfect pitch.

Even when I lived in Abqaiq, those who had been eyewitnesses to "the great unveiling" still greeted the mention, humming, or singing of that tune with raucous laughter.

This colorful bit of camp "history" was amusing, but, as a nondrinker, I didn't see its relevance to my continuing quest for ways to spend my off-duty hours productively and make friends among a broader range of the expat population. My thinking on that subject was about to change. This reversal began a few weeks later during my return flight from Cairo, where I spent the 1960 Christmas break.

CHAPTER FIFTEEN

RETHINKING MY SOCIAL STRATEGIES

NOW THAT I understood the reason for the eclipse of singles' social life in Abqaiq, I could see that my strategy for enlarging my smallish circle of friends needed major revision. "This cannot possibly be as difficult as I'm making it," I told myself. I read the bulletin notices over and over for fresh approaches to building a social life that had thus eluded me.

Wait a minute. I must have been going at this all wrong. Searching for "interesting" people who might or might not share my tastes in leisure pursuits hadn't worked. Maybe I should look for activities that appealed to me—for example, day excursions to nearby destinations of interest—and see who else was participating in them. Surely that strategy for expanding my social circle would be more productive than my previous needle-in-a-haystack system.

I used my new method to filter the bulletin notices in search of recreational opportunities with realistic social potential. Suddenly, it occurred to me that the local Catholic group must have a choir, those being the pre-Vatican II days of the occasional High (choral) Mass. I'd been involved in church music since childhood, so joining the Abqaiq choir might be rewarding in more than one sense.

Willing to try anything by now, I rechecked the bulletin. Mass, I learned, was offered in the movie theater each Sunday—a workday for us—at 7:00 pm. The timing seemed odd, because before Vatican II, Masses were typically celebrated only during the morning hours. Maybe a special dispensation was available to accommodate "underground" congregations like us.

The next Sunday, I set out at 6:40 for the theater, normally a leisurely ten-minute walk—a useful precaution, as it turned out. The theater was packed when I arrived, but I found a seat next to the family of one of my students just in the nick of time.

An acolyte was lighting the candles. And sure enough, a choir occupied the front two rows on the right side of the auditorium. They didn't wear robes, which explains why I hadn't noticed them before.

After Mass, I mentioned to my student's parents that I was thinking of joining the choir and asked them whom I should contact for information. They pointed out the director and the pianist and gave me their names—Sheila and Henry, respectively. They suggested that I try to catch one or both of them before they left for the night.

Taking this advice to heart, I threaded my way down the aisle against the onrush of worshippers bent on hurrying home for Sunday dinner. I reached Sheila just as she was gathering up stray music and putting it into a portfolio for safekeeping. I introduced myself as a newcomer to camp and said I was interested in joining the choir. She welcomed me enthusiastically and explained the rehearsal schedule.

That settled, I looked up at the stage in time to see the ushers folding up the altar. When finished, their handiwork looked like an ordinary, if largish, packing crate. "Fragile, handle with care" was stenciled in English and Arabic on all four visible sides, and "Caution, this side up" was printed in like manner on the top. Two men brought a gigantic dolly onto which they loaded the "crate" and started up the aisle to a lockable storage room off the lobby.

Once the altar-turned-packing-crate had disappeared, I could see Father Thomas packing the lectionary, missal, candles, Eucharistic vessels, and vestments in a very large suitcase. Two women whisked the altar linens away for laundering. Claudio, Father Thomas' houseboy, picked up the "suitcase," and the two of them set off to the "rectory"—a prefab with two bedrooms and a smaller room for

Sun, Sand and Single

the priest's study. I wondered what occupation Father Thomas had declared on his visa application: surely not "Catholic Priest."

I learned later that he wasn't the only member of the Catholic clergy in the country with suspect documentation. One day I was talking with several women outside the theater. A diminutive, dark-skinned man attired in Bermuda shorts and a Hawaiian shirt walked up and joined in the conversation. My confusion must have shown on my face. Finally, one of the women asked, "Have you met the bishop?"

* * *

Joining the choir turned out to be a fortunate decision for social as well as spiritual reasons. I was the only single person in the group, so this was my first chance to become acquainted with married couples since I arrived in camp. They couldn't have been more welcoming. Membership in an "illegal" church must accelerate the bonding process, because I felt like a full-fledged member of that community right away.

A few rehearsals later, I mentioned that I was puzzled by the lack of opportunities to socialize with single employees. Did my choir friends have any ideas on that subject?

They made a stab at finding workable suggestions for me, but then one of them said, "You know, we really don't know much about single employees' social activities. They're working during the daytime, when we do most of our socializing. At night and over weekends, our husbands and children are home, so we pretty much limit ourselves to family things. How about bridge? Most of the housewives play during the day, but one group meets in the evening."

"Thanks for the suggestion. I did notice an ad in the bulletin inviting new duplicate players, but my skills are just not up to duplicate standards, especially if members of the group play everyday from 8:00 to 4:00 and then come back for an encore in the evening. I tried to shape up my game in Venezuela, but life got in the way; I spent my days working for a living. I'd have the same problem here."

After that, the topic of conversation shifted, but I could recognize a blind alley when I'd strayed into one. We went on to discuss the music we'd be singing the next few weeks. Then, just as I turned to leave, Sheila beckoned to me. "Are you free on Saturday nights? That's when Henry practices, so he wouldn't miss me at all." So they're a couple. They mustn't have any children yet, since Sheila didn't mention childcare as her responsibility on Saturdays.

That sounded hopeful. Maybe my social life was on the verge of picking up. "Yes, unless something comes up at school that I have to attend."

"My next-door neighbor, Teri, would make three of us, and Eva Anderson might be interested as well. We've been wanting to play bridge if for no reason other than to get together regularly, but dog-eat-dog combat disguised as a card game isn't our style. Give me your phone number. I'll see what I can work up."

Sheila was as good as her word. At the next choir rehearsal, she asked if I was still available on Saturday nights. I assured her that I was. "Great," she said, "next week, we'll meet at Eva's house; I'll write out the directions for you."

We played serious bridge, but we never let the game interfere with spirited conversation. We became fast friends once we learned that confidences shared at the bridge table would remain there, rather than become grist for the camp gossip mill. Sheila told us that she was expecting her first child at least two months before anyone else in camp had the slightest suspicion she was pregnant.

Our bridge nights were stress-free, win-win occasions all around. However, I was still frustrated that I had made so little progress making friends among the younger singles set, with whom I should have had the most in common.

CHAPTER SIXTEEN

AGAINST ALL ODDS

DATING HAD ALWAYS been a pleasant way for young singles to while away leisure hours anywhere I'd lived before, but it didn't seem to work that way in Abqaiq. A few starry-eyed new hires may have thought they'd arrived at the ultimate happy-husband-hunting grounds, but experienced oil-company expats knew better. If the absolute lack of privacy in singles housing didn't doom budding relationships, transfers and expiring contracts often did. An even greater impediment to dating in Abqaiq—casual or serious—was mathematical.

Five young female teachers and six young single nurses were on the payroll my first year in Abqaiq, but only four of us were dating at all. Given the scarcity of eligible expat women, I was surprised at first that a stag line eager to vie for our attention wasn't a permanent feature of camp life. Reality check: men on single status who were interested in forming couples relationships *and* free to pursue them were in short supply. Second reality check: distinguishing between eligible and ineligible romantic prospects took skillful detective work and a generous dollop of luck.

All too many supposedly single men were actually married. They included employees waiting for family housing, contractors on temporary assignment, or men living apart from their spouses for assorted reasons. Moral issues aside, dating anyone in those categories guaranteed a no-strings relationship, a soul-wrenching breakup for a woman looking for a husband, and the awkwardness of maintaining a cordial social and/or professional relationship with the male partner's wife if and when she showed up in camp. In the worst-case scenario, one of her children might be assigned to the former girlfriend's classroom, or the wife herself might come under the former girlfriend's care at the clinic. Since the whole camp would know perfectly well what had been going on between the bachelorette and the errant husband, all eyes would be glued on the readjustment drama. Occasionally, some incurable blabbermouth just couldn't resist making an intolerable situation worse by enlightening the wife as to just what hubby had been up to.

Another hurdle for those determined to find romance on the sands of Arabia was the relatively large number of verifiably single men who evinced no interest in dating relationships of even the most casual sort. Old Arabia hands, whose service in the oil industry dated to just after WW2, if not before, they must have adapted long since to their status as confirmed bachelors, whatever their natural inclinations.

Indeed, most of them had had no choice even during the heyday of immediate-postwar development. Limited as we were to teaching, nursing, and secretarial work, female employees had never accounted for anything like 10% of Aramco's expat workforce. By the 1960s, that percentage was less than 5%, and declining steadily. Expat women in clerical and semi-professional healthcare positions who had joined the company in 1945 were leaving as soon as they vested in the company pension plan. Almost without exception, their replacements were Saudis.

After I moved to my apartment, I came in contact with several fast-aging men who had joined Aramco in the forties. I knew exactly what their recreational habits were, because all I had to do was look out my living-room window any evening.

My unit faced onto a small open area with a few oleanders scattered randomly about and a row of scraggly date palms along the street. That qualified as a park by Abqaiq standards.

Every day about an hour after quitting time, half a dozen of the perpetual-bachelor crew brought beach chairs and pitchers of alcoholic refreshment out to the "park" in a poignant ritual of *déjà vu*. I know they told the same stories over and over because, as the evenings wore on, the decibel level rose steadily.

Some mornings, when I passed by on my way to work, they were still in the "park," asleep in their beach chairs. Although the "picnic" participants were invariably pleasant to me, I would never have considered any of them suitable date material, even if they'd exhibited the remotest interest, which they didn't.

Then there were the outliers who didn't fit neatly into either the already-married or the not-at-all-interested group. Some unmarried men in their fifties lived openly in company housing with unmarried female employees of similar age and length of service. Perhaps one or both partners were leery of assuming the obligations of marriage. Those who had lost spouses by divorce or death may have had adult children who objected strenuously to a parent's remarriage. Female partners who were not vested in the pension fund may have had second thoughts about legalizing their unions. If they did, they might not be able to continue in the workforce, which would deprive them of their accrued pension rights.

Open cohabitation of unmarried couples raises few eyebrows today, but it most certainly did in the US as the conservative morés of the 1950s fought a losing battle with those of the early 1960s. The Abqaiq social scene astonished many new hires direct from the US. We in the Arabian oilfields were simply a shade ahead of the times or, in the view of some newcomers, on another planet, as the following anecdote illustrates.

* * *

A few serially unmarried men had devised more creative solutions to their lack of intimate female companionship. Harold—who was probably in his late fifties, although the Arabian sun is infamous for its accelerated-aging capability—was a case in point. Edna, my next door neighbor, filled me in about his modus operandi.

Harold and Angela, his wife, lived in a nearby unit with the same floor plan as mine. Angela, a stunning Greek woman barely out of her teens, seemed very lonely and more than a little homesick when I ran into her in the commissary, at the cash office, or on the walkways of our neighborhood. Her English was good, and she was definitely eager to prolong even the most casual conversation. In cooler weather, we used to sit out in front of my apartment on Thursday mornings and have a friendly cup of coffee or tea. She was from Corinth, she told me. She and Harold had been married almost two years.

When I asked Angela how she and her husband had met, her smile faded. I must have stumbled onto some taboo subject, but what was it? Her answer dispelled my ignorance right away. Harold had come to Corinth on vacation, and a "friend" had introduced them. She had known Harold only ten days when they were married. Her husband had been very kind to her mother. Before the newlyweds left, he had given her money to support Angela's younger brother, who was only twelve.

A change of subject was obviously overdue. I asked her how she liked Arabia. Well enough, she replied, but she missed her mother and brother and the mountains and trees of Greece. I told her the profusion of oleander bushes—red, pink, and white—that festooned the camp didn't do much for me either. I still missed the lush beauty of Venezuela's rainforest.

To nudge us back onto what I hoped was a safer conversational topic, I asked if she participated in any of the wives' social activities.

"No. I just don't have the time. My housekeeping chores and cooking the Greek-style dinners Harold prefers keep me pretty busy."

"What kind of work does your husband do?"

"He's a forklift operator—out in the field all day. They don't have refrigeration out there, so he just snacks at lunchtime. Maybe that's why he enjoys my home-cooked dinners so much."

"Do you and Harold have any friends you like to do things with? If not, taking part in some of the married-couples' social activities might help you to expand your social circle."

"Harold wouldn't go out at night. He's exhausted by quitting time. He's worked in the oilfields ever since he got out of the army in 1945. I think it's becoming too much for him now, although he wouldn't like to hear me say that."

"It's none of my business, but have the two of you thought of retiring while Harold's still young enough to enjoy the leisure time? Since your husband's been with Aramco fifteen years, he must be eligible for a very generous pension. The two of you could live in comfort almost anywhere in the world that struck your fancy."

"I really don't know anything about our finances. Harold takes care of all that. I do know that we're going to have a very special summer this year. Harold's contract is up in June, and we're going to spend the three months he has off in the US. I've dreamed of going to America all my life, but I never expected to have a chance to do it. My father died when my brother was only a few days old. My mother has worked long hours as a seamstress ever since to keep a roof over our heads and food on our plates. That's why I'm so grateful to Harold. Now, at least, she has one fewer mouth to feed, which helps some, but not enough."

"Are you and Harold planning to return to Arabia after your stateside vacation?"

"Yes." All smiles now, she added that, like her mother, she had worked as a seamstress in Greece, so she was already planning her wardrobe for their American summer. As for clothing for the next contract, she hoped to buy most of it in the US. She had noticed that the American wives wore an endless selection of fashionably designed and well-constructed garments. "Maybe dressing the way they do would make me more confident about mingling with the Americans."

That comment saddened me, but I couldn't think of anything to say that would help her very much or send the conversation off in a more cheerful direction. I took what I hoped was a more constructive tack by asking her what places she most wanted to see in the US. New York and a place called Disneyland, she replied, which Harold had told her was the greatest sight on earth. "Have you been to Disneyland?"

"No. The last time I was in California, Disneyland was still in the planning stages. Since it's opened, there's never been enough time to make a special trip to Anaheim for that purpose. While I'm on leave, my priorities are completing the ton of shopping for the next contract, getting any necessary medical treatment, and visiting friends and family." Angela promised to bring back photos of this unequaled wonder for me to see.

After Angela went on her way, I couldn't stop thinking about what she'd told me. The scenario didn't add up, or it added up all too well. A few days later, I told my neighbor Edna that Angela and I had had a friendly chat.

Edna's eyes widened. "What on earth did you talk about?"

"Just small talk." I must have strayed further onto dangerous ground than I'd imagined. "She seems so lonely, but my efforts to engage her in extended conversation have mostly fallen flat. Maybe she just misses the companionship of her own age group."

Edna looked thoughtful. "I've invited her to some of the wives' daytime activities, but she always declines on the grounds that she has housekeeping to attend to. I can't imagine how she could fill an entire day with that. If I didn't have other interests, I'd be climbing the walls."

"Angela is really excited about going to the US this summer. She's sewing up a storm to wow American onlookers with her fashion sense."

"She told you that? She'll never get closer to the US than Greece unless she remarries."

"What do you mean?"

"We've lived near Harold for nine years, so we know how he operates. Angela is his *fourth* wife that we know about; there may have been one or two others. Each time he's gone on post-contract leave, he's shed the previous number somewhere in Europe where it's easy to get an almost instant divorce. We don't know where, but we haven't really tried to find out. Then, on his way back to Arabia, he goes to some country where economic conditions are so tough that women are willing to pay almost any price to emigrate, including marrying wholly reprehensible types. Harold definitely has an eye for good-looking women, but it's all about him once he places a ring on his unsuspecting beloved's finger."

As I listened to Edna, I was mentally crossing dating off as a viable component of the social life I was attempting to build for myself in Abqaiq, barring the sudden appearance of a bottled-in-bond Prince Charming with gilt-edged references and a flawless background check. My one experience on what purported to be the local dating circuit not only hadn't had a happy ending; it hadn't even had a happy beginning, or, in truth, any kind of beginning at all. Still, I remained optimistic that something would work out for me eventually. Now, after a couple months of observation of the local social scene, I wasn't so sure.

CHAPTER SEVENTEEN

PSEUDO-ROMANCE AMONG THE DUNES

NEAR THE END of my second week in Arabia, I had a serious problem. My body's loyalty to Mountain Standard Time was unshakable—and inconvenient. It became clearer by the day that changing to Arabian time was not in its plans, even though we'd traveled across twelve time zones to get to Abqaiq. I fought back as best I could, but living in an environment where it never really got dark—those infamous gas flares again—undermined my message. I would lie awake for hours at night and then fall asleep at my desk while I was desperately trying to plan my first trimester's work. Fortunately, I didn't have to explain all this to Andy. He got a live demonstration when he dropped by my classroom one afternoon just after lunch. I was nodding off despite having guzzled a couple of cups of coffee in the teachers' lounge in the vain hope that caffeine would prop up my drooping eyelids.

Always the gentleman, Andy assured me that this was not an unusual reaction among newcomers. He suggested a few days at the Abqaiq clinic for what we would now call light therapy.

"How's that going to cure my time-zone problem?"

"Oh, they'll have you sleep in a pitch-dark room at night and spend your days in a light, bright room. That should do the trick in no time."

"Well, if you say so."

"I do say so. Come along to my office. I'll fill out the paperwork for you to take with you. Stop by the residence for sleepwear, daytime clothes, and toilet articles. The clinic will expect you within the hour."

I did as I was told, although I did wonder how many days I would need clothing for. If I ran out, perhaps the clinic would parole me long enough to bring in reinforcements.

The nurse on duty showed me to my "day" room and told me that if I became sleepy to get up and walk about, which I had to do several times before an aide appeared with my dining-hall-provided dinner tray. At about eight, the evening nurse came to tell me it was time to get ready for bed. She suggested a warm shower to help me to relax and brought me a not-too-ancient magazine to occupy my time until she came back promptly at nine to take me to the "night" room. Once settled in an extraordinarily comfortable bed, I fell asleep immediately and had my best night's rest since leaving New York.

* * *

The morning nurse awakened me at seven and returned me to my "day" room. When I was dressed she asked me if I would like to take my meals with another expat patient. She assured me he didn't have anything contagious. That sounded like a good way to fill in some of the time, so I agreed.

The nurse took me to the dining area and introduced me to Reginald, a very tall, handsome, Scandinavian-looking type. "Do you go by Reggie?" I asked.

"No, I prefer Reginald."

Reginald led me to the breakfast table and seated me with a flourish, all the while peppering me with questions in an overripe Southern accent straight out of central casting. I wanted to ask him which southern state he came from, but I was going to have to watch carefully for conversational openings if I expected to get a word in edgewise.

By lunchtime he had checked out my complete family and educational backgrounds, work history, travel experience, and reasons for coming to Arabia. Was I interested in politics? Only in the general sense, I told him.

"Why aren't you interested in politics? You told me you have a degree in history."

In an effort to excuse my reprehensible lack of civic engagement, I explained that I had been legally domiciled abroad for several years. Consequently, I wasn't eligible to vote under the laws of the time, since I wasn't a resident of any US state. I also protested that, given our lack of access to American periodicals or radio, I would scarcely have enough information to make informed judgments about issues in contention back home.

"Well, of course, I don't vote here either, but I do manage to keep up with the goings on in Washington, thanks to my many friends there." *I wonder. Are your "many friends" regularly subjected to your novel idea of conversation?*

"I can see that you're going to require tutoring." *Oh?*

While I was desperately trying to find a way to stem the flow of this question-and-answer grilling, Reginald pulled a letter out of his shirt pocket and thrust it at me. "Read this."

A form letter from a senator thanked him for his contribution (kind not specified) to the legislator's reelection campaign. *The senator must have had a veritable factory of secretaries pumping out hundreds or even thousands of similar messages to anyone who had handed out a few fliers or contributed pocket change to his effort to retain his seat.*

"What do you think of that?"

You don't want to know what I really think or what I really want to know. How did you happen to bring a vaguely worded letter from a public official who probably wouldn't recognize you if he met you on the street to a clinic where you are a patient? "It's nice that he took the trouble to sign the letter personally."

I had originally planned to stick with this "conversation" because I thought it might help me to stay awake until time for me to go to the "night" room. Unfortunately, listening to Reginald's monologue was having the opposite effect. I would have dozed off long since had he not stopped to interrogate me on this or that at regular intervals. I excused myself after dinner by saying that I had a few things to attend to before bedtime.

When the night nurse came for me, I gave her an abridged version of the day's events and suggested that the Reginald time in my program should be severely curtailed. "By the way, what's he in for? He doesn't seem sick or sleep deprived."

"Sorry, I can't tell you that. However, since you slept through the night yesterday, I think we might limit your contact to mealtimes unless he chances on your 'day' room. I'll leave a note for the doctor."

"All right, but please put instructions in my chart that no one is to tell him where I spend my days."

"Will do," she promised, as she turned the lights out.

* * *

The next morning at breakfast, Reginald began the day's lecture with the news that he had a surprise for me. "Nancy, I have thought this over very carefully, and I have decided that you are the woman I'm going to marry."

I had just taken a swig of coffee. After a freeze-frame moment, I started to choke. I don't think he even noticed when I spewed coffee all over my breakfast plate, reducing my remaining toast to a heap of unpalatable mush.

He continued with his prepared remarks. "I think a Christmas wedding would be best. We'll have a couple of extra days off then. What do you think about that?"

I opened my mouth to point out the inappropriateness of even discussing marriage at this stage, but he was already elaborating on his vision for our wedding before I could goad my choking-damaged vocal cords into action.

"As you know, Christian services are not permitted in Arabia, so we'll take the shuttle to Bahrain." Then in a startling non sequitur, he asked, "Have you ever been married?" I started to shake my head, but I was too late again. He apparently took my lack of response for no, because he said, "That's good, because the one Christian clergyman on the island isn't keen on marrying divorced people."

Whoa! How do you know that? Have you worked this scheme on someone else or several other women before?

Reginald scarcely stopped for breath. "Now, as for your wedding dress, since we'll be married at Christmas time, I think a sheath dress in red Damascus silk brocade with gold thread would make for very attractive wedding photos." *Tell me. Do Damascus silk merchants run a mail-order business? Who is going to pay for this undoubtedly expensive item of couture?* Reginald's bride—who was not going to be me unless he had me abducted and held in close confinement—would never be allowed to express an opinion on any subject, let alone utter a single word of objection to anything.

The sound track continued in the same vein. Reginald's vision of married life seemed to be that we would travel constantly. That might have held some appeal for me as long as it didn't involve being accompanied day and night by somebody clearly out of his mind. As an apparent afterthought, Reginald informed me that we would also maintain an apartment as a home base between trips. We would decorate it with our travel trophies. *I hope you're not a big-game hunter. I wouldn't take kindly to a full-sized stuffed elephant in the living room.*

The apartment would have a wood-burning fireplace. I would sit by the fire doing needlework. *Fat chance.* Two prize-winning Irish setters would snooze at my feet. I wanted to ask who would pay the kennel bills we'd amass while circumnavigating the globe, but I never got a chance. I bolted my breakfast and excused myself, pleading a fictitious doctor's appointment.

At lunch, Reginald took up the marriage theme again. He was planning a jaunt to Jerusalem over the King's Accession Day holiday in November. I would accompany him as his fiancée. When he finally paused for breath, I was ready. I pointed out that I wouldn't be eligible for an exit permit until February. He scowled. "I'll see what I can do about that." I never learned whether he could arrange exit visas—a useless skill in this case, because that issue was going to be moot within twenty-four hours, if I had anything to say about it.

The rest of the lunch conversation was a blur. No response from me was expected or desired, so I spent the time plotting my escape from the clinic. I should be safe then. I doubted that Reginald had any easy way to find out where I lived. His endless stream-of-consciousness chatter had been a good thing in one way. He hadn't bothered to ask where I worked.

* * *

Later in the afternoon, the doctor dropped by. He remarked that I had slept two full nights without interruption and had stayed awake both days. If that trend continued, he planned to discharge me the next day to see how I would fare in the less favorable environment at the residence. I had to restrain myself from falling on the floor and kissing his feet.

"You really should give Reginald a wide berth," he advised me. "That guy has problems."

"No kidding! I'm trying to keep my distance, but that's not easy. I'm doomed to eat all my meals with him. You must have had something to do with that. Couldn't you inflict him on someone else for a change?" I vowed to sleep through the next night if I had to hit myself over the head to do it.

The clinic declared me cured just before lunch the next day; the nurse promised to bring me the paperwork as soon as the doctor signed it. With the end of my mealtime ordeals finally in sight, I set matters straight with Reginald at lunch. I interrupted his soliloquy to tell him, quite untruthfully, that I had enjoyed our chats, but I was sure he would understand that marrying anyone I had known for less than 72 hours was out of the question. He looked both surprised and hurt. He must have imagined himself quite a catch.

I had my things ready to go when the nurse brought my discharge papers about two o'clock. As I walked back to the residence, I heaved a mighty sigh of relief, confident that that was the last time Reginald's and my paths were likely to cross. On this, my day of liberation, all was right with the world—except for the omnipresent hydrogen sulfide gas. I didn't even notice the heat, which was hovering near 120°.

CHAPTER EIGHTEEN

AMATEUR "SPIES" IN CAIRO

The Tarut excursion had whetted my appetite for travel farther afield, like to another country. The perfect opportunity for an international trip—our Christmas break—was less than a month away. I was fully engaged in deciding where to go and what I wanted to see when some spoilsport reminded me yet again of the terms of my visa. Bottom line: I wouldn't be eligible for my first exit permit for another couple of months.

Then it occurred to me that I might have an ace in the hole in the travel-documentation game. On the Tarut trip, I'd met Gregory, who told me he worked in the Passport Office. I phoned him to ask how I could get a permit to leave the country in time to travel in late December.

Just go ahead and submit the paperwork right away, he said. Exit permits sometimes came through even if applicants were technically ineligible for them. How long the process would take was anybody's guess. Editing out the parts of that I preferred not to hear, I leaped to the questionable conclusion that everything would work out to my complete satisfaction. If I had my paperwork on his desk by Saturday, Gregory promised to walk it through channels right away.

"What's your destination? You'll need a visa, and those take time, too."

"I think Cairo, but I'll let you know on Saturday."

We were getting an extra day off, so our break amounted to all or part of four days including the two weekend days (Thursday and Friday). I could take an evening flight to Cairo the previous Wednesday evening and return to Arabia on Sunday (Christmas Day). With the necessary stamina, I should be able to visit the city's most memorable sites within that timeframe.

My destination settled, I phoned Ginette to see whether my Egyptian safari would work with any Christmas plans she already had in place. I neglected to mention that my ability to come by the necessary travel documents in time depended on a figurative roll of the dice.

Ginette's enthusiasm for the project was unbounded. She wasn't sure she'd return to Arabia at the end of her home leave, so this might be her only chance to visit Egypt, something she'd dreamed of doing since childhood. I asked her who else might be interested. She mentioned Karen, a colleague who had recently ended a rocky relationship with her boyfriend. Ginette thought Karen would grab any excuse to get out of town over the holidays. Otherwise, she'd be alone nursing her wounds. Ginette promised to get in touch with her and let me know her decision as soon as possible.

Early Saturday morning, Ginette called to say that Karen wanted us to count her in. Their paperwork would be in Gregory's hands before the day was out.

Salvaged Kuwaiti-Ware Teapot, Copper on Brass

After work, I headed for the home of a housewife who did outside sales for a Beirut travel agency. After she made our flight reservations, we looked for a suitable hotel. Based on location and ratings, the three viable choices were the Nile Hilton, the new Shepheard's, and the Semiramis. The Nile Hilton would have been pure luxury, but pricey. That left the new Shepheard's, which I rightly suspected had retained scarcely any trace of its predecessor's fabled charm, and the Semiramis, an older hotel more likely to match our vision of traditional Cairo ambience. I reserved a triple room at the last, which included full English breakfast, whatever that might mean in post-colonial Egypt.

The fate of the original Shepheard's Hotel—the unofficial clubhouse of colonial society during the British Protectorate—was a major disappointment; I would gladly have paid extra to stay there. My aunt had told me all about the glories and senseless destruction of that legendary property. She and her future husband had stayed there during the 1951 Christmas break. Barely had they exited Egyptian airspace before bands of rioters, angered by British attempts to disarm Egyptian security forces at Ismailia (in the Suez Canal Zone), burned the old Shepheard's and several hundred other iconic Cairo buildings to the ground in a startling outburst of pent-up anti-colonial rage.

* * *

During our three full days in Cairo, we managed to visit the Pyramids, the Sphinx, the Egyptian museum, and several major Muslim and Christian sites in a marathon of sightseeing that left us absolutely exhausted. Back at the Semiramis the last full day of our stay, we ordered tea, put our feet up, and tried to decide what to do about the evening meal. In the end, we walked across the street to the new Shepheards, where, we had heard, the Soviet mission overseeing the construction of the Aswan Dam had established its headquarters. Penetrating an enemy base camp at the height of the Cold War sent cold chills up and down our spines without putting us in any real danger.

About halfway through dinner, Karen, who was seated across the table from me, suddenly exclaimed, "I can't believe what I'm seeing!"

"Neither can I," Ginette chimed in.

"What is it?" I was seated opposite the window, the better to absorb Cairo's most flattering view, which is to say too far from the street to see the abundant litter undoubtedly marring an otherwise picturesque scene.

"Don't turn around. They'll know we're watching them."

Stifling my annoyance at being left out of whatever was happening, I reached into my handbag for my compact. I positioned its mirror so I could see a group of men filing into the dining room. They were uniformly pudgy, or maybe it was just their baggy suits that gave that impression. They sat down at a table several rows behind us. Despite our Cold War biases, they looked harmless enough.

A waiter appeared at once with one copy of the menu, which he handed to the man at the head of the table—their leader, or at least the one of their number who spoke English. Without any consultation at all with his companions, the man with the menu placed their orders. Instructions to the waiter took scarcely a minute for a dozen diners, so I inferred, correctly as it turned out, that they were all having the same thing.

When the food arrived, the leader picked up a drumstick and announced, "Cheekin."

They all repeated, "Cheekin."

The language lesson continued with potatoes, peas, and bread. The Russian mission didn't plan to starve in Egypt, even if their diet was limited to those four foods.

Having solved the immediate mystery, we refocused our attention on the baklava and tea the waiter had just brought. Then, just before we asked for our bill, I took out my mirror again to see what the Russians were having for dessert, but they were gone. Making no effort to conceal my annoyance at being left out of the excitement a second time, I asked when the Russians left.

Karen looked puzzled. "I never saw them go. They just disappeared."

A likely story, but with nothing more out of the ordinary to see, we returned to the Semiramis to pack for our Christmas-morning flight back to Dhahran.

CHAPTER NINETEEN
A BUSINESS PROPOSITION

WE COLLECTED OUR boarding passes and cleared passport control. In the departure lounge, a woman came up to me and said, "I haven't seen you since Venezuela." I hoped I remembered her name (Leila) quickly enough to avoid suspicion that I had forgotten her after only a few months. Leila told me that her husband had been transferred to Abqaiq early in December. Their shipment of household goods was still in its crates, so she'd seized the opportunity to visit her family in Cairo for the holidays. Meanwhile, her husband was batching in a *barasti* and supervising the unpacking crew.

"Are you traveling alone?"

"No. These are my friends—Ginette, in the window seat, and Karen, on the aisle."

"Where are you sitting?"

"5C. Across from my friends."

"I'd like to continue our conversation during the flight. I'll see if I can change my seat." With that, she circulated through the room inquiring bilingually who held seat 5D.

She was in luck. The holder of seat 5D was an Egyptian agronomist who ran an agricultural station somewhere up-country from Abqaiq.

Leila turned on the charm and came back flashing a self-satisfied smile and the agronomist's boarding pass.

The PA system announced boarding for our flight. We trooped onto the plane, stowed our gear, and took our seats, Leila beside me. When the roar of the engines no longer drowned out all attempts at conversation, Leila asked how long I'd been in Arabia. I described my arrival in the August heat and told her she was lucky to have come in December, when the weather was at its best yet.

I asked if she'd had an opportunity to meet any of the other wives. She said that she'd met several and had joined a bridge group to expand her social circle. In response to her question about camp-wide gatherings, I warned her that those were essentially nonexistent in Abqaiq, and told her why.

Leila asked if I was still baking bread and pastries for sale as I'd done in Venezuela. I explained that my housing arrangements during my first month in Arabia would've precluded that. Since then I'd been busy settling into my apartment, getting my teaching plans in order, and waiting for my US shipment.

Leila waved all that aside. "Really, you must take advantage of this potentially lucrative business opportunity. Commissary bread has absolutely nothing to recommend it. Customers would be swarming around your door if they even suspected you were about to open a bakery."

"I'm not so sure about that. Personally, I find Arab flatbread a satisfactory substitute except for the trek to the *suq* to buy it during the hot season."

"Remember, I'm an Egyptian. I'm thoroughly familiar with Arab flatbread and quite like it in its place. However, I don't plan to subsist on it exclusively for years on end unless I have no alternative." She added that she had also tasted dining-hall cakes and cookies and had found them seriously wanting. "I promise to be your first customer and to recommend your work to the members of my bridge group."

"Leila, I'd have to address several logistical issues before I even considered going back into the food business."

"Like what?"

"I'd need a houseboy. If I were teaching full time and running a bakery on the side, someone else would have to do the washing up, laundry, and general housekeeping."

"So hire one, or two, if you need them." Her expression made it clear that I must surely have more brains than this conversation suggested.

"All right, then, how am I going to find a reliable one?"

She volunteered to check the references of applicants and screen them for suitability, after which I could interview the finalists. If my Arabic gave out before the questions I needed to ask the jobseekers did—which was more than likely—she would serve as my interpreter.

Having lost that round, I trotted out the last objection to the bakery idea I could come up with at the moment. I protested that my modest-sized apartment didn't provide adequate space for a commercial food-preparation business. The mere thought of trays of bread and pastries cooling all over my living room and on my bedroom dresser was enough to send me running for the exit. Besides, I would have to locate reliable sources for key ingredients, which might not even be available in the emptiness of the Arabian Desert.

Leila glared at me and seemed primed to launch into a lengthy rebuttal. To buy time, I promised to think about her suggestion and let her know my decision.

In a tone that brooked not the faintest whisper of argument from me, she put an end to the discussion—for the time being. "Fine. Think about it until the end of the week." I wondered if she meant the Muslim or the Western week. The latter would give me two additional days to develop a strategy to wiggle out of her plan for my future.

No such luck. Leila had the Muslim weekend in mind. She called on Thursday to announce that she had three qualified houseboy candidates ready for me to interview. "What date would be convenient?"

"I'll need to check the school calendar to rule out conflicts. That won't be finalized until after New Year's."

"Oh, all right. I'll expect to hear from you during the first week in January." Catering was to be my destiny whether I liked it or not.

I had to admit—but not to Leila—that the idea of setting up a food-preparation business was beginning to grow on me, despite the difficulties I knew it would present. Catering is hard physical labor. If successful, the business would vacuum up my free time like a wind tunnel. "Well, you're always complaining about not having enough to do after work," my rational self pointed out. "Think about it this way. The additional income would ease the pain of financing your overly ambitious international-travel agenda. Otherwise, without a transfusion, your bank balance will soon be on life support."

* * *

As I was chewing on that unpleasant truth, another income-producing opportunity came my way. Miriam, the wife of one of my coworkers, begged me to give her eight piano students lessons while she was on home leave. My qualifications were minimal, and I had no piano, but I had given lessons in Venezuela for the same reason she was approaching me now. No one else wanted to take on the chore.

My first inclination was to tell her I was too busy with other projects to help her out just then. Still, the extra income would come in handy. Then I had a sobering thought. Lest I get myself into an awkward situation by inadvertently taking on students so advanced that they played better than I did, I asked about the levels at which her students were working.

"First, second, and third."

Well, that would be all right, but I would need suitable music for the third level. (I had enough leftovers from Venezuela for levels one and two.) I told her I'd let her know.

Much depended on whether I could buy a piano without breaking the bank and defeating the whole purpose for going back into business. I delegated the piano matter to the parents of the students I'd tentatively agreed to teach. Find me a piano, I promised, and I'll give your child lessons. In no time at all, one of the mothers called to say she'd located a piano for my inspection. She admitted that the instrument wasn't exactly a thing of beauty, but the tone sounded all right to her.

She was right about the aesthetics. The piano looked as if it had seen better days or had never had any in the first place. However, the action worked without a hitch, and none of the ivory caps on the keys were missing. It needed tuning, but Miriam's husband tuned pianos. I plunked down 175 *riyals* (about fifty dollars), and the piano was mine.

CHAPTER TWENTY

A WELCOME SURPRISE

WHEN I RETURNED from Cairo, I found an official-looking memo in my mail box. My US shipment had cleared Customs. Better yet, delivery was scheduled for December 27—two days hence.

Now that my reunion with my possessions was imminent, I had to admit that the delay in the shipment's arrival had been a blessing, despite my recurrent jitters about its safety enroute. It might have arrived in Dammam—our nearest port—while I was still cooped up in my miniscule residence room. I would have had to move out—to a Bedouin tent or similar, as they say in the travel brochures. Meanwhile, my clothing, other personal effects, and household goods would have luxuriated in Aramco's best efforts at climate control.

On second thought, probably not. My shipment wouldn't have fitted into a residence room regardless of what I'd done to accommodate it. My theater-style wardrobe trunk, which was approximately the size of a walk-in closet, would have left no room for anything else.

Now, all I had to worry about was whether the shipment had been looted by persons unknown in places unknown for reasons unknown, as had happened to my recent shipment direct from Venezuela. Even as I packed that trunk, I doubted I'd ever see its contents again. I'd steeled myself for what I thought was the worst-case scenario, but my idea of "worst" fell well short of reality. My trunk arrived nearly empty, the lock broken, the hinges loose, anything of value gone, one shoe of a pair missing, and odd bits of torn clothing protruding from what was left of the carelessly closed container.

To my immense relief, I need not have worried about my shipment *this time*. I was one lucky Aramcon. Every week, the camp bulletin carried plaintive notices inquiring if anyone had received certain items—listed in detail—missing from someone else's shipment. At least all of my containers were accounted for and structurally intact, although Customs officials eager to plow through my goods and chattels had obviously opened each and every one of them.

Despite my eagerness to see which of my possessions had come through unscathed, I let the wardrobe trunk sit unopened for a couple of days. I was so terrified that my cold-weather clothes might have gone missing that I couldn't bring myself to look. It may have been 122° in August, but nighttime lows had fallen to near freezing in December, despite the now helpful heat from the gas flares. Without my warm clothes, I would be stuck watching "edited" sitcoms in the forced-air-heated comfort of my apartment every evening for the remainder of the cool season.

On the third day, practicality triumphed. That trunk was obstructing the path between my bed and the bathroom, a major inconvenience. I reminded myself that if any items were missing from my shipment, someone had probably filched them long before the trunk landed on my doorstep.

I turned the key in the lock and peeked under the lid. The trunk seemed full, although someone had obviously pawed through my underwear. I tossed items hit-or-miss onto my bed in my anxiety to see which of my possessions had successfully completed the trip.

When I saw my warm clothes at last, I heaved a mighty sigh of relief. All were present and in good condition.

I checked my shoes against the inventory I had so painstakingly compiled in the US. Apparently no one in Arabia could cram her feet into 9AAA shoes.

Then I had an even more disturbing thought. What about my cosmetics and hair-care products? If sticky fingers had made off with those in Customs or anywhere else, I'd be out of luck. I knew for certain I couldn't replace them anywhere in Arabia—and probably not in any nearby Arab state either.

While I was still assembling my shipment, I came in from a grueling day of searching for several elusive items still on my shopping list. A special-delivery letter from the New York Office of Aramco lay on the hall table. I opened it to find that it contained three single-spaced pages of products that couldn't be imported into Saudi Arabia legally because they were made by Jewish-owned firms. *Now* they were telling me!

With a sense of foreboding, I examined my recent purchases and unpacked those already in my trunks awaiting shipment. All of my two-year supply of cosmetics and hair-care products and the majority of the clothing items I'd chosen so carefully on the basis of their mix-and-match potential fell within the prohibited category.

After a sleepless night worrying how I was going to cope with this "surprise," I came up with a workable solution. Since I was still in the hunt for several essential items, I enlisted the help of my grandmother. Her task: remove the offending labels by any means necessary, including scraping them off cosmetics containers with a razor blade.

I'd packed my personal-care contraband in plastic icebox containers and sealed them with generous amounts of duct tape. I counted twenty-four containers, one for each month of my contract. So far, so good. The tape was undisturbed. Wrestling it off the packages must have been too much work for Customs. It almost was for me.

* * *

The timing of the shipment's arrival was opportune for another reason. Several crates contained kitchen equipment urgently needed for my soon-to-be-opened bakery business. I didn't really think anyone would have made off with a blender or an electric skillet on the high seas, but best to be sure. A borrowed crowbar in hand, I set to work liberating the crates' contents.

All the small appliances were present and apparently undamaged. I lined them up on the kitchen counter, plugged them in, and switched them on one by one. The reassuring whir of their motors was one of the sweetest sounds I've ever heard.

I set out for Al-Khobar the next Thursday to see which of my remaining bakery needs I could satisfy locally. I headed for the smithy I'd observed on my first trip to the *suq* and asked to see samples of kitchen utensils their shop had crafted.

The cookware's quality was amazing for hand-wrought work. All the lids fitted snugly; the pieces were well balanced; and baking pans were sturdy enough to resist warping. I gave the head smith an eighteen-inch ruler I'd "liberated" from school, the measurements for each piece, and crude drawings to show what the items should look like. Much to my relief, he agreed to deliver the finished merchandise to Abqaiq at no additional cost.

* * *

Since I planned to open the bakery and begin my stint as a piano teacher simultaneously on April 1, I scheduled a trip to Beirut over Id al-Fitr, which fell in March that year. The holiday would give me an extra day to find suitable music for my level-three piano students, complete my catering shopping, and sightsee in what my expat neighbors assured me was the Paris of the Levant.

My travel-agent friend booked me on Middle East Airlines (MEA) flights and made a reservation for me at the Normandie Hotel, which she recommended highly. After I stayed there, I always recommended it too, even though newer deluxe hotels were springing up in central Beirut every day. The high-rise newcomers just didn't have the panache of the Normandie, which had opened for business during the French Mandate.

CHAPTER TWENTY-ONE

LEBANON: PROGRESS, INTRIGUE AND DIVERSITY

BEIRUT WAS BEAUTIFUL during that brief and all-too-fragile interlude between the governmental collapse of 1958 and the bloody and destructive civil war—exacerbated by foreign intervention—that broke out in 1975. Superb hospitality was the unvarying hallmark of luxury hotels of all sizes. World-class restaurants lined the streets of the central area. Fascinating natural, cultural, and historical sites abounded throughout the city. For those who preferred manmade wonders, the Casino du Liban up the coast offered entertainment and meals of unfailing quality seven days a week. Visitors intent on lightening their wallets at the tables needed look no further.

Most of us—Lebanese and foreigners alike—took it for granted that this paradise of tolerance, prosperity, and gracious living would somehow escape the religious/ethnic/ideological tensions already besetting its neighbors. For the time being, the Lebanese model of successful diversity and welcome for immigrants regardless of their countries of origin did seem to be working. In addition to ethnic Lebanese, Beirut was home to a vibrant mix of French citizens who had stayed on after independence and an assortment of Palestinians,

Syrians, Iraqis, Kurds, Greeks, Assyrians, Cypriots, Armenians, and White Russians—the majority of them refugees or the offspring of refugees. Although the 1943 constitution declared Arabic the country's "official" language, French, the language of the former Mandatory Authority, was the *lingua franca* that made communication among all segments of the country's polyglot population possible.

A perceptive reading of history might have tempered Lebanese optimism about their country's long-term chances of steering clear of internal conflict and/or foreign interference. But, for the time being, the Lebanese gloried in the country's seventeen years of successful independence and wanted to believe it would never end. What they and those of us who wished them well failed to take into adequate consideration was the historical pattern of economic and geopolitical attraction of Lebanon for more powerful foes. That history was writ large in ancient and not-so-ancient stone.

For thousands of years, Lebanon had never been left to its own devices for long. The country's superabundance of archeological sites chronicled a millennia-long saga of peoples who defeated their predecessors and were in due course supplanted by others as the turbulent history of the Levant played itself out. Phoenicians, Egyptians, Seleucids, Romans, Byzantines, Muslims, Crusaders, Mamluks, Ottomans, and French had all left traces of their presence. When Lebanon separated from Syria in 1943, the country began its first recorded experience as an independent nation. In the 1960s, it was trying very hard to remain one.

From my base at the Normandie, I took early-morning walks along the Avenue des Français—the coastal promenade with its achingly beautiful mountain views and seascapes—before returning to the hotel for a delicious Levantine breakfast.

Since I expected to have more than enough time for shopping, I began my stay with a morning of sightseeing. I headed for St. George Cathedral (Greek Orthodox) in Parliament Square and St.-Georges Cathedral (Eastern-Rite Catholic) nearby. Two cathedrals dedicated to the same saint virtually across the street from one another would have been unusual anywhere else, but not in Beirut. The legend of

St. George's slaying of the dragon (thought to be an allegory of the triumph of Christianity over paganism) originated along the coast of Lebanon. St. George was a home-town hero.

* * *

After a stroll through the historical sector of central Beirut, I hurried back to the Normandie, where, according to my expat informants, the smoked salmon and baguettes, with or without a glass of beer, would make the whole trip worthwhile. On my way to the dining room, I stopped by the desk for help finding the items on my shopping list. Georges, the concierge, gave me a map with several locations circled and labeled.

While I was looking at the map to see if I had any questions, I overheard a snippet of conversation that meant nothing to me at the time. The man next to me at the counter had come for his mail, although I didn't hear him ask for it. Without audible prompting, Georges went to the vault and returned with a manila envelope about three inches thick. He handed the envelope to the man at the counter and said in English, "Here you are, Mr. Philby." "Mr. Philby" tipped him with what I managed to identify as British pounds and headed for the Normandie bar.

This transaction piqued my curiosity, but not for what later turned out to be the most significant reason. That day, I merely tried to imagine how a guest or Beirut resident who did not even need to give his name or indicate the purpose of his errand could have received so much mail unless he had been out of town for months. If so, why hadn't he asked Georges to forward his mail to him wherever he planned to be? If this man lived in Beirut but used the hotel as his permanent address, why had Georges addressed him in English rather than French?

I had also noticed that the envelope was closed with sealing wax. That meant it must have been full when it arrived at the hotel. Georges wouldn't have opened the envelope to insert newly delivered correspondence and then resealed it with wax over and over again.

Not until I was reconstructing the events of my first visit to Lebanon for this book did I realize the full significance of what I had witnessed in 1961. Kim Philby, the former high-ranking British-intelligence official and notorious double agent, had worked in Lebanon as a journalist since the mid-1950s. His real purpose in Beirut was to run a network of Soviet spies. (Philby himself defected to the Soviet Union in 1963, when Western intelligence agents were fast closing in on him.) Further research revealed that he used the Normandie as his mail drop. No wonder his mail arrived in a wax-sealed envelope, probably by courier. He must also have asked that the mail repose in the hotel vault until called for—surely an unusual request—although I suspect Beirut hotel staffs were used to just about anything.

Philby could hardly have been the only intelligence operative active in Beirut at the time. As the financial center of the Middle East, the city was a superb vantage point for monitoring significant events and policy shifts in Egypt, Syria, Iraq, Jordan, Israel, Turkey, and Lebanon itself. The numerous communities of refugees in Beirut must also have been prime sources of information about the politically tinged activities of their fellow émigrés, including plots to infiltrate anti-Communist spies into the Soviet Union.

Philby, it seems, received his agents' reports in the Normandie bar, a well-chosen venue to avoid curious ears' overhearing much of substance. Doubtless his informants spoke to him in French, so his use of English with hotel staff must have been part of his cover.

* * *

Over lunch, I decided to look for piano music first, because that was the only item on my list with which Georges had been unable to help. If I had to allocate additional time on another day for that purpose, at least I'd know that in advance. Out on the street, I asked a shopkeeper who sold phonograph records if he handled sheet music. He didn't, so I asked if he knew of anyone who did. He scratched his head for what seemed like an eternity. Then he said that a couple who owned a rug shop a couple of blocks down the street had two musically talented children. They should be able to tell me where they bought their music.

That was my only lead, so I continued down the street in the direction he indicated. Sure enough, I came upon a rug shop in approximately the right location and went in. I complimented the merchant on the high quality of his merchandise and said I would certainly keep his store in mind when I was ready to make a purchase. Then I shifted the conversation as smoothly as I could by saying that I had heard that his children had exceptional musical talent. Beaming with fatherly pride, he described the many prizes they'd won in young-pianist competitions.

"They must be very gifted. I'm wondering where you buy their music."

His wife spoke up. "That isn't easy to find in the central area. The luxury hotels and restaurants in this quarter cater mostly to the tourist trade, but I'll give you the address of a woman who sells used sheet music at bargain prices."

* * *

I asked the concierge at a nearby hotel for help finding the address. He confirmed my guess that it was in East Beirut (the traditional Christian quarter), circled its approximate location on my map, and warned me that it was much too far to walk.

CHAPTER TWENTY-TWO

NATALYA (1)

I ENGAGED THE FIRST taxi in the rank, showed the driver the address, and asked him to circle the nearest bus stop on my map in case I couldn't find a taxi to take me back to my hotel. My destination turned out to be a small house, rather than a shop. When the driver saw that, he offered to wait to see whether anyone was at home. If not, he would take me back to the central area. Grateful for his concern, I climbed the stairs from the street to the front door and rang the doorbell.

A slender, sprightly woman probably in her mid-eighties opened the door immediately. She had bright blue eyes, wavy white hair, and a delicate, rather pale, complexion. She introduced herself as Natalya.

I asked whether she preferred English or French. In perfect French, she said she knew only a few words of English. I told her my name and stated my business. Natalya confirmed that she did indeed have sheet music for sale, but first, we must have tea. She disappeared into the kitchen and returned with a steaming teapot on a tray with two cups and saucers, teaspoons, yellowed lace-edged napkins, a sugar bowl and a pitcher of milk. She set the tray down and made one last trip to the kitchen for some obviously homemade cakes and small salmon sandwiches. I assured her they were exactly what I needed to revive myself after an exhausting morning of shopping and sightseeing.

We made amiable small talk for several minutes. In my by now thoroughly mystifying role of guest rather than customer, I showered her tea cakes and sandwiches with compliments and asked where she had obtained such delicious pastries. Smiling with pleasure, she confessed that she had made them herself. She found the quality of the baked goods at the neighborhood *pâtisserie* unreliable.

The longer this tea party went on, the more perplexed I became. Natalya couldn't have known I was coming, and yet here she was, fully prepared to play a *grande dame* right out of Tolstoy. If I went along with her script, maybe I would eventually understand why someone who had sheet music to sell didn't seem to be in any hurry to close the deal. I praised her exquisite china and got my first clue what she really wanted to talk about.

The china was a vibrant shade of forest green with ornate gold edges and handles. As I had already guessed, she identified it as Limoges. Now I was more puzzled than ever. While Tolstoy might have used a tea set like that as a prop in one of his novels, one would hardly expect to see anything of the sort in a simply furnished house in a working-class district of Beirut.

As if she had read my mind, Natalya solved that mystery for me right away. She had bought the china a few years earlier from a White Russian couple who had finally secured visas to rejoin their son in North Dakota. They hadn't seen him since he left St. Petersburg following the Bolshevik Revolution, so they could hardly wait to be on their way. Natalya's eyes grew moist.

She was Russian, she said. Amid mounting signs of stress, she went on to relate the terrifying details of her escape with Vladimir, her husband, from Bolshevik-controlled territory. They had had an estate near Voronezh, but they were forced to leave almost everything behind except a few gold coins to finance their journey wherever fortune took them. At an exorbitant price, they traveled on a freight barge down the Don until they found temporary refuge behind a White Army unit still operating in the Crimea. However, they couldn't stay there for long. The Reds were pushing the Whites back relentlessly. The couple risked almost all the money they had left to pay for passage on a fishing boat to a Turkish port near the Russian border. With a bitter edge to her voice, Natalya commented that people with boats were taking atrocious advantage of refugees. They knew that people like them had no choice but to pay or suffer a worse fate.

The couple spent several reasonably happy years at Adana in southeastern Turkey. Vladimir found work as a warehouseman for a company that exported cotton clothing, but he developed a breathing problem in the late 1920s, probably from exposure to cotton dust in the warehouse. He couldn't find more suitable employment in Adana, so they came south to Beirut. He died in the mid-1930s. Since then, she had been alone.

"We were so happy here at first. The White Russian community was much larger then. We even met several families from Voronezh. We treated the sprinkling of Russian restaurants and cafés in East Beirut like clubhouses. On major holidays, restaurant and café owners decorated their places of business with the red and blue of the Old Russia, and we all joined in the singing of the traditional songs, including, at the end of the evening, *God Save the Tsar*. We compared notes about escaping from Bolshevik Russia and mourned the fate of friends and relatives who had not been so lucky."

"Do you still do that sometimes?"

"No. All that is finished now. The restaurants and cafés are long gone. So are most of the people. Vladimir and I were among the younger members of the émigré community. One by one, most of the refugees to whom we were close have passed on. The familiar liturgy at the neighborhood Orthodox Church was such a comfort when we first came. Over the years, though, I've attended so many funerals there—including my husband's—that just walking by that church now makes me cry."

"Have you any friends left in Beirut from the old days?"

"A very few still live here, but most have moved away. Some refugees of my generation like the couple who sold me their china were lucky enough to locate younger family members and rejoin them elsewhere."

Her answer provided a perfect lead-in for a question I'd hesitated to ask. Now, I was virtually certain she wanted to tell me the rest of her story, so I decided to take a chance. "Were any of your kin able to leave Russia before the Bolsheviks sealed the borders?"

Natalya wiped her eyes with a handkerchief embroidered with what looked like a family crest. She glanced briefly at a photo on a nearby shelf and then faced me again. "We had two sons. We knew what happened to Andrei, the older one. He was killed in 1914 during the rout of the Russian Army at the Battle of Tannenberg. That was three years before the Revolution, so the army notified the families of officers killed in action promptly. I just couldn't stop crying for months. I lit a candle for Andrei every day and prayed that the notice of his death was all a mistake. Vladimir tried to remain stoic about Andrei's death, but he would sometimes sit silently and look at his son's photograph for hours on end."

I wondered if I should even ask about the younger son, but failure to do so after hearing about Andrei almost seemed to imply that the fate of his younger brother was less important. "And your younger son? What was his name?"

"Yevgeny. We never found out what happened to him. That's almost worse than knowing that one of your sons is buried in an unmarked grave on a foreign battlefield. We last heard from him early in 1919 during the Russian Civil War. He was an officer in General Yudenich's army fighting the Reds in Estonia. For several years, we kept hoping he'd been able to escape into Poland or Finland after the White Army's defeat. That would explain why he hadn't contacted us; he couldn't have known where we were. I used to dream that Yevgeny was looking for us just as the two of us were looking for him. Sometimes we were very close to each other, but we just couldn't connect."

"It must be hard to quit searching for a loved one if you don't know what became of him."

"It is, but we finally had to give up. We traveled clear across Turkey to Istanbul to see if anyone in the émigré community there had any information about Yevgeny. We finally found one ex-soldier who had served in the Baltic States who remembered him, but he had no idea what became of him. On the way back to Adana, Vladimir said that we had to stop looking for Yevgeny; we were just making ourselves miserable without having anything positive to show for our efforts. We had looked for him for ten years, and we would have found him by then if he was to be found. It wasn't easy, but I concentrated on imagining that he was somewhere doing great things and leading a rewarding life. That comforted me somehow, even though I knew that story was just make-believe."

This had been a gripping tale, but it seemed in her best interest to move on before she broke down completely. In any case, I really needed to shift the conversation back to the sheet music she had for sale. I asked her if she could show me what she had in stock. With a sigh, she opened the piano bench and took out a thick stack of music, almost all of it classics, with titles and dynamic markings in Russian. The only pieces that would do for my level-three students were some relatively simple arrangements of Russian folk tunes, so I bought those.

The financial details taken care of, I took my leave. Natalya seemed reluctant to see me go. She urged me to call again the next time I was in Beirut. I did return to see her and buy music from her three more times, always with a bouquet of flowers in my hands. She obviously needed the money—and someone to talk to.

CHAPTER TWENTY-THREE

VISIT TO THE GOLD SUQ

SATURDAY WAS ANOTHER peerless day—deep blue skies and a deeper blue sea. Several Abqaiq expats had warned me that the winter rains sometimes lingered into March, but this time the weather gods must have misread their calendars. With any luck, they wouldn't discover their error until I was safely out of Lebanese air space.

After breakfast, I asked Georges for ideas for my last full day in Beirut. He asked if there was anything I especially wanted to see. If so, he could help with location and/or transportation. I reminded him that this was my first trip to Beirut, so I didn't know enough to have anything particular in mind.

"Have you done any shopping other than for your catering needs?"

"No, I've spent most of my free time visiting historical sites and admiring the city's magnificent setting."

"Do you know the tale of Ali Baba and the Forty Thieves?"

"Yes, but you've lost me. How did we get on that subject all the sudden?"

"I was going to suggest that you visit the gold *suq*, and I thought that intro might give you a hint about what you would see there."

"There's still a missing link somewhere, even though gold—and murder—figure into the Ali Baba story. The gold *suq* must sell gold, or it would be seriously misnamed, but surely you're not recommending that I risk life and limb just to see a bunch of trinkets I can ill afford?"

"Of course not. The gold *suq* is perfectly safe except for the occasional pickpocket, but I suspect you know how to defend yourself against those types. It's just that the objects for sale in the gold *suq* rival the loot in the thieves' cave in the Ali Baba story. Here, let me show you where it is on your map. Be on the alert, or you'll miss it entirely. The X marks a tobacco shop located a few steps from the gold *suq's* entrance. When you see that, you'll know you're almost there."

Who could resist a sales pitch like that? I did, however, take the warning about pickpockets seriously. I was carrying a large amount of cash and travelers' checks to settle my hotel bill. I told Georges that I had a few valuables to place in the hotel vault before I set out. He nodded his approval and handed me an envelope.

Upstairs in my room, I placed most of my remaining cash and all my travelers' checks in the envelope. I couldn't do the same with my passport. I had to carry that for identification in case the police stopped me for a random check, so I put it in the zippered inside pocket of my jacket and hoped for the best.

Back downstairs, I handed the envelope to Georges, who sealed it with glue—apparently wax was a Philby special—and we both signed across the flap. He walked to the vault, and I witnessed in writing that I had seen him place my valuables therein. Beirut apparently had its shady side despite its beauty, glamour, great hotels, opulent restaurants, and reputation among Aramco expats as R & R Central.

Following Georges's instructions, I found the entrance to the gold *suq* on my first pass. He wasn't joking about its dimensions. The passageway was so narrow I had to wiggle through it sideways. Nor did he exaggerate the dazzling effect of the sunlight on gold items of every description everywhere I looked. The merchandise may not have been quite as awe-inspiring as Ali Baba's legendary haul, but it came close.

I picked a shop at random and went in. The display cases were stuffed with jewelry to fit every taste and pocketbook. A sign advertised gold bars for sale. No thanks for the latter. I couldn't imagine carrying gold bars through the streets, even if I'd the money to pay for them, the muscles to heft their weight, and a Brink's truck to follow me.

Since I was doing a lot of looking but no buying, the proprietor, who introduced himself as Boghos, offered to help me find what I was looking for. I explained that this was my first trip to Beirut from Arabia. I was just familiarizing myself with the merchandise available, with an eye to making future purchases. To establish myself as a bona fide potential customer, I added that I was especially interested in earrings. He showed me two or three trays. The pieces were magnificent, but with most of my money in the Normandie vault, my unreliable will power didn't get much of a workout this time.

Boghos spoke excellent French, although I detected the faintest hint of a foreign accent—probably Armenian, since Boghos is an Armenian name. I didn't want to come right out and ask his ethnicity, because I didn't know how sensitive that question might be in Beirut, so I said I was looking for a church for Sunday Mass. Did he happen to know what language was used in the liturgy at Sts. Elie and Gregory (an Armenian Catholic church in the central area)? He replied that since his wife was more comfortable speaking Armenian, they attended a Mass in that language, but one of the other Masses might be in French. I should call the church to find out.

Boghos told me that local people bought gold for reasons I hadn't thought of. When the victors dismembered the Ottoman Empire after WWI, they created several perennially unstable successor states—including Syria, Palestine, Transjordan, and Iraq—without consulting the preferences of the populations destined to live in any of them. In fact, the "peacemakers" displayed a rare talent for assigning mutually antagonistic ethnic/tribal/religious groups to the same new countries.

Minorities who suddenly found themselves living as barely tolerated interlopers in countries not of their choosing had every reason to fear that they might be forced to flee again, as some had had to do as recently as during the involuntary exchange of populations between Turkey and Greece in 1922-24. Gold, the traditional reserve currency of the Middle East, was portable, freely convertible, and relatively stable in value. It provided a measure of security in an insecure world. Georges was right; the trip to the gold *suq* had taught me a lot, even thought I hadn't bought anything this time.

* * *

The next morning, after a brief farewell walk along the Corniche and a dependably delicious Normandie breakfast, I stopped by the concierge desk to see whether Georges had or could find out the Mass schedule at St.-Louis des Capuchins. With a name like that, the lessons and homily would surely be in French. (The rest would be in Latin anyway.) He made a quick call. The church had an appropriate Mass at 9:30.

I turned to go, but then I thought of another way Georges could help me. "Would you please reconfirm my 1:15 flight to Dhahran today on MEA?"

Georges dialed the number and talked briefly in Arabic with the person on the other end. He frowned. A bad sign? I gesticulated wildly to get his attention. Seeing my frantic gyrations at last, he covered the receiver and announced, "They can't find your reservation." I fished out my ticket and pointed to the ticket number. Maybe that would help.

Georges spoke into the receiver again. His tone was insistent. He wasn't taking no for an answer. Finally he turned to me and laughed. "You'll never believe this. They had your reservation filed under "N" for Nancy. Everything is in order now."

CHAPTER TWENTY-FOUR

BACK IN BUSINESS

THE HOUSEBOY FINALISTS arrived promptly for their interviews. I had turned down Leila's offer to serve as interpreter. She would not be around all the time after I hired one of them, so I needed to assess each candidate's communication potential before making my selection.

All three applicants really wanted—and needed—the job. Without exception, they were clean, neatly groomed, and bright-eyed. Leila had interviewed them in Arabic and had checked references from previous employers. I was momentarily sorry I wasn't in a position to hire all three. None had any baking experience, but that wouldn't matter. I planned to do all the cooking myself. I could teach the one I hired selected culinary skills, if necessary.

Two applicants were Saudis and the other, Kenyan. I'm not sure what the Kenyan's primary language was, but I don't think it was Arabic. The trio's English was limited, although they did understand most words associated with everyday household tasks. Whomever I picked, we would manage somehow.

In the end, I hired Jomo, the Kenyan. He had served briefly in a colonial unit of the British Army during the suppression of the Mau Mau insurgency in the early 1950s, so his English was slightly better than that of the Saudi applicants. He also had a longer history of successful houseboy employment. Once he was on the job, Jomo put a lot of effort into improving his English and learning kitchen skills for his next job hunt. Meanwhile, we made do with mangled Arabic.

* * *

The bakery business began operation on schedule and grew steadily without my doing anything to promote it, much as Leila had predicted. The best selling items were doughnuts, bread, and cakes for children's birthday parties. My customers included both married and single employees—no surprise, given the lack of competition—but another byproduct of my business venture was. Operating a bakery turned out to be my best strategy yet to meet a broad range of camp residents. Odd. My direct efforts to achieve that goal had fallen flat. Now that I was offering a much-needed service to the community, my circle of acquaintances was expanding rapidly. There had to be a message in that.

Within a few weeks, requests from family-housing customers for me to expand my services to catered dinners were pouring in. With some reluctance, I agreed to accept bookings for weekend nights. My chief reservation about branching out in that direction was that unless I could find dependable sources of fresh produce and other ingredients only sporadically available in the commissary, my best efforts would look—and taste—suspiciously like dining-hall food.

Then I thought of Mohammed, the gardener assigned the unenviable task of keeping the sparse vegetation in our neighborhood alive. He lived in Al-Hasa Oasis and commuted to Abqaiq by company shuttle bus. Early on, he told me he could buy fresh vegetables, dates, and eggs at the Hofuf *suq* and deliver them to me each week when he reported for his yard-maintenance duties. Mohammed's offer was a godsend, although I wasn't so sure about the eggs. Local eggs had a shaky reputation because of occasional salmonella contamination.

Al-Hasa vegetables were huge and flavorful, regardless of variety—like color photos in gourmet-cooking magazines. With more than three hundred sixty days of sunshine per year and plentiful water for irrigation, those vegetables lived a life of luxury in a vegetal Eden. They had nothing to do but grow and develop prize-winning flavor.

The first consignment of produce Mohammed delivered to my door included two splendid-looking eggplants, a bunch of gigantic but sweet and tender carrots, and a cauliflower the size of a dishpan. I had a liberal serving of the last every day for a week, and shared some with Edna next door, but I still had to discard a portion of it when it succumbed to mold.

A visibly nervous Mohammed handed me a closed bag. Inside the bag were a dozen eggs small enough to have been plucked from distraught pigeons' nests—but where? I'd never seen pigeons in or about our camp, or many birds of any description for that matter.

Birds were more common in the great oases, where they could find plenty to eat and trees to roost in. Abqaiq, on the other hand, was not a place where anyone was likely to awaken to the cheerful chirping of our feathered friends. No self-respecting bird would have chosen our camp for anything but an emergency stop. Even then, it would have had to consider whether its predicament was serious enough to risk perching on an oleander bush—not a suitable place for an avian snack.

By this time, Mohammed was standing first on one foot and then the other. Frantically, I consulted my Arabic dictionary and inquired, "*Jaaj* (chicken)?"

"*Na'am.*" His expression of relief exceeded mine.

Well, I'd have to measure those eggs for recipes rather than count them in the shell, but I could do that. The possible health consequences of using them were another matter; no one in the food-preparation business would dare risk making anyone sick by using questionable ingredients. Those "pigeon eggs" should be safe enough in pies and cakes, though. Both log lengthy time in the oven. Nonetheless, I felt duty-bound to verify this assumption by using myself as an experimental subject.

Feeling exactly like the taster for some profoundly unpopular monarch, I hardboiled an egg for lunch. One bite—and the absence of unfortunate health problems the next day or two—convinced me of the advantages of "buying local." Those eggs were fresh from the nest, in stark contrast to those available in the commissary. I had recurrent nightmares about the latter. What if I cracked a well-traveled commissary egg open one day, and a fully formed chick hopped out?

CHAPTER TWENTY-FIVE

PRODUCT-LINE EXPANSION

THE DINNER TRADE led me in a direction I'd never planned to go, or even considered. My customers favored showy menus. When they entertained two or three dozen guests, most hostesses envisioned a buffet table laden with faithful copies of menu items served at top-tier Beirut eateries. I wasn't yet fully conversant with the unique features of de luxe Beirut cuisine, so I asked for descriptions of clients' preferred dishes. With the help of my trusty *Larousse Gastronomique*, I could usually field reasonable approximations of their favorites.

My customers were especially enamored of flaming entrées and desserts, which were very popular during the fifties and sixties. I always reminded those requesting such concoctions that a liquid suitable to flame the food was absolutely essential, and that I had nothing to use for that purpose. Such naïveté reduced most of the ladies to stunned silence, but not one of my most outspoken customers. "How ridiculous can you get?" she exclaimed, eying me for early-stage mental illness. "Just use hooch!" So that's how I, one of the few unreconstructed teetotalers in camp, backed reluctantly into the unlikely business of operating a still.

* * *

My neighbors told me how and where to obtain the necessary equipment. Ray, they said, was the best still maker in camp; I contacted him to discuss my needs and solicit his suggestions about how best to satisfy them. He recommended a forty-gallon electric still made from what looked like a large steel milk can with a copper-tubing superstructure. He also brought along a copy of *The Blue Flame*, which he left with me.

This mimeographed pamphlet (of unknown, but probably local, authorship) was an owner's authoritative guide to safe still operation. It even outlined the procedure to follow in case of a still fire—*i.e.*, call a special number (provided) immediately. Two expat employees in fire-retardant suits would arrive posthaste to remove the "evidence." Then, and only then, was it safe to call the Arab fire department in an attempt to salvage anything not already reduced to smoke and ashes.

Safety was a non-negotiable requirement as far as I was concerned, so I pored over the contents of the *Blue Flame* until I could recite its admonitions like the catechism. That exceedingly useful pamphlet did not, however, tell me all I needed to know about the practicalities of making drinkable alcohol. For example, what was the standard Abqaiq "recipe" for mash? How should I store the raw mash during fermentation? How long did the fermentation cycle take? How much mash would I need for a full run? How many gallons of distillate at what proof would a fourth run—the gold standard for home-based distillation in Arabia—yield? I would need sufficient containers of appropriate size to receive the output.

My experienced neighbors cheerfully assumed responsibility for guiding me through the intricacies of do-it-yourself hooch production. Empty acid jugs from the refinery were the preferred containers for fermenting mash. Upon request, these arrived cleansed of any residual acid and encircled with strips of duct tape to guard against a showering of glass shards in case of breakage. The usual fermentation cycle was twenty-one days. Ray would place a mark on the still to show the maximum load permissible. A fourth run would produce about ten gallons of approximately 176-proof alcohol, which could then be cut with distilled water to the desired potency.

* * *

Refined sugar was the invariable basis for mash in the oil camps. Regular purchases of large quantities of grain would have attracted unwanted attention, since they could only have been obtained in the *suqs*. Sugar offered two other advantages. It yielded the highest concentration of alcohol from a given quantity of mash—important because of our limited storage space. Sugar mash also left very little residue to scrub out of the pot before the next run, a deal maker for me. The other ingredients of mash were water, brewer's yeast, and raisins. I was initially puzzled by the last. Then I drew upon my childhood memories of making bread on Indian reservations far from any commercial bakeries. Yeast works most efficiently in mildly acidic environments, which the raisins provided.

Compared with stills pictured on the Internet today, our pot stills were quite primitive. Their chief advantage was ease of use by the untutored like me. On the other hand, they had one major disadvantage, at least for those who had run out of hooch and were desperate for a quick fix. "First run," the only choice for time-pressed thirsty souls, came off our pot stills with a maximum alcoholic content of about 60%. Guess what the other 40% was. Yep, liquid mash. No one with intact taste buds would touch hooch containing 40% raw mash unless they were truly desperate. A perennial inside joke about first run invariably elicited roars of laughter from the old guard, regardless of how many times they'd heard it. The story went like this:

Sam retired to the US after many years in Arabia. Since Arabia was not exactly a consumer paradise in the early days, he had accumulated a sizable nest egg, some of which he used to buy a large dairy farm. Bill, another retired Aramcon, dropped by for a visit. Bursting with pride in his recent investment, Sam took Bill to view the farm's thoroughly modern barn. After demonstrating his milking prowess, Sam set the bucket in front of the cow he had just milked, and the cow proceeded to drink the contents. Bill was dumbfounded. "Sam," he blurted out in his best Saudi slang, "I know you have *wadjit flus* (a lot of money), but the idea is to sell the milk, not to use it for cattle feed."

Sam shook his head in astonishment. "Man, don't you know first run'll kill you?"

*   *   *

After the umpteenth hearing of this quintessential bit of oil-camp humor, I realized that I had found the marketing niche to differentiate my output from like products in a community in which still operation was a cottage industry, and I do mean in virtually every cottage—and *barasti*. I would sell only fourth run, the oil-camp premium grade. In the interest of consumer safety, I would cut it with distilled water to a non-lethal 90 proof.

Fourth run was virtually tasteless, so it would also lend itself to the addition of several kinds of flavorings to simulate commercially produced alcoholic beverages. Limiting production to fourth run would require longer run times, during which I would have to remain at home for safety reasons, but that wouldn't be a problem. I would be busy cooking anyway. With a timer set for critical points in the distillation process, I could check the still as needed.

Flavorful liquors would also allow me to achieve the purpose that had gotten me into still operation in the first place: flaming menu items for the dinner trade. After all, the purpose of flaming entrées and desserts is to infuse dishes with flavor, not to keep the food warm. There are less complicated ways to do the latter. I turned my thoughts to suitable flavorings I could obtain locally or on my next shopping expedition to Beirut.

To get a sense of the preferences of potential customers for flavored hooch for use in cocktails, neat, or on the rocks, I did an informal marketing survey. Vodka, gin, bourbon, and scotch all had their fans. Vodka would be easy enough to supply; that was essentially what came off the still at the end of the fourth run. My *Larousse Gastromique* clued me about juniper berries, the conventional flavoring for gin. That left bourbon and scotch for me to figure out for myself.

The husband of one of my catering customers stepped forward with an ingenious suggestion for making reasonably convincing "bourbon." First, chop hickory clothespins into pieces similar in size and shape to those used to smoke barbecued meat. Next, roast the wood chips in a slow oven until they turn a dark golden brown. Then, place the roasted chips in a mash jug full of fourth run for several weeks. The result satisfied most bourbon aficionados. They had no alternative source for their favorite tipple anyway.

Approximating the flavor of scotch proved more challenging. A wag suggested that I import charred oak casks from Scotland. I passed on that on the grounds of expense, awkward questions in Customs, and the time required for the casks to arrive by ship. In the end, it took me a couple of months, but I finally came up with a solution. Why not make a strong batch of lapsang souchong tea, which is cured by smoking black tea leaves over pine fires to produce the tea's distinctive smoky flavor and scent? I could then mix enough of the tea into a jug of fourth run to come as close as possible to the color and taste of genuine scotch. This seemed to satisfy hard-core "scotch" customers, but vodka, gin, and "bourbon" remained my best sellers.

Making drinkable cordials that could do double duty as flaming media was a cinch compared with making believable liquor for mixed drinks. Enough people in camp had pioneered production of the former that I had only to follow their user-tested recipes. The first step in making cordials was to sweeten fourth run with bar syrup (three parts sugar and one part water) and then infuse the sweetened hooch with flavorings in concentrations that would yield the most pleasing and readily identifiable tastes and aromas. For example, instant coffee powder produced a cordial that could pass for crème de café or Tía María. Added almond extract made for an acceptable amaretto. An orange in a cheesecloth bag suspended above hooch in a closed container drew enough peel oils out to turn sweetened "vodka" into a Cointreau-like potion.

*   *   *

Since I would need attractive containers for market-ready beverages, I walked out to the *suq* in search of a starter set of suitable glassware. Almost at once, my eyes lit upon a display of hand-blown bottles with a faint bluish cast at one of the stalls. They looked so classy that

I wondered momentarily if I could get away with charging a bottle deposit. On second thought, that would be more trouble than it was worth. Better to add the cost of the container to the asking price for the hooch. The vendor assured me that the bottles would be at my apartment at 4:00 the next day, when I could be home to receive the delivery.

Sure enough, at 3:59 the next day, the merchant's truck was pulling up. Over the time I lived in Arabia and did business with *suq* merchants, I learned that Arab businessmen were exceptionally reliable. If they said they would do something in a certain way by a certain time, they kept their word—no written contract necessary.

Saudi Ceremonial Serving Tray, Brass

Before long, my hooch clientele expanded to members of the singles set whose liquid inventory had failed to keep pace with the demands placed on it. A poker game reputed to have operated around the clock since 1947 became a fertile field for business expansion. Regulars raced to the poker premises immediately after the ends of their shifts to claim their seats at the table, so calls for sustenance and/or liquid refreshment peaked just after 8:00 am, 4:00 pm, and midnight. With a stack of pizzas always at the ready in my freezer, I could toss one or more into the oven and deliver orders within thirty minutes.

My bakery department even broke into the institutional market when Andy hired me to cater the spring open house, scheduled for the third week in June. I was thrilled—but also nervous—to have a chance to display my work to a broader clientele. The possibility of being hailed as the toast of the town on the basis of my cakes, cookies, and French pastries was exciting. The thought of botching a job like that in full view of the camp's most influential residents was terrifying.

I checked and rechecked my ingredients inventory. To my dismay, the larder wasn't exactly bare, but close to it.

CHAPTER TWENTY-SIX

THEFT PREVENTION

THE ISLAMIC CALENDAR came to my rescue. The *Id al Adha* holiday was only two weeks away. I made a reservation at the Normandie for May 17-21 and booked my flights.

Most of the items on my shopping list were routine, so I knew exactly where to find them. The one exception, a hydrometer, was a piece of equipment I'd previously resisted buying, but some of my best customers convinced me that I was courting disaster without one. Should Jomo be caught with hooch traceable to me—and that could happen, although I didn't think it particularly likely—the company would fire me and place me on the next aircraft leaving Dhahran.

"Don't press your luck too far," they warned. "Some houseboys aren't above siphoning hooch out of storage vessels and refilling the containers with water to mask their theft. A hydrometer would be a major deterrent to that sort of thievery if Jomo saw that you tested the water content of your inventory *regularly*."

Much as I regretted the necessity for that rigmarole, I could see their point. Better safe than sorry. Jomo seemed trustworthy enough, but the stakes were too high to take a chance. As far as I knew, nothing of consequence had been missing from the apartment since I'd hired him, but one curious incident early in his employment might have been a trial run. Scarier still, I might have missed a tell-tale sign of theft in the making entirely if my neighbors hadn't filled me in about pilfering, Arabian style. They explained that if a servant planned to steal something, he moved the article to a location where it obviously didn't belong and waited to see whether his employer noticed. If not, the loot disappeared after a couple of weeks.

The only thing I'd known Jomo to swipe was an occasional cookie. He was addicted to sweets, so I allowed him a certain latitude to satisfy his craving.

Then one day, I went to the linen closet for some towels. Nothing seemed amiss at first, but then I noticed a stack of sheets leaning precariously to the left. I investigated and found my flute—still in its case—wedged against the right-hand wall.

"Jomo," I called, "come here at once." What looked suspiciously like an apprehensive expression clouded his face. "Do you know how my flute ended up in the linen closet?"

"Oh, memsahib, so sorry. I forgot I put it there. I was cleaning up sand after the last *shamal*. I didn't want it to get into the instrument, so I thought the flute would be safer in the cupboard. Here, let me put it back where it belongs."

"Great catch," I thought. Of course, he might have been completely innocent, but I wasn't entirely convinced. I wondered if he'd had his alibi ready in advance. Jomo was quick-witted, and he'd worked in expat houses for several years. He would know when and how to cut his losses. He would also know that if I blackballed him for theft, his chances of getting another job anywhere near Abqaiq would be subzero.

So here I was in Beirut in search of a hydrometer. I had no idea who sold them, so I dropped by the concierge desk to see if Georges could point me in the right direction. He assured me that I need give the matter no further thought. He would have the apparatus delivered to the hotel by noon the next day and charged to my hotel bill. I suppressed the urge to ask whether it would come in a plain brown wrapper. I couldn't think of any way to translate that expression into French without losing some of its juicier connotations.

CHAPTER TWENTY-SEVEN
SIDETRIP TO DAMASCUS

LATER THAT DAY, Georges beckoned to me as I was on my way to tea in the Normandie lounge. "Since you seem to have finished your shopping, do you have any plans for Saturday?"

"Not yet. What do you suggest?"

"How about a full-day excursion to Damascus, with a brief stop at Baalbek? The ruins would be at their most awe-inspiring in the early-morning light."

"Georges, I don't have a Syrian visa, and there's no way to get one before Saturday."

"You can buy a visa at the border."

"Tell me. If I 'buy' a visa, will it be real or fake? An indeterminate jail term in a Damascus prison would ruin my holiday."

"It will be real. The collapse of Nasser's pipe dream of a United Arab Republic—to which Syria signed on as a founding, if junior, member—hasn't done the Syrian economy any favors. The country is desperate for hard currency, so the welcome mat is out for Western tourists."

"Well, if you're sure about the visa..."

"Trust me. Have I steered you in any questionable directions yet?"

"No, but how am I going to get to Damascus and back? I draw the line at traveling by camel or any other member of the animal kingdom."

"Leave the details to me. A French-speaking driver-guide will pick you up at 7:00. I will arrange for two box breakfasts for you to take with you."

The next morning, my driver, Jean-Paul—a retired high-school-history teacher—awaited me in the lobby. We set off at once in an immaculate black Citroën. An hour later, we were eating our breakfasts amidst the ruins of Baalbek's magnificent temple complex. Georges was right; the early-morning light enhanced the beauty of what would have been an impressive sight at any hour under any weather conditions.

Jean-Paul explained that recent architectural evidence suggested that Baalbek's prominence as a Phoenician/Canaanite religious shrine dated to about 6000 BC, if not earlier.

"Are you sure about that date? These temples look like Greco-Roman architecture to me. The Roman Empire didn't come into existence for more than five thousand years after that."

"You're right about the architectural style. The Romans conquered this area in 64 BC and almost immediately went on a building binge. Most of the surviving Baalbek temples date to the period between the reigns of Augustus Caesar and Septimius Severus (31 BC to 211 AD)."

"Baalbek seems like an out-of-the-way location for a religious complex of this size and importance. Why here, rather than in some more densely populated region?"

"The defeat of the Phoenicians near Baalbek was a major strategic victory for the Romans. Control of Egyptian-Mesopotamian trade routes promised significant economic *and* military benefits, provided the defeated didn't rebel as soon as the Roman legions turned their backs. To make that less likely, the Romans launched an intensive public-relations campaign to sell their new subjects on the advantages of coming within the Roman orbit.

"In polytheistic cultures, there was always room for additional gods, especially if a people had just suffered a major military defeat or other catastrophe. In the ancient world, losers in battle regularly attributed their misfortunes to the powerlessness or, worse still, capriciousness, of their gods. Switching to (or adding) more reliable deities to their pantheon was an appealing option in such situations."

Sun, Sand and Single

"Do we know how the Romans chose the gods to honor at Baalbek?"

"Not directly, but most of them are easy guesses. The Romans dedicated the first temple they built here to Jupiter, their supreme god and father of all their other gods. Jupiter was a one-for-one replacement for Ba'al, who played the same role in Phoenician mythology. Venus and Bacchus were the Roman protectors of female and male fertility, respectively—functions critical to ethnic survival in the violence-plagued ancient world.

"Mercury was the messenger of the Roman gods. Building a temple to him at Baalbek may have been a left-handed attempt to court support among the local population by merging his identity with that of the legendary Phoenician hero Cadmus. Cadmus was the traditional bearer of the alphabet—a Phoenician innovation—to Greece, whence it was disseminated throughout the known world."

* * *

Back on the road through the foothills of the Anti-Lebanon, we were soon at the Syrian border. As Georges had predicted, the guards were happy to sell me a visa. A quarter of an hour later, we entered the outskirts of the Syrian capital. Jean-Paul gave me a quick course in Damascus history as we drove through the city's suburbs.

The self-renewing supply of water from the nearby Barada River must have seemed like a miracle to the desert tribes who founded the first Damascus settlement more than 11,000 years ago—soon after the end of the last Ice Age. Those first Damascenes must have been eyewitnesses to and participants in one of the most dramatic transformations of Middle Eastern life ever: the transition from a pastoral to an agrarian economy.

For innumerable generations before they settled down in the Barada Valley, the pioneering Damascenes' ancestors had pastured animals when and where they could, while fighting off attacks by tribes covetous of oases they controlled. The erstwhile nomads must have been delighted to exchange their hardscrabble desert lifestyle for the collaborative environment and more reliable food and water supplies of village life. As an additional benefit, they soon discovered they could trade their surplus agricultural commodities for items they couldn't produce themselves—a process that eventually transformed Damascus into a major commercial hub. The city was already well enough known to rate a mention in *Genesis 14:15*.

> *He [Abraham] and his retainers deployed against them under cover of darkness, defeated them and pursued them as far as Hobah, north of Damascus.*

The Damascenes' nomadic ancestors must have been skilled in the arts of desert war, or they wouldn't have survived for long. Lacking that martial experience, their farmer descendents employed a different strategy to protect their stored harvest and trading activities. They built a city wall. They also developed a mindset that classified outsiders as dangerous and unreliable, an attitude that led them to insist on uniformity of culture and ethnicity within the Damascus settlement.

"Were their walls an effective method of defense?"

"Yes, as long as the raiders were smalltime desert marauders like the Damascenes' ancestors. Since Damascus was situated in the midst of a vast desert that offered few natural barriers to attack, walls made up for what geography failed to do for the city—for a while, anyway.

"But, as the Damascenes were to learn by the 4th century BC, they could be a double-edged sword for cities dependent on wide-area trade for their living. Blockaded within the walls they relied on to protect them, they had no alternative but to surrender to the armies of Alexander the Great, Pompey, and the Islamic invaders of the seventh century AD, which had the manpower and other resources to surround a city, camp outside the walls for an indeterminate period of time, and let no one in or out.

"Alexander the Great's army looted Damascus and left; their brief stay had minimal impact on the culture or lifestyles of ordinary Damascenes. Empire builders like the Romans and the Islamic conquerors were different. They considered a long-term stream of income from Damascene commerce more valuable than a one-time windfall of plunder. To achieve their economic goal, they needed local cooperation.

"Since the Romans and the Islamic conquerors stayed on in Damascus for centuries, they had to overcome the Damascenes' ingrained bias against foreigners in their midst. Both were successful in accomplishing this by redefining uniformity in terms of commonality of economic and security interests. The Romans and the Islamic governors kept taxation at manageable levels, provided effective protection for goods caravans, and improved the city's infrastructure. The Romans even sold citizenship to those able to pay for it."

* * *

"Jean-Paul, I understand all that, but contemporary Damascus still looks remarkably homogeneous to me. Why didn't its various conquerors leave more obvious traces of their presence here, as happened in Lebanon? The French left Syria fewer than twenty years ago, but I haven't seen a single sign in that language so far. In Beirut, there would have been dozens, if not hundreds, by this time."

"You're right about the linguistic homogeneity of Damascus's modern population. Almost all the inhabitants of Damascus today are native speakers of Arabic. They don't need another language for informal or official communication. A *lingua franca* is a strategy for dealing with high levels of linguistic diversity, which play a negligible role in modern Syria.

"The linguistic picture is very different in Lebanon and has been for untold centuries. Lebanon today has a very high percentage of citizens and long-term residents who are not proficient in Arabic or who barely speak it at all, let alone read it. Ever since our independence in 1943, our *lingua franca*, French, has been absolutely essential for us Lebanese to work toward our goal of an inclusive national conversation.

"Even in ancient times, our ancestors had to look outward to the sea to make a living. The Lebanon and Anti-Lebanon Mountains made trade with inland areas difficult, expensive, and subject to frequent attack by bandits. The Lebanese coastal plain is fertile, but too limited in size to produce commercially profitable surpluses of agricultural commodities. What we did have, in addition to the famed cedars of Lebanon, was several ports suitable for seagoing vessels: Sidon, Tyre, Byblos, Tripoli, and (later) Beirut. Our forebears, the Phoenicians, went into the business of transporting and marketing other peoples' goods, while collecting commissions on every shipment.

"Lebanese commercial outposts once ringed the Mediterranean Basin, so our traders had to learn other languages, adapt to unfamiliar customs, and develop tolerance for other people's religions. Even in ancient times, our ancestors regarded cultural diversity and multilingual skills as assets; they were good for business. That tradition has lived on in our present policy of opening our doors to refugees and other immigrants."

"How exactly did the seventh-century Islamic invasion differ from previous conquests of Damascus? The Jihadists came from central Arabia, so they couldn't have been too far removed from their desert-raider roots."

"You're right about the cultural background of the Islamic invaders, but they had learned a thing or two since the days when their remote ancestors made a living by hijacking passing caravans. The Islamic victors must have studied Roman policies carefully; they showed every sign of realizing that dismantling the economies of conquered regions was not in their own best interest."

"Still, the Damascenes must have remembered tales of the indiscriminant looting and gratuitous violence their city suffered at the hands of the armies of Alexander the Great. Did they really believe that an Islamic conquest would be so different? I still don't understand why a local population known for its mistrust of outsiders offered only token resistance to the Jihadist assault."

"The Damascenes were heartily weary of constant attacks that threatened the viability of the city's commercial activities. The Islamic conquest promised to put an end to that game in Syria for centuries. The Jihadists weren't about to put up with amateur military escapades within or against their rapidly expanding empire. That stance alone was enough to ensure the support of Damascus traders."

"What post-defeat changes were less agreeable to the local population?"

"The religious composition of Damascus's population changed almost overnight, and a disproportionate loss of affluent families by emigration temporarily undermined the stability of the local economy."

"I've never given much thought to Syria's pre-Islamic religion. What was it?"

"At the time of the conquest, Damascus was over 85% Christian. Remember, the city already had a thriving, if persecuted, Christian community by the middle of the first century AD. After the Islamic conquest, the percentage of Christians dwindled rapidly. Christians today [1961] make up less than 10% of the Syrian population."

"Why were the Damascenes so willing to switch religions almost en masse?"

"Christians and adherents of other non-Islamic religions who refused to convert faced three possible consequences, none of them very appealing."

"What were they?"

"They could leave all their non-portable assets behind and emigrate, risk intensive religious persecution up to and including death, or pay the *jizya* (a special tax on non-Muslims) in gold. Emigration with the intent of settling beyond the borders of the expanding Islamic Empire required significant resources and/or established foreign connections—not a realistic option for the overwhelming majority of post-conquest Damascenes. For those who declined to convert but wished to remain in Damascus, the sole alternative was to pay the *jizya* year after year, but fewer still had sufficient annual revenues in gold to do that. Except for the well-off few, the prudent choice was conversion."

CHAPTER TWENTY-EIGHT
DAMASCUS CITY TOUR

DESPITE THE NUMEROUS tourist attractions in Damascus that dated to the city's golden age as the seat of the Ummayad Caliphate, tours for the relatively few Western visitors in the 1960s focused on locations associated with early Christian history. Since we had only about six hours of daylight for sightseeing, we followed a similar itinerary. Jean-Paul parked the car near *Bab Touma*, named for the Apostle Thomas, who lived in Damascus briefly before departing on his missionary journey to India.

"Where did most of the early Christians live?"

"Remember, the city was much smaller then. The Old City was about all there was to Damascus in the first century AD. The growing Christian community lived in the quarter we're walking through now. *Bab Touma* is behind us and the East Gate (*Bab Sharqi*) lies ahead. You'll remember that a man named Saul came to Damascus to persecute Christian converts. He reputedly stayed near *Bab Sharqi* during his pre-conversion visits."

"Oh yes. On the road into the city at the time of his conversion, Saul had some kind of seizure and lost his sight. The men with him led him into the city to a house located in 'the Street called Straight.' [Acts 9:11] Did such a street actually exist?"

"Yes. It still does, although with an Arabic name. *Via Recta* was its Latin name. Did you do Latin at school?"

"Yes, but that was a long time ago."

"I'm sure you've spotted 'Straight Street' as a literal translation."

"Yes. At least I remember that much."

"The Romans built *Via Recta* to provide an 'express route' to connect *Bab Sharqi* with *Bab al-Jabiya*, a Roman gate on the west side of the Old City that has not survived. Military convenience, rather than city planning, must have been the Romans' primary motive. *Via Recta* enabled them to move troops quickly to defend the city against threats from either the east or the west. Today, the Roman route still eases transport across the Old City for peaceful purposes, thanks to its superb construction and extraordinary width. The Romans designed *Via Recta* for two-way traffic down the center of the street, with pedestrian walkways flanking the roadway on either side. The modern street follows the two-thousand-year-old route; we'll see the tops of some of the columns that lined it in Roman times shortly."

"If we have time, I'd like to walk down that street."

"We'll make time. That way you'll see a number of other attractions that will give you a sense of the Old City's history."

We stopped briefly to examine *Bab Sharqui* more closely. I remarked to Jean-Paul that it reminded me of the Arch of Triumph of Septimius Severus in Rome and those at Orange and Arles in France, except that the Roman and French arches are freestanding.

"I've never seen any of those, but the architecture of *Bab Sharqui* confirms that military functionality was its designers' primary purpose. See how they embedded the arch in that very thick city wall. In peacetime, the arch was simply an entrance to Damascus that gave direct access to *Via Recta* and hence to the Old City as a whole. However, when an attack from the east was imminent, the narrowness and low ceiling of the arch made it easy to block. Attackers then had two choices. They could scale the walls and risk high casualties; fighting men attacking walled cities were especially vulnerable while climbing. Or they could use sappers to undermine the walls. That method was far from foolproof. Not only did the tell-tale sounds of digging sometimes alert defenders to an imminent attack, but sappers' tunnels were prone to collapse in Damascus's sandy soil."

Sun, Sand and Single

* * *

We turned left onto *Via Recta*. As we walked, Jean-Paul pointed out a number of people wearing new clothes in honor of *Id al-Adha*.

"Are they wearing new clothes because they're going to special religious observances?"

"I'm a Christian, so I'm no expert on customs associated with the *Id*, but I do know that another name for *Id al-Adha* is the Feast of the Sacrifice. I'm not sure about the rationale for it, but custom requires Muslims to dress in their best clothing on this occasion. That means new garments if their finances permit."

"What sacrifice does the *Id* commemorate?"

"According to the Koran, Allah ordered Abraham to sacrifice his son. Once Abraham showed his willingness to obey the divine command, even at such a shattering emotional cost, Allah intervened to halt the sacrifice."

"That sounds a lot like the Old Testament account of Abraham's journey up Mount Moriah to sacrifice his son Isaac." *[Genesis 22]*

"That's no coincidence. Islam, like Christianity, has roots in Judaism. Muslims accept many Hebrew prophets, including Abraham. The spiritual meanings of the sacrifice story in the Koran and the Hebrew Scriptures are similar, despite a few differences in the details.

"Remember, Abraham had two sons: Isaac, by his wife Sarah; and Ishmael, by Hagar, the Egyptian slave. According to the account in *Genesis*, Abraham loved both his sons. The Koran doesn't specify the name of the intended victim, but Muslims believe it was Ishmael, rather than Isaac."

"How else do Muslims commemorate Abraham's obedience to Allah's command?"

"Muslims participate in special prayers at the end of the *hadj* period that emphasize sharing and community building. In pastoral times, the affluent sacrificed unblemished first-born sheep or goats to share with the poor. That wouldn't be practical in today's predominantly urban environment, so the well-off simply buy meat and cook it. They divide the cooked meat into three portions: one for the family, another for friends and neighbors, and the third for the needy. If even that approach is impractical, they donate what they can to charities that serve the poor."

"Very interesting. Skipping ahead to New Testament times, does the house where Paul was staying when Ananias came to baptize him still exist?" *[Acts 9:10-19]*

"No, but tradition places it near that arch in front of us. As you can see, there's a mosque beside the arch today, but Damascus Christians insist that the mosque stands on the site of a first-century church honoring the baptism of Saul (who subsequently took the name of Paul). Just beyond the arch, near the site of the vanished *Bab al-Jabiya*, is the place where Syrian Christians believe local disciples lowered St. Paul over the wall in a basket to save him from a lynch mob. I must warn you, though, that the details of these traditions may or may not be reliable. Significant incidents sometimes become linked to specific locations with only the slightest justification, or none at all."

* * *

As we approached the *Bab al-Jabiya* site, *Via Recta* merged with *Suq al-Tawil* (the long market). Vendors of similar categories of merchandise were grouped together to resemble a combination supermarket and big-box store. For example, the staples of the Syrian diet were on sale just a few steps from one another. The day we visited, appetizing-looking grilled-eggplant sandwiches were available as take-out at one stall.

The *suq* was solution central in other ways. Your shoes showing serious wear? A shoemaker could remedy that in record time. Cloth to make new pillows for the living room? Textiles hand-woven by Bedouin women might be just the ticket. Piles of miscellany cluttering your home? Baskets in all shapes and sizes might bring that problem under control. For small but precious objects, perhaps one or more meticulously inlaid wooden boxes might meet your needs.

For upscale customers with special occasions in the offing, the silk textiles on display were irresistible. Despite my no-purchasing vow, I just had to have a length of red brocade interwoven with silver thread, which I subsequently made into a jacket for formal occasions. In time, the silver gave convincing evidence that it was genuine by tarnishing. I had to find a specialist to clean the jacket once I was back in the US.

When we exited the covered *suq*, we realized it was later than we'd thought. To save time, Jean-Paul suggested we make our way back to our car by taxi. That was fine with me. I still had to pack for my flight to Dhahran the next day.

CHAPTER TWENTY-NINE

THE CLIMATE'S REVENGE

SOON AFTER MY return, Andy's secretary called me to the phone for what she described as an urgent message. A clerk at the Passport Office greeted me with the unwelcome news that my passport would expire in a bare two weeks. My marching orders: report to the Abqaiq photographer at once to have the required photos taken. Then proceed immediately to the Consulate in Dhahran to begin the renewal process.

Terrific. The mother of all *shamals* was blowing, but I couldn't afford to be without a valid passport. I called a taxi and fought my way out to get into it. Visibility was about ten feet and dropping steadily.

At the photographer's studio, things went from bad to worse. When I was younger, my hair had some natural wave, but the near-zero humidity in Abqaiq regularly overwhelmed that genetic trait, especially during high winds. The resulting photographs showed a singularly unhappy subject with her hair—styled by gravity—hanging straight down in an incredibly unflattering bowl cut. I was stuck with that passport for the next five years, during which time I entered at least two dozen countries. Each time I cleared Immigration, suspicious officials stared at the passport photo in bewilderment and then at me and asked, "Is this you?" As long as they let me into their countries without a hassle, I considered their questions reassuring. I'd hate to think that I looked like *that* picture.

Once underway to Dhahran, I watched with mounting apprehension as the driver fought what looked like a losing battle to keep the taxi out of the ditch. The wind and the low visibility weren't the only problems. The early-summer heat had turned the paving materials into a quagmire. Oncoming vehicles were weaving into our lane regularly. One of them would surely hit us sooner or later. None of that happened, but I lost count of the near misses.

My business at the Consulate complete, a Dhahran taxi returned me uninjured to my Abqaiq apartment. As I was rinsing the remnants of sand out of my hair that evening, I replayed the events of the day in my mind. Outside, visibility had not improved, but my personal ordeal was over. I'd faced the worst an Arabian *shamal* had to offer and, although I couldn't say I'd prevailed, I'd at least survived. My relationship with Arabian weather had nowhere to go but up.

* * *

Nothing robbed me of that comforting illusion for nearly a year. Then April 14, 1962 dawned on the still unsuspecting Abqaiq public. At first, it seemed like an ordinary mid-April day—warm, but not yet suffocating.

Then, at about ten o'clock, each staff member received a memo from Andy in a sealed envelope. We all tore our envelopes open right away to see what time-sensitive emergency had occasioned this unusual administrative behavior.

According to the memo, the UN Food and Agriculture Organization (FAO) had been tracking a gigantic swarm of locusts since they left Eritrea. At their present rate and direction of travel, we could expect them to hit both Abqaiq and Dhahran about noon. Since this would be a once-in-a-lifetime experience for the children, Andy encouraged us to take our students out to the playground to watch the locusts' approach.

I told my class as much as I could about swarms of locusts. That didn't take long, since I knew virtually nothing about the subject. Then I took them outside to await the arrival of our six-legged visitors.

With any luck, the swarm would descend on us on time. I wasn't exactly enchanted by the possibility of a drastically curtailed lunch period.

I needn't have worried about locust punctuality. Airplanes should adhere to their schedules as conscientiously as those locusts did. Right before noon, there they came—millions strong—through the air and on foot. The book of Exodus was right; they blackened both the earth and the sky. *[Exodus 10:14-15]*

Later, as I walked home for lunch past groups of Arabs catching locusts in blankets, I crushed a couple hundred of them each time I put a foot on the ground. The popping noises reminded me of the sound produced by pouring milk on Rice Krispies.

The locusts wiped out the camp's pathetic bits of greenery in less than an hour. Abqaiq just wasn't a user-friendly destination for their species. A far better choice for them would have been to have made a sharp left turn when they reached the Red Sea shore and settle down in the Nile Delta. Still, they must have been smarter than I thought. They gave the temptingly green oleander bushes a wide berth.

Back at school after lunch, I asked my longer-serving colleagues why the Arabs were catching locusts in blankets. The science teacher seemed fully informed, although he admitted that this was the first swarm he'd ever witnessed in action. "The Arabs roast them. Like other arthropods (shrimp, crayfish, crabs, and lobsters, for example), locusts are a great source of protein. I've heard they make a tasty snack food, too, although I haven't had a chance to try any. Sometimes people grind them up and mix the locust meal with flour to boost the latter's nutritional content. If that doesn't appeal to you, beware of any grayish Arab bread you spot during the next month or so."

CHAPTER THIRTY

JOMO THE BUDDING TYCOON

BUSINESS SURGED AFTER the spring open house, but the boom was unlikely to last much longer. Employees with enough seniority to schedule home leave in July and August were departing in droves. I wondered why I wasn't feeling quite the pinch in the pocketbook I'd expected. Then I discovered that, unbeknownst to me, my baked goods were on sale in the general camp on a limited basis.

My houseboy was responsible for this unplanned business expansion. A couple of months earlier, Jomo had approached me with an odd request.

"Memsahib, I want cake Wednesday."

"What kind of cake?" I asked, wondering if we should be speaking Arabic so both of us would be at a similar level of linguistic disadvantage.

"Chocolate cake."

"Jomo, are you going to eat a whole cake? That might make you sick."

Bewildered at first, he suddenly grinned, and, evidently thinking he had figured out the reason for my hesitation, hastened to reassure me. "I paying."

That still made no sense, but I agreed to do as he asked. When he was ready to leave for the weekend, I handed him his pay envelope and his "order." He fumbled with the envelope and took out enough money to pay for the cake.

"*La, ya Jomo. Mo lazim flus.* (No, Jomo, no need for money)," I explained in my always defective Arabic. "*Tafaddal* (please)," I added, waving my hand toward the cake.

Despite my unwise flight into Arabic, Jomo had the good sense to stick with his English, of which he was inordinately proud. "No, memsahib, I paying." Thoroughly mystified as to why he thought it so important to pay for the cake, I took the money, if only to humor him.

Every Wednesday for five weeks, Jomo ordered at least one chocolate cake, always with the assurance, "I paying." Finally, my curiosity got the better of me.

I fixed a beady eye on him and inquired in my most forceful memsahib voice, "Jomo, what are you doing with these cakes? You're not getting fat."

He hesitated for a moment and then admitted, "I go up and down streets in labor camp, and I say, 'My memsahib make good cake. You buy one slice?'" His expression was enough to tell me he half expected me to fire him on the spot.

"*Fikra tayyiba* (good idea)," I assured him, hoping he wouldn't take that as a cue to switch to Arabic. "How much do you charge for a slice of cake?" From what he told me, he was making a tidy profit. His "franchise" was serving as an additional retail outlet for my business. I baked him his "Wednesday cake(s)" until I went on short leave in August and then resumed the practice after I returned. By that time, he was ordering two, or even three, cakes per week.

I tried periodically to persuade Jomo to vary his order, but chocolate cake seemed to have become legendary in the general camp. He even sprang for a taxi occasionally to transport his bulky "inventory" to his quarters. Through it all, Jomo always paid me the full "retail" price for his merchandise.

CHAPTER THIRTY-ONE

A WELCOME CHANGE OF SCENE

By early July, I was hankering for any break at all from Abqaiq's mid-summer heat. I was prepared to be flexible as to destination—as long as it promised to be dependably cool. I finally chose Austria, with a brief stop in Istanbul on the way back.

I had not been in Vienna since that memorable day in 1955, when the post-WW2 four-power occupation came to an end. The Viennese press screamed "*Neutral wie die Schweiz* (neutral as Switzerland)" in three-inch-high headlines. The gray cards of yore (once mandatory to transit the Soviet sector to occupied Vienna) had been consigned to the dustbins of history by four strokes of the pen. I was eager to see how the ever-resilient Viennese had adapted to life in the free world in the intervening six years.

Businesswise, August was the perfect time for me to take time off. My piano pupils were on summer vacation. The catering business was bound to be slack even with Jomo's energetic marketing in the general camp. Most of my best customers and closest friends had taken off for more temperate climes.

I requested short-leave for August 3-18, with an exit permit for the 2nd. My evening flight arrived in Cairo right on time. My travel agent had booked me on an SAS red-eye flight to Vienna due to leave within the hour. Like two other Vienna-bound passengers, I didn't need an Egyptian visa, because I was in transit.

The gods of the airways had other plans. Our flight was delayed until morning for unspecified reasons.

That didn't sound too bad at first. In those days, when only a few flights operated with jet aircraft, and mechanical problems were more frequent, a guesthouse on the airport property stood ready to take care of just such emergencies. However, Egyptian officials weren't disposed to be accommodating this time, probably because of the unsettled political conditions following the recent collapse of the Egyptian-sponsored United Arab Republic. The bottom line from a surly Immigration official: no visa, no exit from the terminal. He directed us to the bar, which, he assured us, would remain open all night.

The bit about the open bar seemed unlikely, but that, at least, turned out to be true. The barkeep's expression soured rapidly when he discovered that none of us drank alcoholic beverages. The poor guy had probably agreed to work an extra shift in anticipation of fat tips unlikely to be forthcoming. His expression brightened considerably when we surprised him with a generous *bakshish* when the PA system announced boarding for our flight the next morning, but by then he had suffered through a tipless night. Meanwhile, the four of us had endured ten hours of compulsory wakefulness.

I learned two things that night. Barstools are not suitable accommodation for snoozing, and if three total strangers plus a reluctant barkeep are corralled together overnight, it helps to have a common language and something of mutual interest to talk about. Whether we could manage to come up with either by dawn was problematic.

We were a linguistically ill-matched lot. One of our stranded threesome was Ethiopian; he was pretty much limited to his native Amharic, with occasional bits of English, French, and Arabic thrown in. In functional French, the other passenger identified himself as Maltese. His English promised to be almost comprehensible if I could manage to slow him down. When he tried Maltese with me, I detected a few isolated words that resembled the Arabic I had learned in my east-of-Suez classroom, but I couldn't make sense of them when I tried to string them together. By default, French seemed to be our most promising medium of communication, although that excluded the barkeep, who spoke only Arabic and the English he had learned in school during the British protectorate.

The last hardly mattered; the barkeep's participation in our hijinks was limited to bewildered observation. I was just happy that we three passengers had finally hit upon a way to stay awake and communicate semi-comprehensibly during time when we would otherwise have been catching some Z's.

Having stumbled upon a marginally workable means of expression, we struggled to come up with something—anything—to talk about. By sheer chance, we hit upon a most unlikely subject. The Maltese had studied acting, and he was passionate about Shakespeare. The Ethiopian also seemed familiar with Shakespeare's works, although apparently only in Amharic translation. I had read a number of the bard's plays at school, and that had not been so many years ago that I had forgotten absolutely everything I'd ever known about them.

Shakespeare got us through the night. When all else failed, the Maltese wannabe actor recited lengthy passages in heavily accented Elizabethan English, complete with gestures and pacing about the "stage." He was particularly enchanted by Macbeth and gave us a heartfelt rendition of the "sleep that knits up the raveled sleeve of care" speech. (He skipped over the part about the capacity of the innocent for sleep; maybe he thought we three were guilty as charged.) For my part, guilty or innocent, I thought all three of us would have been better off if sleep had swung into action with those knitting needles then and there. I quailed at the prospect of translating that passage into French for the benefit of the Maltese, let alone trying to get any meaning at all across to the Ethiopian, who was making an earnest effort to be a full-fledged member of our little troupe.

When the Maltese persisted in seeking my "expertise" about the exact meaning of certain passages, I told him that Shakespeare's metaphors didn't translate very well into French. Visibly disappointed but not really discouraged, he suggested that we do the witches' scene in Act IV that begins, "Round about the cauldron go; in the poisoned entrails throw." Relieved that he had moved on from the raveled sleeve of care to a translatable portion of Shakespeare's work, I complimented him on his choice. As an added advantage, that scene had three speaking parts, one for each of us. On second thought, though, I suggested that it would perhaps be best for him to assume responsibility for the "solo" parts of all three witches, since he did Shakespeare so meaningfully. The Ethiopian and I would join in with "Double, double, toil and trouble; fire burn and cauldron bubble" after each of the witches' speeches. The Maltese outdid himself, and the scene was a roaring success. I don't know what we'd have done without him.

On the plane the next morning, I managed to remain conscious just long enough to savor a superb Scandinavian breakfast before wrapping myself in a blanket and reclining my seat as far as it would go. I awoke when we began our final descent into Vienna, so I'm unable to comment on the flight itself, but I have every confidence that it was just about perfect.

CHAPTER THIRTY-TWO

MIRACLE ON THE BOSPHORUS

Customs clearance in Istanbul for passengers from the Vienna flight was anything but routine. It called to mind border crossings throughout much of Europe immediately after WW2, when black-market trading in weak currencies was a persistent problem. But in 1961, and in a country that had remained neutral throughout the conflict?

Had I misunderstood the Customs official's order? He insisted that I take out all the cash and cash substitutes—*i.e.*, traveler's checks—I was carrying and count them in his presence. Then he noted the amounts by currency on my visa page.

This puzzling ritual completed, I assumed I had hurdled the last obstacle between me and the arrivals hall. I was mistaken.

The official demanded to see any gold jewelry I had with me. I handed him a pair of studs and pointed to the hoop earrings I was wearing. He put out his hand for the earrings. Did he have a device nearby to melt them down as soon as he'd declared them property of the Turkish State? False alarm. He inspected my quite ordinary baubles with a loupe to confirm the percentage of gold in them and noted his findings below my currency declaration. When he finally dismissed me with a wave of his hand, I hightailed it through the door to the arrivals hall before he could change his mind.

* * *

First-time visitors to semi-legendary cities like Istanbul often have vivid memories of what they saw when they first arrived. Not me. Aside from the dreary interiors of the Customs area and the arrivals hall, all I saw that night was the glare of oncoming headlights.

My first glimpse of an Istanbul street scene from my hotel window the next morning more than made up for the missing sensory input the night before. Even after several return visits to Turkey, I still remember how much what I saw and heard that first time reminded me of Agatha Christie's mysteries with Middle Eastern settings. Teeming crowds spilled into the streets. Occasional donkey carts and more numerous motor vehicles wove their way around incautious pedestrians. Horns blared. Street vendors hawked their wares.

Ms. Christie herself would have had little difficulty recognizing the Istanbul of 1961, even though she had written her novels with splashes of Middle Eastern local color nearly thirty years before. Reminders of the city's storied past were everywhere. The Emperor Justinian left behind an expertly engineered, city-block-sized, underground cistern built to supplement the stingy water supply of a stubbornly arid climate. Later Byzantine Emperors and Crusaders dotted the old city with sturdily constructed churches and defensive installations that still stood as integral features of Istanbul's 1960s skyline. Expansion of the city after its fall to the Turks in 1453 added a hefty dose of decorative grandeur, thanks to the opulent tastes and ample resources of the Ottoman Sultanate. New mosques sprang up almost overnight to accommodate the religious needs of what soon became an overwhelmingly Muslim population.

One surprising exception to Turkish religious homogeneity lingered on into the 1960s at the *Grand Suq*: I encountered a few descendents of Jews expelled from Spain in 1492 among the vendors. They still spoke Ladino—an antique dialect of Spanish I could almost decipher—and told me harrowing tales of their ancestors' involuntary migrations until they at last found sanctuary in tolerant Istanbul.

Sun, Sand and Single

Hammered Copper Serving Vessel, Grand Suq, Istanbul

As a sometime resident of the Middle East during the interwar period, Ms. Christie would not have been surprised by the continuing lack of a bridge over the Bosphorus. The only link between the European and Asian sides of the city in 1961 was the same perilously overcrowded ferry that had chugged across the strait for decades.

On the other hand, several changes still in the planning stages when she first came to the city would have astounded Ms. Christie had she revisited Istanbul in the early 1960s. They certainly came as a shock to me.

Turkey had not just turned over a new leaf; it had rewritten the entire book. In no way did the Turkey of the 1960s resemble the exotic remnant of backward-looking, decadent Ottoman grandeur I had been led to expect. The so-called "Sick Man of Europe" of the nineteenth and early twentieth centuries I had read about in school had somehow made a miraculous recovery and appeared to be bursting with health.

Signs in the elevator and on the breakfast menu startled me as much as they would have Ms. Christie. They were all in the Latin alphabet, rather than Arabic script—a powerful indicator of Turkey's determination to become a user-friendly partner with as many nations as possible within the broader international community.

Out on the street, the use of the Latin alphabet on all signage and maps filled me with boundless gratitude. I wandered about the central city at will without having to worry whether I could find my way back to my hotel without the help of passersby with whom I shared no common language.

*   *   *

I signed up for a city tour, complete with a short cruise up the Bosphorus to the Black Sea. Our guide's flawless English came as a pleasant surprise.

On the cruise portion of the tour, the woman next to me was chatting nonstop with a couple across the aisle. I thought they were speaking Arabic—although not the Saudi dialect. I recognized occasional words, but most of what they were saying sounded like pure gibberish.

During a lull in their conversation, I smiled at my seatmate and asked "*Min wayn inti* (Where are you from)?"

"*Min Haifa* (from Haifa.) We are Israelis."

I gaped, I hoped only mentally. How had three persons who were almost certainly Jewish secured visas to enter a Middle Eastern country that was more than ninety-five percent Muslim? To get a Saudi visa, I had had to present a baptismal certificate—an odd entrance requirement for a country that banned any and all non-Muslim public worship. Only much later did I figure out that the certificate was an indirect method of ascertaining that I was *not* Jewish.

I asked what I thought was a safe question. "Where did you learn such perfect English?"

"I was born in Prague, but I spent the war years in England."

"Oh, was your father in the diplomatic service?"

"No. After the Munich Agreement and the German annexation of Austria, we were obviously next on Hitler's list. My parents managed to secure seats for my younger brother and me on a children's evacuation train. Within a few years, the Nazis would be killing every Jewish child they could lay hands on, but in 1938, they allowed trainloads of Jewish children to transit Germany to Vlissingen in Holland, where we boarded a ferry to England.

"No one in our family believed that any war could possibly go on for very long. The occupation of Austria had been complete within seventy-two hours. We were confident as we embraced our parents on the railway platform in Prague that we would all be together again within a few weeks. We were wrong. We were never to see our parents again."

I had dozens of questions about the children's evacuation program—who sponsored it; what qualified children to participate; how often the trains ran; from where; etc.—but I never got a chance to ask them. Just then the guide bore down on me and scolded me for inconveniencing the other tour participants, who were already on the bus, just waiting for me. (Gilda—the lady from Haifa—had apparently signed up for the cruise portion only, so he ignored her.) I apologized meekly, but the guide still marched behind me as if to restrain me if I attempted to bolt.

Gilda rushed up to lend me moral support. As we struggled to keep up a pace that would discourage the guide from running over us, she told me she came to Istanbul every year or two just for the shopping. "Have you been to the *suq* yet? Turkish jewelry is a tremendous bargain. The *suq* is a great place for rugs, too, but they're a nuisance to carry on the plane." At that, the guide seized me firmly by the arm and propelled me toward the bus.

* * *

Nothing my expat friends had told me had prepared me for the hundred-eighty-degree difference between adamantly modern Turkey and its ultraconservative neighbors. Not a single *abaya* or veil was in sight, even on elderly women. The cartoon-generated image of Turkish men in fezzes and baggy pants belonged to another age. Young boys and girls in neat school uniforms chatted amicably on their way to school.

The Middle East was definitely not as homogeneous as I had supposed. The difference between Turkey and Lebanon on one hand and Syria, Egypt, and Saudi Arabia on the other was startling. So what could account for this dissimilarity? Whatever it was, it didn't seem to be sectarian-religious affiliation. Both the Turks and the Saudis were overwhelmingly Sunnis, yet the Turks had embraced comprehensive modernization as a national goal, while the Saudis clung tenaciously to a lifestyle that had served their ancestors well, albeit more than a millennium ago. I asked our guide what he thought accounted for this difference.

"Turkey and Saudi Arabia have had very different historical experiences even in this century. Our great leader, Mustapha Kemal Ataturk, worked tirelessly until his death in 1938 to bring a modern, forward-looking Turkey into existence. He believed that unless we updated and reoriented the social, political, and economic structures of our country, we risked an even more catastrophic defeat in the future than the one we suffered in 1914-18. No one wanted to go through an experience like that again, so the Turkish public paid close attention to Ataturk's proposals for change.

"Saudi Arabia was neutral in WW1, so it was largely untouched by the peace treaties' consequences. Not having suffered through the bitterness of defeat and the difficult postwar adjustments that the Turks had to accept, today's Saudis see no reason to change their familiar lifestyle."

"You speak of Ataturk as the architect of the new Turkey. I learned in school that he abolished the veil, but that must have been a mere footnote to a much longer list of his innovations."

"Yes. Ataturk did much more than that. When he came to power in 1922, he managed to pull off two unimaginable political feats, given the cultural context of the Middle East of his time. He abolished the Caliphate and official Islamic organizations—thereby putting an end to religious interference in Turkish politics. While we Turks were still in a state of shock over the de facto secularization of our country, Ataturk stunned Turkish conservatives with another unprecedented bit of statecraft. He got rid of the Sultan—whom he considered to have been hand in glove with the Caliph. In so doing, he eliminated the two most powerful sources of opposition to the implementation of his modernization program."

"How did he persuade the Turkish citizenry to accept such radical changes? Disturbing long-established religious arrangements can be very risky political business."

"Ataturk had immense credibility with the Turkish public. He was one of our few successful generals in a losing war. Without his brilliant defense at Gallipoli, Istanbul—our capital then—might have fallen to the Allies. No one knew this better than his former army colleagues. They backed all his measures enthusiastically.

"It helped that Ataturk was much too clever to attack Islamic authorities and their opposite numbers in the Sultanate on religious grounds. His couched his objection to their influence solely in terms of their unfortunate habit of meddling in political and military decisions. The public and the army were left to read between the lines: if army leaders had been free to act as they thought best, the Empire might have staved off outright defeat."

"Ataturk must have had spectacular public-relations skills. How did he persuade the Turkish man in the street to go along with his political and religious arguments?"

"It helped that Ataturk was building a nation from scratch. The multinational Ottoman Empire that had spanned parts of three continents as recently as the late nineteenth century was finished. Everyone knew it wasn't coming back. Ataturk took full advantage of every opportunity to remind us Turks what defeat had cost us. But, he declared, all need not be lost permanently if we followed his plan for avoiding similar disasters in the future."

"What was the public response to that message?"

"Reaction was mixed. No one wanted another defeat, but most Turks still felt considerable nostalgia for the supposed glories of the vanished Empire. Ataturk used constant repetition to sell his message to the public at large."

"Which aspects of Ataturk's program aroused the greatest opposition?"

"Beyond a doubt, the emancipation of women. Turkish men found that a bitter pill to swallow. The old way allowed men to divorce their wives at will, but that is no longer permitted. Not only that, but Turkish women can now divorce their husbands, and their rights to equitable division of property and inheritance are enshrined in Turkish law. Ataturk also banned polygamy. While he was at it, he made civil marriage mandatory and thus subject to state regulation. Those were stupendous changes in a country still emotionally tethered to traditional ways."

"Did women receive equitable access to education? Without that, they couldn't have taken advantage of their new marriage rights. They would have had to stick with even the most abusive marriages for want of any way to support themselves as single persons."

"Yes, ever since Ataturk's modernization program, admission to Turkish universities has been gender-neutral. And Ataturk's educational-access reforms didn't stop there. Under the Empire, high fees denied most children and youth opportunities for even the most rudimentary schooling. Ataturk explained that limiting instruction to the economic elite in the past had contributed to the nation's loss of the 1914-18 war. The country just didn't have enough technologically trained workers to hold its own against more up-to-date adversaries. As long as that continued, Turkey would remain a backward country unable to compete in the modern world. To that end, he made primary education free and compulsory *for both boys and girls* and ordered comprehensive reform of secondary schools' and universities' curricula to stress science, mathematics, and foreign languages. My own sister benefited from these changes. She is a university graduate and a practicing pharmacist."

* * *

The highlight of my last full day in Istanbul was a visit to the fabled Hagia Sophia, the sixth-century Byzantine cathedral erected by order of the Emperor Justinian. American geography and world history textbooks in my youth often featured pictures of that very photogenic building, so I thought I knew what to expect. And I did, insofar as its exterior appearance was concerned, but the role assigned to the Hagia Sophia in Ataturk's Turkey was a major surprise.

After Constantinople (later Istanbul) fell to the Turks, the victors converted the erstwhile cathedral to a mosque. The Sultan's workers installed a gigantic crystal chandelier to replace the individual candles that had lit the interior of the Hagia Sophia in Christian times; carpeted the floor to accommodate the postures of Muslim worship; and installed a *mighrab,* the niche that indicates the *qibla* (the direction of Mecca).

It had never occurred to me that the Hagia Sophia might no longer be operating as a mosque, but Ataturk had another role in mind for that venerable structure. He funded restoration of Byzantine mosaics plastered over in Ottoman times and reopened the Haiga Sophia as a museum of architectural design from the Emperor Constantine's founding of Byzantium to the 1930s.

Considering Ataturk's stellar success in transforming the lumbering remains of the Ottoman behemoth into a modern state, there must never have been any doubt that this museum project would meet with public approval. But why secularization of a major *mosque* justified a sizable financial commitment from a Muslim country that had just suffered a disastrous military defeat continued to puzzle me.

Such public largesse might have been a bid for Christian support for Ataturk's secularization policy had it occurred in 1900. However, after the 1915 expulsion of Christians from Anatolia (the territory that became post-WW1 Turkey), followed by the involuntary exchanges of populations with Greece in 1922-24, very few Christians remained in Turkey to support any government initiatives, including Ataturk's.

* * *

Ataturk's public statements demonstrated that he had learned his lesson about the folly of alliances with countries whose interests and goals did not coincide with Turkey's. As he saw it, the Ottoman Empire's involvement in WW1 was unwise and unnecessary. Neither Germany nor Austria-Hungary was willing or able to come to their Ottoman allies' aid when needed. Chastened by that experience, Ataturk declared Turkey a neutral state like Switzerland, which had profited handsomely for centuries by standing apart from international conflicts.

Realist that he was, Ataturk knew that an official proclamation of perpetual neutrality was an essential first step in clarifying Turkey's place in the modern world. However, even self-declared neutral nations must be prepared to defend themselves against aggressors and resist the inducements of belligerents to draw them into shooting wars.

As a serving general in WW1, Ataturk was also acutely aware that the backwardness of the Ottoman Empire's transportation system, its recurrent water shortages, and its meager domestic energy resources had impaired Turkey's efforts to resist attacks by the more economically advanced Allied countries. He reminded the public that these deficiencies would cripple Turkish defensive capabilities in the future in the absence of effective corrective measures.

Thus, infrastructure-development projects—which offered the side benefit of meaningful employment for jobless Turks—began as soon as Ataturk solidified his political position. By the mid-1920s, workers were already laying new rail lines and preparing modern roadbeds. Construction of dams to capture and store flood waters in Turkey's mountainous regions and supply the hydroelectric power needed to fuel Ataturk's economic-modernization initiatives proceeded in tandem with the rest of his infrastructure-improvement program.

CHAPTER THIRTY-THREE

KUWAIT AND BACK TO ARABIA

My Istanbul-Dhahran itinerary required a change of planes in Kuwait, so I came away with at least a superficial impression of the oil-rich, strategically located territory so coveted by the Iraqis. My connecting flight from Beirut was not due for another couple of hours, so I hired a taxi to take me on a brief tour of Kuwait City.

A Dhow
(Traditional Arab Sailing Vessel for the Coastal Trade)

Kuwait City was no seaside resort, surrounded as it was by alluvial swamps, but it would have been hard to miss the plentiful evidence of the city's wealth and forward-looking spirit in 1961. New-model cars whizzed about on expertly paved roads. Newly constructed buildings in the city center betokened an ample flow of investment capital and confidence in Kuwait's economic future.

The territory had been a British Protectorate for sixty-two years until two months before my visit. Public excitement about independence went a long way toward making up for the city's lack of aesthetic appeal. The taxi driver, a product of Protectorate-era schools, spoke fluent English, so I asked him about rumors of Iraqi designs on Kuwait.

"We don't take their scare tactics too seriously. We're used to their bullying. We know the Iraqis are worried about their navigation rights along the Shatt al-Arab from Basra to the Gulf. If their tankers couldn't travel that waterway, they'd have no way to export oil at all."

"Is there any realistic danger of an Iraqi attack on Kuwait any time soon?"

"Kuwaiti territory sits on one side of the waterway and the Iranian oilfields near Abadan front it on the other. We wouldn't close the Shatt al-Arab to Iraqi shipping unless they attacked us, but it's hard to predict what the Iranians might do."

* * *

The conventional flight pattern from Kuwait to Dhahran followed the Gulf shore. Window seats on the right side of Dhahran-bound flights were highly prized; they gave passengers an unobstructed view of the main attraction along the route. Aramco was flaring natural gas all along the Trans-Arabian Pipeline, which delivered Saudi crude to the tanker terminal in Sidon. Unlike the flames of Abqaiq's gas flares, which cleared the tops of their pipe chimneys by a few dozen feet at most, the Gulf-shore version leaped thousands of feet into the air.

While I was enjoying the nearest thing to a fireworks display we Aramcons were ever likely to see until we traveled to suitable foreign destinations, I thought about Turkey's and Saudi Arabia's dissimilar approaches to economic modernization. Ataturk's reform model had produced spectacular results in Turkey, but would his strategies work in a much more conservative country like Saudi Arabia?

As the successful defender of Gallipoli, Ataturk had a lot going for him besides a well-designed economic-development plan. He was a national hero, one of the few left standing in post-defeat Turkey. The public perception that the Caliph and the Sultan, the traditional authority figures of the Ottoman Empire, had mismanaged the war effort ruled them out as potential leaders for postwar reconstruction. Getting rid of them entirely was an inspired coup on the part of Ataturk.

Ataturk was able to convince his public that Turkey's status as a new nation was actually an advantage rather than a punishment inflicted by the victors. Unhampered by antiquated traditions, their country was free to set out on a new path that would bring Turkey prosperity and international respect. Ataturk's modernization plan did exactly what he promised. It improved the quality of life for all Turkish citizens, and it did so rapidly enough to discourage more than token opposition.

* * *

While Ataturk was working his magic in Ankara, the Al-Saud were engaged in the gritty business of building a nation out of an assemblage of unruly desert tribes and scattered urban populations that had initially resisted incorporation into the new Saudi state at all. Unification might well have been impossible without the common religious beliefs and practices of the diverse peoples of the Arabian Peninsula to hold the new state together.

But the Saudi government knew, even if its subjects didn't, that technological modernization was imperative if the country was to take control of its economic destiny. Many more Saudis with the skills needed to keep the oil flowing would be indispensable if and when the government bought out Aramco. Even before I left Arabia in 1962, we expats were convinced that that was exactly what the Saudis had in mind. As we saw it, they were simply biding their time until they accumulated sufficient cash to consummate the deal and developed the human resources necessary to exploit the economic opportunities that the takeover would offer.

We also thought that shrewd financial management would be the easier of the two pre-buyout tasks. Educational preparation for a technologically oriented economy was going to take time—and a major change in the attitudes of some of the Al-Saud's most ardent and innovation-resistant supporters.

The rare non-private schooling that existed in Arabia during the 1930s and earlier focused almost exclusively on religious education, with rudimentary literacy and computational skills thrown in. Neither science nor mathematic problem-solving figured into instruction at all.

Shifting the orientation of schooling to preparation for employment in a technologically oriented industry would require a comprehensive overhaul of the curriculum, pedagogy, and duration of instruction. It also risked trampling on the toes of the powerful religious establishment—core supporters of the Saudi regime.

In the late 1950s and early 1960s, the Saudi leadership was obviously doing its best to straddle the chasm between the ultraconservatism of much of the country's population and the urgent need for workforce development. Their first step—a school-building campaign—wasn't particularly controversial, probably because official statements about it were few and far between and exceptionally short on detail. It also helped that the public wasn't asked to tax themselves to pay for school construction; oil revenue would do that.

When I arrived in Arabia, the crash campaign to train a more highly skilled oilfield workforce had been in full operation for half a dozen years without noticeable public outcry. A government-Aramco joint venture had built dozens of new primary schools to address the high rate of illiteracy in Eastern Arabia. Promising Saudi boys who graduated from the new primary schools were then channeled into the few secondary schools in operation or the vocational-training schools run by Aramco.

However, both the government and Aramco recognized that even a secondary-school education or task-specific vocational training would not be enough to qualify young Saudis for higher-skilled oil-company jobs. The solution: send especially talented secondary-school graduates to colleges and universities abroad to complete science-, math-, or technology-oriented degree programs.

What no one was talking much about then was that limiting educational opportunities to oil-production specialties would do nothing to diversify the Saudi economy, which was subject to the random ups and downs of the country's commodities-based one modern industry. Nor would young men who had spent several years in the West find it easy to readapt to the strictures of traditional Saudi lifestyles. We often speculated about the long-term consequences of this obvious economic-social mismatch.

CHAPTER THIRTY-FOUR

A DIFFERENT KIND OF DESTINATION

WHEN MY FLIGHT landed in Dhahran, the August temperature wasn't quite the shock it had been the year before. I was soon on my way to Abqaiq, which I could smell several miles before the camp came into view. Welcome home—for now, anyway.

As I loaded my dirty clothes into the washer, I grieved for what had once been my favorite white blouse. I wondered what it would look like by the end of my contract. Corrosion in Abqaiq's plumbing system stained toilet bowls and wash basins deep reddish brown over the months between acid treatments to dislodge rust deposits. Meanwhile, light-colored clothing underwent the same undesirable dyeing process as the plumbing fixtures.

While the washer did its thing, I updated my to-do list. Unless I planned to wrap up my catering business before the month was out, replenishing catering supplies and setting mash for a new still run had to be major priorities. Preparing for my "day" job was also urgent. So much to do, so little time. Funny, last year about this time, I was tearing my hair out trying to come up with something—anything—to do during my off-duty hours. Now, "the faster I went, the behinder I got" summed up my time-management predicament perfectly. Maybe once I plowed through a few of the most urgent items on my work agenda, I wouldn't feel so much pressure.

"If you believe that," my hectoring rational self protested, "I have a nice piece of underwater Florida real estate to sell you at a bargain price. The things on today's to-do list will be history in two or three weeks. What about those longer-term issues you've been so studiously avoiding?"

"I haven't the remotest idea what you're talking about."

"Don't you? How about whether you're planning to return to Arabia for another contract? If not, you need to be researching transfer possibilities and/or looking for appropriate jobs in the US right away."

"There'll be plenty of time to think about that later."

"You mean there'll be plenty of time to procrastinate later?"

"Stop badgering me. I have enough to do just now without nonstop harassment from you. When I have time, I'll think about next year. Right now, I have a whole year of second-year French curriculum to plan for my third graders. Besides, I don't know what my choices will be at the end of my contract."

"You don't? Let me help you. Why don't you consider the three options you had when you were pondering whether to leave Venezuela? You could stay where you were, transfer to another oil-company job, or return to the US. What's so difficult about that?"

"Cutbacks in production in Eastern Venezuela made staying there too risky. Fewer professional staff with elementary-school-age children meant lower enrollments. Oil companies lay off or terminate redundant employees. It's different here. I feel certain I can return for another contract if I want to."

"That's probably true, but would your teaching assignment be the same? I don't know how much attention you've been paying to camp gossip, but I keep hearing whispers that all students will have to take Arabic next year. Do you really think they'll have room in their schedules for French as well?"

"No one has said anything about that to me."

"Why should they? Remember the Girl Scout motto and be prepared. Meanwhile, let's consider the second option for the moment.

How about transferring to an affiliate in another country? Does that appeal to you?"

"Not really. You never know what you're getting into when you take a flier on one of these jobs."

"You've noticed. I see you're more cautious now that you're a mature thirty. Here's my advice. Cull the list of Aramco affiliates down to those most likely to have teaching vacancies and decide whether living and working in any of those locations would suit you. You can probably disregard Aruba and Iran, because you chose Arabia over them when you signed your contract with Aramco.

"As for the others, how about searching your house for a cobra before you go to bed each night? My spies tell me that's standard procedure in the Straits Settlements. They may exaggerate, but still . . . Or how about Iraq? Rebels there took a few Americans hostage three years ago and killed off the Prime Minister and most of the royal family. Would that be to your taste? Libya would be another option, but the fields there are so new that going there seems a bit premature, unless you long to be a sand-dune pioneer."

"You're just trying to scare me."

"Well, let's consider the other option. You could always return to the US. It's a big country, so you wouldn't have to settle too near the parental nest unless you wanted to. However, if you're even thinking of going back to the States, you should be researching suitable jobs in desirable locations *now*. Stateside applicants will be snapping up the best teaching jobs fairly early in the spring."

"Have you checked a calendar recently? This is August. Last time I looked, spring didn't begin until March. That's eight months away. Besides, I'm not sure I want to leave Arabia. If I decide not to renew my contract, I'll have plenty of time to apply for a stateside job later."

"Really? Never underestimate the difficulties of finding work from halfway around the world. Intercontinental mail is painfully slow, especially if the sender uses boat mail. An interview—a standard part of the hiring process—is out of the question until you get back to the US. By then, jobs that appeal to you might already be filled. Then there's the little matter of a valid teaching certificate."

"I have a teaching certificate."

"For which state?"

"New Mexico. That's where I taught between France and Venezuela."

"Are you considering returning to New Mexico?"

"No, they don't pay enough."

"You must surely know that each state has its own licensing requirements. You might even have to take a correspondence course or two to qualify for the job you want. That alone could take months."

"I hadn't thought about that. Another two years in Arabia is sounding better all the time. I still have a longish list of Middle Eastern locations I'd really like to visit while I have a chance."

"Tell you what. Think about it, but set yourself a firm deadline. You can't afford to wait till March."

CHAPTER THIRTY-FIVE

MODERN AND HISTORICAL IRAN

JUST IN CASE I decided not to renew my Aramco contract, I checked the Middle Eastern must-see agenda I'd put together with the help of an out-of-date atlas before I left Venezuela. I hadn't the faintest idea whether travel to some of the destinations I'd highlighted would be feasible, let alone what I'd see if it was.

So far, I'd been to Egypt, Lebanon, Syria, and Turkey, plus that brief between-planes stop in Kuwait. That left Bahrain, Iran, Jordan, and the Palestinian territories to fit into the second year of my contract. Iraq had been on my original list, but I'd deleted it for reasons of safety. Saudi troops armed to the teeth had passed through Abqaiq in late June on their way to reinforce the Kuwaiti and Neutral-Zone borders. Someone with better sources of information than I had must have been expecting trouble.

I would have liked to visit Israel, too, but that was out of the question. Despite the uneasy Arab-Israeli armistice in force since April 1949, Israel and its Arab neighbors were still technically at war. Neutral-passport holders, which included American citizens, could cross into Israel from neighboring Arab countries only at the Mandelbaum Gate in Jerusalem. Even that option wouldn't work for me. Israeli entrance and exit stamps in my passport would bar me from returning to my employment in Arabia until I had a new passport. Not too practical for the job-dependent.

"Cramming visits to three countries and what's left of Palestine into the remaining months of your contract will demand better planning than you usually manage," I told myself sternly. "And don't forget the two or three additional shopping trips you'll have to make to Beirut just to keep the catering business afloat, although you won't need vacation days for those. Just follow your usual system. Leave on Wednesday evening, do your shopping on Thursday, and return to Abqaiq on Friday."

I looked up the dates of Muslim holidays scheduled to fall within the remaining months of my contract and perused *Sun and Flare* each week for notices of employee- or DOG-sponsored trips to destinations of interest. This might be my last year in the Middle East. It only made sense to pursue my travel agenda aggressively.

The next opportunity for international travel that required a long weekend was the King's Accession Day, which fell on November 12, a Sunday, in 1961. Aramco had already announced that the 11th would be a bonus vacation day. Counting the Thursday-Friday weekend, we would have a four-day break.

Luck was with me. A Dhahran housewife was organizing an excursion to Iran. Fearful that I might already be too late, I called her immediately and was relieved to learn that seats were still available on the tour.

* * *

Thirty-two of us boarded our flight to Shiraz early on November 9. My assigned roommate, Nedra, a teacher at Ras Tanura and a recent transfer from Aramco's Peruvian affiliate, was my seatmate. I'd spent Christmas in Lima in 1959, so that gave us something to talk about.

We landed in Shiraz at about 10:30 local time. After checking into our hotel, we went down to lunch. Anyone who had dozed off as a result of our early-morning departure must have awakened with a start at the sight of our first course. The contents of the icy-cold soup plates the waiter placed before us were unidentifiable. The room was abuzz with guesses, some less probable than others. Elementary detective work—*i.e.,* the absence of other cutlery—revealed that we were supposed to eat whatever it was with large soup spoons.

The main component of the dish was a white liquid, very possibly milk to which a mild thickening agent had been added. That put us all on guard. Even newcomers to less developed countries, which included Iran at the time, learned from bitter experience that dairy products that hadn't been cooked or otherwise treated to ensure their safety could be sure tickets to days or even weeks of misery.

Nearly submerged in the liquid was an equally puzzling dark green object that looked like a zucchini, except that it had slightly tapered ends. Tiny bits of greenery floated randomly on the white base.

None of us could speak Farsi, so one of the men flagged down the waiter and resorted to pantomime. Nice try, but veteran charades players soon concluded that asking "what are the ingredients of this dish" with gestures alone was virtually impossible. When the waiter looked absolutely nonplussed by this performance, the group member who had summoned him kept pointing rapidly at the contents of the soup plate. Finally, the waiter seemed to catch on. He smacked his lips and said, "*mast.*" Then he showed us that we should eat whatever it was with the big spoons. Since we had long since figured that out, our score at the mystery-food-identification game stood at zero.

While we were still trying to come up with a more effective communication strategy, the maître d' appeared, seemingly having been summoned by the waiter, who must have thought these foreigners were either extraordinarily picky eaters or rather thick in the head. In flawless English, the maître d' announced that the dish was an Iranian specialty. The white liquid was yogurt; the solid green object, a Persian cucumber; and the green bits, chopped mint. Grateful that the concoction wouldn't do us irreparable harm, we peppered the maître d' with questions, most of them variations of "Where did you learn such excellent English?"

"My father worked for the Anglo-Iranian Oil Company in Abadan. I went to the company school there."

Restrained by their wives, who were eager to eat the first course to see what would come next, the petroleum engineers among us refrained from following up that information with a barrage of questions about the tedious details of operations at Abadan. The maître d' assured us that he was at our disposition and returned to his station.

Now all we had to do was to figure out how to eat a whole cucumber immersed in liquid yogurt with a soup spoon without sending the dish flying across the room like a demented Frisbee. I would give us a rather generous grade of C-. To this day, the only word I know in Farsi is "*mast*."

* * *

After lunch, we boarded a bus for our afternoon tour. We were all hoping the maître d' would double as our tour guide, but no such luck. The young man assigned to guide us delivered a canned spiel about the attractions of "greater" Shiraz. We succeeded in deciphering most of it.

Winter was coming, he said. We were wise to have come while the flowers in the parks were still in full bloom. A profusion of roses lined every street in central Shiraz, so maybe he was right about our timing. The roses' heavenly scent was a special treat for the Abqaiq contingent, inured as we were to less pleasing aromas. With justifiable pride, our guide pointed out the many varieties of autumn flowers used to add color to several of the parks.

We heard him, but by now, most of us were fixed on a humbler form of vegetation: acres and acres of unbelievably green grass. "Do you suppose he would stop the bus for a few minutes so we could roll in it?" someone behind me asked in a stage whisper. About the only green we saw on a regular basis in our part of Arabia was on the Saudi flag.

The lavish use of water in the pools and fountains in Shiraz parks astounded us. Seeing a single sprinkler in action would have made our day. Water conservation obviously hadn't caught on in Shiraz despite the desert-like appearance of the surrounding countryside.

At the edge of the city, fields of flowers of every kind surrounded us. What a treat for desert rats like us, who hadn't seen flowers other than oleanders for months on end. But where did those farmers get all that water? Inquiring minds really wanted to know, but deterred by the language barrier, we didn't try to find out.

A little farther on, we caught sight of what we thought at first must be a mirage, despite the garden-spot appearance of the surroundings. Row after row of vines, meticulously trellised and cut back for the coming winter, must have yielded tons of grapes in season. Were table grapes that popular in Iran? One of our more diplomatic tour members asked a carefully framed question that boiled down to "are the grapes sold as fruit or dried to make raisins?" Of course, that wasn't what he really wanted to know, so his indirect-information-gathering technique impressed the rest of us mightily.

"Neither. Those are wine grapes. Farmers here have grown them for thousands of years to make the famed Shiraz wine. The oldest wine in the world—about seven thousand years old—was recently discovered at a nearby archeological dig."

The bus was all ears now. Our spokesman continued, "Do you produce wine for export only?"

"Oh no. Wine-merchants sell it throughout the country. You can order wine with your dinner tonight, if you like."

I could well imagine what was going through more than a few fevered brains. "Pass on wine inadvertently aged for seven millennia, but could I figure out a way to sneak a bottle or two of the modern stuff into Arabia? No, too risky. Maybe I could order a glass or two or three with breakfast, lunch, and dinner. Well, maybe not breakfast, but definitely for a nightcap."

* * *

As we continued on our way to the town's famous bazaar, our guide pointed out a synagogue and an Armenian Orthodox church. Both buildings looked well cared for, so those religious minorities must have been living in the city then or until shortly before our visit.

"Are there other religious minorities living in Shiraz now?" I asked.

"Yes, the Baha'i. They are the largest local minority group."

"How is it that so many Baha'i live in Shiraz?"

"Siyyad 'Ali-Muhammad, called the '*Bab*' by his followers, founded the Baha'i faith here. The Baha'i believe that the *Bab* had some sort of spiritual revelation about ultimate truth that he passed on to all who would listen."

"So his followers considered him a prophet?"

"Exactly. However, this got him into serious trouble with local religious authorities. They imprisoned and executed him as an apostate. Mirza Husayn 'Ali Nuri took up his work and fared only slightly better. The authorities expelled him from the country, but he escaped execution."

"Is the modern Baha'i community growing?"

"No, it's declining. Life is hard for them here. Orthodox religious authorities consider their beliefs heretical. Many of them are emigrating."

Hand-Wrought Iranian Vessel for Liquids,

By this time, we were approaching the last stop on our tour, the Vakil Bazaar. The merchandise was of extraordinary quality: gorgeous rugs and brass work, silver, ceramic tiles, mosaics, and textiles. I was severely tempted by all of them, but I averted my eyes as best I could and wandered over to the produce section.

It's hard to explain why fresh fruit and vegetables are such an attraction to anyone who has never lived in a place where both are exceedingly difficult to come by. Fresh fruit other than dates was seldom available in Eastern Arabia except during a couple of summer months, when quite tasty melons from Al-Kharj appeared now and then in our *suqs*.

My eyes lit up at once at the sight of great heaps of Fuyu persimmons (the kind that are shaped like tomatoes and can be eaten hard). At that moment, I would rather have had those persimmons than anything else in that well-stocked bazaar. Heedless of the logistical challenges of carrying them around, I bought half a burlap bagful. Fuyus keep for weeks and are almost immune to bumps and bruises, so I figured they could survive bouncing around in the overhead compartments of our two remaining flights.

I did wonder what Saudi Customs would do when they opened that burlap bag. I need not have worried. I offered a few persimmons to the Customs officer before he had a chance to say or do anything. He took about half a dozen and passed my suitcase without even opening it. That must have been the most unusual "bribe" he'd ever received.

* * *

The next day, box lunches in hand, we boarded a bus for the two-hour drive to the ruins of Persepolis—the ceremonial capital of the Empire of the Medes and the Persians. The guide surprised us with the welcome announcement that fruit juice and filtered water would be available on the bus all day. We veterans of the Tarut trip waited with bated breath for him to address the restroom issue, but he didn't mention it, and we were afraid to ask. We weren't naïve enough to expect anything but holes in the ground without plumbing or toilet paper, but we dared to hope for a little more privacy than we'd experienced on Tarut.

The guide, a professor of archaeology at a nearby university, had participated in excavations at Persepolis for nearly a decade. His English was good—a relief, because most of us had never heard of Persepolis until our tour escort broke the news that a visit to the ruins was on the schedule for the following day.

Even from a distance, we marveled at the immensity of the site. The complex was the work of three successors of Cyrus the Great—

the Persian king who encouraged, financed, and provided a military escort for descendents of the Jews of the Babylonian captivity to return to Jerusalem to rebuild King Solomon's temple.

Construction of Persepolis began in 518 BC under Darius I, a distant relative of Cyrus. From the guide's description, Darius was a thoroughly amoral opportunist. Not only was he suspected of plotting against Cyrus during the latter's lifetime, but he killed one of Cyrus's sons and may have been responsible for the death of another.

Like most usurpers, Darius had to watch his back. He spent most of his reign putting down revolts in his far-flung Empire and executing underlings at the faintest whiff of disloyalty. The magnificence of Persepolis must have been intended to remind restive subject nations—and his own people—of his overwhelming power and the futility of challenging it.

Our guide pointed out several architectural characteristics of Persepolis unique in the ancient world. The architects took ingenious advantage of the topography of the construction site. They used manmade terraces sparingly and only when absolutely necessary. Three defensive walls of increasing height encircled the complex, a useful feature for a pitiless tyrant like Darius, whose outsized political ambitions ensured that he would never lack for a full complement of enemies. An immense cistern hewn out of the side of a cliff caught and stored rainwater to accommodate the needs of the hundreds of court officials in residence. So how did the Persians pay for all this?

That, our guide assured us, was an easy question. Empire builders in the ancient world had no way to occupy extensive and/or distant conquered territory, given the transportation and communications limitations of the time. Their usual procedure was to loot everything not nailed down and carry off the able-bodied for use or sale as slaves. The rest of the defeated were left to their own devices, but poverty-stricken. One of the few well-preserved sections of Darius's palace shows a procession of ambassadors from subject nations come to present their annual tribute to the king.

Alexander the Great, who brought the Persian Empire to an end in the fourth century BC, used similar intimidation tactics with his potential and actual conquests. Perhaps his tutor, the great philosopher Aristotle, had taught the young Alexander about the gratuitous destruction perpetrated by the Persians during earlier invasions of Greece.

We asked the guide why Alexander detoured to such a remote site as Persepolis with so many equally rich and more accessible targets just ripe for the picking. The guide pointed to an empty space between two sets of ruins. That, he said, was where the palace of Xerxes the Great, Darius's son, once stood. Xerxes planned and carried out a particularly brutal invasion of Greece in 480 BC that forced the evacuation of women and children from Athens. The victorious Persians went on a rampage during which they vandalized several Athenian temples, including the Parthenon, before they finally departed and left the Athenians to pick up the pieces.

Alexander was apparently not a man to forgive and forget, even after a century and a half. He turned his soldiers loose on Persepolis after an alcohol-soaked victory gala. They burned everything they could and hacked away at anything they couldn't. As our guide commented, this horde of amateur arsonists sent a clear, but subversive, message to subject nations: even tyrants are vulnerable.

* * *

We flew to Tehran the next morning. The beauty of the Iranian capital's setting came as a surprise. The sky was deep blue, and the mountains to the north were already dusted with snow. Our local guide announced that since our stay in the capital would be so brief, we would drive through central Tehran's major neighborhoods on our way to our hotel to give us an overview of the city.

Tehran came across as a hit-or-miss conglomeration of architectural styles. The modern and the traditional coexisted, but uneasily. Sleek, multiple-story buildings towered over graceful Persian-style palaces.

The physical/social layout of Tehran resembled that of large cities throughout the world. The poor were relegated to South Tehran. The upscale housing of North Tehran accommodated the needs, tastes, and convenience of more affluent Iranians, prosperous members of ethnic-minority groups, employees of foreign companies, short- and long-term residents of international hotels, and the diplomatic community.

Armenians, Jews, and Turks were the principal ethnic minorities in the Iranian capital at the time of our visit. Most of the first two groups lived in ethnically homogeneous neighborhoods in North Tehran for linguistic, cultural, and religious reasons. Turks lived on both sides of town, depending on their socioeconomic status.

Manufacturing, artisans' workshops, and small retail establishments were concentrated in South Tehran, where most of their predominantly Iranian workforce lived. Many of the more prosperous businesses in South Tehran belonged to minority businessmen who lived farther north in the city.

* * *

After our orientation tour and lunch at our hotel, we embarked on a memorable visit to the bank that housed the Iranian Crown Jewels. The jewels are so valuable, we were told, that they were once used to back the country's currency.

They made the jewelry in the Beirut's gold *suq* look like dime-store baubles. The most valuable individual pieces included crowns set with gemstones the size of pigeon eggs, an enormous canary diamond reputed to weigh almost 60 carats, and a solid-gold globe set with more than 50,000 individual gemstones. Thousands of smaller stones encrusted lesser items. The solid-gold flat surfaces of the Shah's throne were inlaid with innumerable precious gems. Sitting on that throne without thick cushions for more than a minute or two must have been pure torture.

We celebrated the end of our Iranian trip with a world-class banquet featuring local specialties—and Western-style cutlery. The cucumber salad reminded us of the first course that had so mystified us in Shiraz, but this time, the chunks of cucumber were of manageable size and weren't swimming in a yogurt bath, much to our collective relief. The banquet's main course consisted of roast lamb and a rice pilaf studded with nuts and dried fruit. Thirsty Aramcons—who were only too aware that they would be back in the land of homemade hooch the next day—kept the wine steward very, very busy.

On our flight back to Dhahran, I asked Nedra if she had plans for any other travel that year. She said she really wanted to see Riyadh, but she had just learned that the Saudi capital was closed to tourists. If that ever changed, she planned to be the first to sign up.

"Maybe, but you'll have to be quick on the draw to beat me."

CHAPTER THIRTY-SIX

THIRD-GRADE THANKSGIVING

AS A VACATION-ENRICHMENT activity for my third-graders, I scheduled an optional ten-day colonial-life workshop in honor of Thanksgiving—a holiday that seldom generated a groundswell of enthusiasm among cooks in Aramcon Land. Searching for the traditional ingredients of the November repast in the commissary and *suqs* was a thankless and only partially successful task. Our workshop would have to work around supply problems of our own, and my classroom had its limitations as a kitchen, but a modest project seemed doable.

I planned five major learning activities. After reading stories about the challenges of living in a new land more than three centuries ago, the children would (1) write and perform skits illustrating key aspects of colonial life; (2) fashion costumes for their skits from tag board and crepe paper; (3) make candles; (4) finger-weave Indian-style belts; and (5) assemble an afghan from squares woven on cardboard looms of their own design. As a culminating activity on the last day of our workshop, we would prepare as authentic a replica of the limited-menu first Thanksgiving celebration as we could manage with what we had to work with. (The meal would be vegetarian to avoid a head-on collision with Muslim dietary laws.) The children would at least learn that seventeenth-century cooks faced supply problems, too.

Our menu comprised Boston baked beans; steamed brown bread with raisins; Indian pudding (a custard-like dessert made with milk, butter, eggs, molasses, sugar, cornmeal, and cinnamon); and frozen spinach (in lieu of the unavailable wild greens) with an oil, vinegar, and minced-onion dressing. I used my electric roaster and borrowed three more from obliging mothers, and we were good to go.

I readied my roaster with the ingredients for the beans at home and took it to my classroom by taxi at about 6:00 am so that they could begin to cook at a suitably low temperature. When the children arrived at 8:30, the aroma of baking beans pervaded the entire building. That heightened their enthusiasm for the day's activities considerably.

A student committee measured the ingredients for the bread (cornmeal, whole wheat flour, baking powder, molasses, evaporated milk, and raisins), mixed the batter, and greased and filled No. 2 cans two-thirds full. I placed the cans on a rack to steam over simmering water in another roaster.

Next, we tackled the Indian pudding, because it had to bake for two hours and then cool before serving. We needed two large puddings to accommodate the expected number of diners, so we put one pan in one roaster and the other in another.

We used my hotplate to cook the spinach. Since I didn't want little fingers using a grater on the onion, I made the dressing for the spinach at my apartment. When not otherwise occupied, the children practiced their songs, rehearsed their skits, and decorated the serving table.

The party was going full tilt when I noticed the same two Arab heads peering through the glass pane in the classroom door for the umpteenth time. They must have been trying to figure out what these foreigners were up to now.

I beckoned to two boys and told them to fill two plates and follow me. The nearest girl brought napkins and plastic cutlery for two.

I opened the door. The two janitors started to flee down the corridor. "*Ogaf* (stop)," I called after them. "*Tafaddal* (please)," I said, waving my hand toward the plates of food. The janitors looked dubious. I thought I knew why. "*Halal* (in keeping with Islamic dietary laws)," I assured them. They took the plates, grinned from ear to ear, and set off down the hall with their culinary loot. We saw their empty plates later when we dumped our own trash, so they must have found third-grade cuisine more than acceptable.

CHAPTER THIRTY-SEVEN
REGINALD REDUX

WHEN MY CHRISTMAS travel documents arrived from the Passport Office, I was already packing my smallest suitcase for three very different climates within six days. Beirut was likely to be rainy, with a brisk wind blowing off the Mediterranean. Jerusalem is approximately 2,500 feet above sea level, so it would be colder there, but not so damp. Jericho is 853 feet *below* sea level—warm and sunny year round. In the end, I took mostly woolens, my all-weather coat, and cotton slacks and a blouse for the Jericho side trip.

I ordered a taxi for 2:00 to take me to Dhahran to catch my 4:00 pm flight to Beirut. To occupy my time until boarding, I brought along my copy of *Our Jerusalem* by Bertha Spafford Vester. I had met Mrs. Vester earlier that fall when she came to Arabia to market needlework done by Palestinian refugees—one of her many Middle Eastern charities.

She was only three when her parents and several like-minded companions—all of them survivors of the Great Chicago Fire of 1871—moved to Ottoman-ruled Jerusalem. They mission: service to the people of the Holy Land, irrespective of race/ethnicity or religious tradition. Their Palestinian neighbors soon christened their enclave near the Damascus Gate "The American Colony."

The founders of the American Colony began their work with

skimpy finances; the Chicago fire had consumed most of their net worth. Nevertheless, their soup kitchen and clothing-distribution center opened its doors to the needy almost before the newcomers had had time to unpack their own suitcases.

Before long, they realized that food and clothing were not the only needs of the underserved poor of Jerusalem. American Colony workers established the first school in the country for Muslim girls and implemented several vocational-training programs to qualify Arab adults to enter the skilled trades.

* * *

The PA eventually interrupted my reading with a boarding announcement for the Beirut flight. I gathered my possessions, climbed the ramp, and settled myself into my window seat. Shortly thereafter, I heard a vaguely familiar voice. "Nancy, I haven't seen you in ages. May I join you?"

I looked up and saw . . . Reginald, of Abqaiq Clinic infamy. "I don't think so, Reginald. This seat must surely be assigned to someone else." *Anyway, I hoped so, but no such luck.* When no one else claimed the seat and a flight attendant was securing the door for departure, Reginald eased himself in beside me. That sealed my fate, at least for the next three and a half hours.

"Where are you going?"

I weighed my options for responding, but without knowing his destination, I was at a loss what to say to avoid unwelcome entanglements for the entire Christmas break. "I have some business to take care of in Beirut. How about you?" Best to know what I was up against.

"Jerusalem. I've resigned from Aramco effective February 1. I wanted to visit the Holy City while I still have the opportunity." Anyone that tall and blond would stand out in any Middle Eastern crowd. Surely I would have time to take evasive action if we ended up at the same sightseeing attraction at the same time. I made an abortive attempt to return to my reading, but Reginald was having none of that.

"Are you staying in Beirut the whole time, or are you going on to another destination?"

"I'm flying to Amman on Friday." Hoping to divert his attention from me to him, I asked the question I assumed he was waiting to hear. "You said you are leaving Aramco. Are you returning to the US, or are you perhaps taking another foreign job?" The answer to that would surely last until we passed Kuwait, if not longer.

"I have accepted a position with the US government." Reginald named a country I couldn't place—apparently some nation's newly independent former colony. In a maneuver reminiscent of the form-letter-from-the-senator caper at the Abqaiq clinic, he whipped out his passport. "Look," he commanded.

"It looks like a passport to me."

"Nancy, you aren't very observant." *Or very interested, either.* "What is different about the front of it?" No need to reply because he would almost certainly answer his own question at prodigious length.

He handed the passport to me for closer inspection. "Notice the gold border on the cover. It's a special passport for employees of government agencies."

It occurred to me that the graphic arts shop might have given him the gold foil to alter an ordinary passport himself. However, I went along with his explanation for the time being. I asked what he'd be doing in his new position.

"I've been hired to shape up the relief-distribution system to ensure that American aid goes where it's most needed." Maybe Reginald had more political pull than I thought. Surely no one at Aramco would have recommended him for employment that entailed that level of responsibility.

While I was still lost in that train of thought, Reginald asked the question I'd been dreading. "What's the nature of your business in Beirut?" *Is this a job interview?*

"I have some catering trivia to attend to." *Well, sort of.*

"How long will you be in Amman? Surely you're not planning to spend three days there. Whatever are you going to do for that long in Jordan?"

Caught like a rat in a trap. "No, I'm going on to Jerusalem."

"Where are you staying, and how do you plan to get to Jerusalem from the airport?"

"I'll solve the lodging problem when I get there. I wasn't sure which hotels were located on the Palestinian side. As for the trip from Amman to Jerusalem, I plan to take a taxi." Not quite accurate, but the best I could come up with on short notice.

"Well, your worries are over. I will arrange everything."

No, my worries are just beginning, and I have a sneaking suspicion there'll be nothing I can do about that. "What do you mean?"

In an unbearably pompous tone, he announced that he was staying in pilgrim quarters at the Anglican cathedral. "I will ask reception to reserve a room for you. I also have a car and driver at my disposal for the duration of my stay in Jerusalem, so I will meet your plane at Amman. What time does it arrive?"

"Reginald, it seems rather presumptuous for me to arrive at the cathedral unannounced and expect the staff to care for my needs for three days."

"But you won't be unannounced, because I will let them know right away that your arrival is imminent." Then he inserted the deal maker. "Besides, they have tickets for Midnight Mass at the Church of the Nativity in Bethlehem. Without a ticket, you'd have to hunker down in the cold in Manger Square for the entire service."

"Well, all right." I'd already realized that the only way to avoid spending three days with Reginald was to cancel the Jerusalem trip, and I had no intention of doing that.

"We'll follow this sightseeing itinerary. Friday afternoon, the driver will take us to the Dome of the Rock and Al Aqsa Mosque and show us where Solomon's Temple stood. We'll also visit the Western Wall during that stop. Next, we'll cross the Valley of Kidron to the Mount of Olives for a superb view of the skyline of the Old City. After that, we'll return to the cathedral in time to hear the choir at evensong." That didn't sound too bad. Maybe he should have applied for a job with a tour company instead of a relief agency. "I need to do a little more research before I decide what we'll be seeing on Saturday."

"Reginald, count me out for Saturday evening. I plan to visit friends of my parents—Willard and Christina Jones—and Saturday seems like the most convenient day for me to do that."

"Where do they live?"

"I'm not sure, but I intend to find out. They're well known in Jerusalem. Willard is the Executive Secretary of the Near East Christian Council Committee for Refugee Work. Someone at the cathedral can surely supply contact information. The Archbishop is undoubtedly a member of the Committee."

"All right. On Sunday, we'll attend the Christmas Eve service at the Shepherds' Fields. In keeping with centuries-old tradition, we'll walk from Jerusalem to Bethlehem."

"Reginald, I don't know about that. How far is it?"

"My guidebook says it's seven miles."

"Count me out for that, too. I don't have shoes with me that could possibly withstand a seven-mile hike."

"We can buy you a pair of shoes."

"No, we can't. There's not a pair of shoes in the entire Eastern Hemisphere that would fit my long, skinny feet."

"Can't you stuff tissue paper in your shoes if they're too wide?"

"And walk seven miles? Are you out of your mind?"

The captain announced—not a moment too soon—that we were beginning our final descent into Beirut. Deliverance was at hand, albeit temporarily.

CHAPTER THIRTY-EIGHT
NATALYA (2)

AFTER LUNCH AT the newly opened Phoenicia Hotel, I raced to the Normandie to collect the flowers and Christmas card I'd asked Georges to have waiting for me. I grabbed a taxi, gave the driver Natalya's address, and prepared myself for an unsettling ride through the byways of Beirut. Suddenly, a disturbing thought struck me. What if Natalya had died, become too ill or disabled to live alone, or moved nearer to a White-Russian community for emotional support?

Then I saw that we were already bearing down on her house. It looked the same as before. When I rang the bell, Natalya opened the door immediately. "I'm so glad to see you looking so well," I exclaimed, as I presented the flowers and the card. "The card is for Western Christmas. With Russian Christmas still two weeks away, I couldn't find anything that reflected the traditions of the Eastern Church."

She embraced me European style with kisses on both cheeks and admired the flowers extravagantly. Her eyes were moist with tears she was making a valiant effort to conceal.

"Nancy, *quel plaisir* (what a pleasure)! You're just in time for tea. Have a seat; I'll be back in a moment." She reappeared almost at once with a tea tray, a basket of freshly baked pastries, and a crystal vase. Baccarat? Probably. How was she always prepared to serve tea and homemade pastries with such elegance and flair? Did she have a bakery business on the side? I didn't dare ask. People of her social background didn't "go into trade." Natalya had lost everything but her pride. I wasn't going to rob her of that.

Natalya took the card out of the envelope and examined it more closely. "The picture on the front reminds me of the icons in our church in Russia when I was a girl. I wish you were going to be here for our Christmas so I could serve you some of our seasonal dishes. Then we could go to the liturgy together." She wiped her eyes with a linen handkerchief.

"I'm sorry I can't be here. The oil company I work for operates strictly on the Western calendar. But tell me, what was Christmas like in the Old Russia?"

"Christmas festivities began the day before. We cut a tree in our forest and made new decorations each year. They weren't at all like the ones for sale in Beirut these days. After we decorated the tree, we could hardly wait for the first star to come out. That was the traditional time to break the Christmas Eve fast. We had been smelling *kutia* simmering on the stove for what seemed like hours, so we were famished."

"What's *kutia*? Several Russian families lived near us in North Dakota when my father was stationed on the Standing Rock Sioux Reservation, but as far as I can remember, no one ever mentioned *kutia*."

"It's a thin porridge made with cracked wheat, dried fruit, honey, and poppy seeds."

"That sounds delicious. Did other dishes follow the *kutia*?"

"Yes, but only meatless dishes were permissible that night. Christmas Eve was a day of abstinence, as well as a fast day. Otherwise, Christmas Eve menus reflected the tastes of each family, although various regions had their traditional specialties. Vegetable pies with potato filling were popular in the Voronezh district.

"Borscht and sauerkraut were customary everywhere because their ingredients were readily available even in December, when most other vegetables were unobtainable. During the long, cold Russian winters, everyone stored root vegetables like beets, parsnips, potatoes, and onions for months on end, so even the poorest families could make borscht for the Christmas Eve supper. Cabbage is a summer vegetable, but everyone had sauerkraut on hand throughout the year. The acid it contains preserves it from spoilage."

"What did you have for dessert on Christmas Eve?"

"Gingerbread and dried fruit were traditional in most parts of European Russia."

"What did you drink with the meal?"

"Our traditional Christmas Eve drink resembled sweetened hot tea, but we made it by boiling dried fruit, honey, and water together."

"Honey was a key ingredient in your Christmas recipes, wasn't it? Was that because it was the only sweetener readily available in Russia then?"

"That was part of it, but honey had been a symbol of happiness in Russian culture as far back as anyone could remember. Christmas was a joyous season, so honey seemed especially appropriate then."

"Was there a ritual to accompany the Christmas Eve meal?"

"Yes. Father led us in the Lord's Prayer. Then we gave thanks for our good fortune during the past year and prayed for happiness in the year to come. Then, Mother blessed us by making the sign of the cross on our foreheads with honey."

"Was that the end of the Christmas Eve ritual?"

"Not quite. We all dipped pieces of bread in honey and grated garlic and ate them."

"Ooh! Why spoil the taste of honey with garlic?"

"Garlic was for disappointment and misfortune. Both are part of every life, even in the happiest of times."

Oh, Natalya, you've surely had more than your share of the former.

"Did you go directly to the liturgy after supper?"

"No, the children opened their presents first. Adults had to wait until New Years' Day—the traditional gift-giving time in Russia."

"What time did you get home from the liturgy?"

"Around two or three in the morning. The Christmas Eve liturgy is long, and thick snow always covered the ground. We went to and from the church in horse-drawn sleighs—not the quickest way to travel."

"Christmas Eve sounds exhausting. Did you sleep late on Christmas Day to recuperate?"

"Oh no. The Russian custom was to call on friends and neighbors and sing Christmas carols as we made our way through the streets of the village."

"What wonderful memories you have of those times."

"Yes, I cherish them, but they are the past, and we have no choice but to concentrate on the present." I wondered if she was thinking about the sons and husband she hadn't been able to bless for so many years, but then she smiled and changed the subject.

"How are your piano pupils doing? Do you need any solo music for them?"

"Probably, but I'll have to see how much progress they make over the next two or three months. I want to be sure that their recital pieces showcase their individual skills to full advantage."

"Will you be returning to Beirut anytime soon?"

"I'm planning to come over *Id al-Fitr*, as I did last year. When I'm running out of hard-to-find ingredients for my catering business, it's time for another trip to Beirut."

I explained that I would be leaving the next day for Jerusalem, where I would spend the remainder of my Christmas break.

Her smile faded. "I've always wanted to be in Jerusalem for our Christmas, but I have to face facts now. The trip would be much too exhausting for me at my age. I found a Russian program on the radio one year that took me back to the Christmases of my youth and early married life, but that was pure luck."

I hated to leave Natalya on that note, but I had no choice. I was taking the bus back to the hotel district, and it would soon be dark.

"Be sure to come by when you're in Beirut for the *Id*," she said, as she walked me to the door.

CHAPTER THIRTY-NINE

JERUSALEM, DAY 1

A S HE THREATENED, Reginald met my flight in Amman. At least I didn't have to figure out how to get to Jerusalem on my own. Elias, his driver, was waiting for us when we exited the terminal.

As we crossed the Jordan, Elias pointed to a pool in the river on the right side of the car. He explained that many people believed that St. John baptized Jesus there, but no one knew for sure.

From Jericho, we began our 3,300-foot ascent to Jerusalem. I was tempted to ask Reginald if he wanted to walk it. Elias and I would be delighted to wait for him at the entrance to the Old City. However, in the Christmas spirit, I let that one pass.

After I checked into the pilgrim quarters, we set out on Reginald's itinerary for the afternoon. I did risk one suggestion, to which he grudgingly acceded. I doubted that we'd be back in time for evensong at 5:00, so I recommended that we transfer that visit to the next day, when we'd be touring the nearby Old City on foot. Returning to the cathedral from anywhere in the Christian Quarter would take only a few minutes.

Our first stop was the Temple Mount. Reginald was too busy reading his guidebook to spare a glance at either the Dome of the Rock or Al Aqsa Mosque, so I took advantage of the silence to ask Elias why Solomon chose this site for his temple.

"David, rather than Solomon, was the prime mover of the temple project. He fully intended to carry it out himself. He designed the temple's layout, accumulated high-value materials for its construction, recruited workmen skilled in the building arts, specified the manner and content of temple music, solicited offerings to supplement his personal contribution to the cost of construction, and designated Levites to offer the sacrifices required by Mosaic Law. *[I Chronicles 29:1-9]* Given the specificity of his plans, he must also have had an exact location for the temple in mind, but we can't be sure where it was. The Hebrew Scriptures are mute on that point."

Reginald laid his guidebook aside with a sigh. "So, if David did all the groundwork, why was the building called Solomon's temple, rather than David's?"

"God forbade David to build the temple 'because he had waged wars and shed blood.' Many Biblical scholars think the latter is a reference to the murder of Uriah the Hittite by sending him to almost certain death in the heat of battle to cover up David's taking of Bathsheba, Uriah's wife, as his own. David gave his plans to Solomon—Bathsheba's son—who completed the construction of the temple as David had envisioned it." *[I Chronicles 22-29]*

Reginald checked his guidebook. "That's all very well, but where did Solomon build the temple? Such a large and impressive building must have left some traces of its existence."

"Sir, in 587 BC, the Babylonians did a workmanlike job of dismantling the temple. They took precious structural elements, temple furnishings of value, and virtually the entire population of Jerusalem who had survived the siege of the city with them back to Babylon. Then they leveled the temple to its foundations.

"That was the beginning of the Babylonian Captivity. *[II Kings 24:13-15]* After the Persians defeated the Babylonians, Cyrus the Great encouraged those who wished to return to Jerusalem to rebuild Solomon's Temple to do so, but so much time had passed that the returnees were grandchildren or even great-grand-children of the original captives. *[Ezra 1:1-5]* In the absence of more reliable sources of information, they had no choice but to turn to tradition, which may or may not have been accurate, for guidance as to where they should build the restored temple and what it should look like when it was finished.

"We know more about the returnee-built Second Temple, but not its exact location. The Romans razed it in 70 AD following the Jewish Revolt. Builders of the Western Wall salvaged whatever masonry they could for their own purposes. Education was more widespread in the first century AD than in Solomon's time, though, so several writers have given us some idea of the layout of the temple."

"There shouldn't be any question about the location of either of the temples—or their layouts—by this time. Couldn't someone just take a spade and start digging?" Reginald, of course.

I admired Elias's patience. "Studies scholars undertook during the waning years of the Ottoman Period were too limited to yield conclusive results. Jews, Muslims, and Christians alike balked at the very idea of turning the Temple Mount into an archeological dig. That objection persists today."

"Surely someone could knock a few heads together. Who's in charge here?"

"You've put your finger on the crux of the problem. Locations sacred to Judaism, Christianity, and/or Islam stud the Old City. At present, an uneasy agreement between Christians and Muslims governs what can and cannot be done on the Temple Mount and who is responsible for what. A Jordanian-Palestinian organization is responsible for religious matters affecting the Dome of the Rock and Al Aqsa. Orthodox and Latin-Rite religious orders manage the Christian sites, but they don't always see eye-to-eye about what should be done or who should do it. For their part, the Jordanians have done a good job of protecting access to Christian and Muslim holy places, but Israelis who wish to pray at the Western Wall [1961] have been barred from doing so since the 1948-49 war. That's an understandable grievance with them."

"Elias," I asked. "Will we be able to see the interior of the Dome of the Rock and/or Al Aqsa today?"

"Unfortunately, no. At this time, only Muslims may enter the Dome of the Rock. As for Al Aqsa, no visiting hours are scheduled for today. As you know, Friday is the Muslim Sabbath."

"Who allowed the Muslims to build on the Temple Mount in the first place?" Reginald again. I cringed. Elias seemed shaken momentarily, but he recovered faster than I did. He must have had experience with "ugly" Americans.

"Remember, sir. Jerusalem was under Muslim rule from the seventh-century Islamic conquest until 1917, with the exception of the Crusader period in the twelfth century. Successive Muslim dynasties had plenty of time to carry out construction projects of their choosing. Besides, Al Aqsa is the third most important holy place for Muslims after Mecca and Medina."

"Why is that?" I asked before Reginald could commit another gaffe.

"Al Aqsa is the legendary starting place of Muhammad's Night Journey. Muslims believe that he ascended to paradise astride a white animal 'smaller than a mule and larger than a donkey' in the company of the Angel Jibreel (Gabriel). When he and his escort arrived at their destination, the gatekeeper asked whether Muhammad had been sent for. Jibreel confirmed that he had been. Once inside the gate, Muhammad conversed with Jesus, John the Baptist, Adam, Enoch, Joseph, Moses, Aaron, and Abraham—all of whom welcomed him as one of their own, thus validating his call to prophecy. Muhammad also spoke with Allah himself and received from him directions for the regimen of prayer Muslims throughout the world follow to this day."

Elias was moving us toward the Western Wall, where he pointed out the sections believed to be parts of the Second Temple. He also explained that when the Jews had unrestricted access to the Wall, they wrote their petitions on bits of paper and stuck them into cracks in the masonry.

All at once, we noticed that the sun was fast slipping below the horizon. Elias suggested that we drive to the Mount of Olives to see Jerusalem's skyline in the twilight and leave our visit to the Church of All Nations until the next day. Even Reginald concurred that that would be wise. I refrained from mentioning that scratching evensong from the afternoon's program had been a realistic move.

CHAPTER FORTY

JERUSALEM, DAY 2

THE NEXT MORNING was sunny, but colder and windier. About three inches of snow had fallen overnight.

Elias was waiting for us when we finished breakfast. He suggested that we visit the Church of All Nations first and then devote the rest of the day to touring the Old City. As we neared the basilica, he pointed out a grove of the oldest-looking olive trees I'd ever seen. Tradition held that these trees were remnants of the Garden of Gethsemane where, according to the gospels of Matthew and Mark, Jesus prayed on the night of his betrayal and arrest. (The gospels of Luke and John identify the site as the Mount of Olives—surely a reference to the same place; "*gethsemane*" means "olive press" in Hebrew.)

The modern architecture and décor of the nearby Church of All Nations presented a striking contrast to the ancient Garden of Gethsemane. Reginald remarked that the design of the basilica was impressive, but out of place in such a venerable location.

"Sir, the Church of All Nations is a post-WW1 construction, but the inspiration for its building is very much in keeping with Christian values throughout the ages."

"Oh? What exactly was that inspiration?"

"A reaffirmation of the unity of mankind and the superiority of reconciliation over warfare as a means of settling national and/or cultural clashes. The generation who financed the construction of the basilica had just lived through four years of carnage that sometimes took tens of thousands of lives in a single afternoon. The architecture and ornamentation of the basilica symbolize both survivors' horror of war and their hope that the world had learned its lesson and would choose peaceful means for resolving even the bitterest disputes in the future."

"But WW1 was a just war."

"The builders of the basilica either rejected the whole concept of 'just' wars or felt that no war was worth its cost in lives lost and long-lasting human misery."

This conversation seemed likely to escalate into a mini-war of its own unless something put a stop to it pronto. "Elias, I think we would all agree that reconciliation is a noble ideal, but one that mankind regularly loses sight of. Does the design of the basilica suggest any steps we might take to improve our record in this regard?"

"Yes, and it does so in a way that demonstrates that human diversity and unity are not mutually exclusive. Come. Let me show you one example."

Outside in the courtyard, Elias pointed to row upon row of stone tablets, each with the Lord's Prayer inscribed on it in a different language. The architects of the basilica hoped that visitors from all over the world would pray the common prayer there in their own tongues and within the frameworks of their personal religious traditions.

* * *

We headed back to Jerusalem to begin our walking tour of the Old City. Just outside Lions Gate, we stopped for a quick lunch of tea and sandwiches. While we were eating, I asked Elias whether he was a native of Jerusalem.

"No, I was born in Jaffa. My family had a prosperous business there."

"What kind of business did your family own?"

"We exported the famous Jaffa oranges. When I was a little boy, I used to pick up fruit that had fallen to the ground, find a nice shady spot, and eat so many oranges that I sometimes made myself sick. I remember my father saying, 'Elias, if you keep stuffing yourself like that, your skin will turn orange, and everyone will laugh at you.'"

"Did that cure you of your orange-eating habit?"

"No. I just tried to be more discreet. For a long time, though, I kept checking my skin to see if it was changing color, but I couldn't see any sign of that."

Elias went on to explain that as the oldest son, he couldn't remember when he hadn't known that he was destined to take over the business when his father retired. As an eight-year-old, he began to do odd jobs around the warehouse to prepare for what he understood was to be his life's work.

All of a sudden, a peculiar popping sound startled me. I looked around and saw ... Reginald cracking his knuckles.

I was eager to hear more about Elias's background and more than grateful for any excuse to put off our slog over snow-covered cobblestones as long as I dared, so I risked asking Elias a series of follow-up questions. "Elias, what else did your family do to prepare you for your career as a business owner?" Reginald switched to drumming his fingers on the table. Better not push this conversation too far. I watched him out of the corner of my eye in the hope of spotting a potential explosion in time to head it off.

"I completed my primary schooling at a parochial school in Jaffa. My father went over my grade reports *very* carefully every term, especially in math, because, as he never tired of telling me, I would be responsible for the financial management of the business. English was the second most important subject. The British held the Mandate then, and we expected that to continue for the foreseeable future."

I glanced at Reginald. Oh-oh, time to defuse this situation before it spun out of control. Turning to the human thundercloud forming on my left, I asked, "Reginald, don't you find Elias's background fascinating?" A slight nod of the head that could mean anything. No surprise that; I hadn't detected much interest in anything else we'd seen or heard. I wondered why he had taken the trouble to come to Jerusalem at all.

Like the celebrity I suspected he craved to be, he must have been thinking of his public. For the rest of his life, I could just hear him telling anyone who would listen how his visit to the Holy City had changed his life. Meanwhile he sulked silently, so I went back to prompting Elias to share more of his life story with us. "Where did you receive your secondary-school education?"

"At the Friends' School in Ramallah. My acceptance letter elated my father. He bragged about it to all his acquaintances and business associates. That school was famous for its success in qualifying students for admission to the American University of Beirut."

"And did you attend AUB?"

"Yes. After I graduated in 1944, I returned to Jaffa to work for my father, who was planning to retire soon for health reasons. The 1948 war upset our carefully laid plans."

"So how did you end up in Jerusalem?"

"By late 1947, fighting around Jaffa intensified to the point that sheltering in place was no longer feasible. My parents took refuge in Beirut, but I headed for Ramallah, because I knew the people at the school. I thought they might help me to find a job in the Palestinian sector. That way, I could avoid going to a refugee camp." Reginald opened his mouth to say something, but I beat him to the draw.

"Elias, not only has hearing your life story moved us, but your connection with the Friends' Schools is an unbelievable stroke of luck for me. I want to visit Willard and Christina Jones this evening. Bertha Vester told me they're living somewhere in Jerusalem, but I don't know where. You must know them. They would have been at Ramallah during your student days." Reginald was just aching to change the subject, but I had no intention of letting him. Nor did Elias.

"Of course I know the Joneses. They do live in Jerusalem. They're leaders in relief services for Palestinian refugees. They found me my job at the cathedral and helped me locate affordable housing for my family in Bethlehem. I don't know exactly where they live, but I can definitely find that out by the end of the afternoon."

"Speaking of our afternoon activities, we shouldn't waste any more time here." Reginald's patience was obviously exhausted, but I was thankful he had managed to sit through more of Elias's and my conversation than I'd expected.

"Quite right, sir, but we won't have any trouble covering the two remaining sites on the itinerary you gave me. We still have at least four hours of daylight, and in view of the cold and snow, I doubt the lady will want to do more." I put my hand over my mouth to cover an unseemly smirk.

"All right, but we absolutely must have time to do justice to those two sites." He was not pacified, but he could hardly fire Elias on the spot. That would leave him without a car, a driver, or tickets to Midnight Mass in Bethlehem.

We entered the Old City via the Muslim Quarter and began our walk along the Via Dolorosa, traditionally thought to be the route Jesus walked from the Antonia Fortress to Golgotha, the site of his crucifixion, burial, and resurrection. "Lady," Elias inquired solicitously, "the Via Dolorosa extends about half a mile beyond this point, and the ground is fairly level. However, the streets are cobbled and still snowy. Will that be all right with you?" *He had Reginald's number all right.*

"Thank you for asking, Elias, but I'm sure I can manage."

"Just tell me if we're walking too fast, and we'll slow down." Reginald opened his mouth to say something but closed it again.

As we neared the Church of the Holy Sepulchre, Elias pointed to a ladder leaning against a wall of the church. "How long do you think that ladder has been there?"

Reginald opined that that was irrelevant. The ladder was unsightly, detracted from the appearance of the church, and should be removed at once.

"Elias, that sounds like a trick question. You tell us. How long has the ladder been there? It almost seems to invite a break-in."

"A workman left it there in 1757. As far as I know, no one has used the ladder for any purpose, legal or illegal, since."

"The caretakers of the basilica should be replaced at once on the grounds of negligence in the performance of their duties." Reginald again.

"Unfortunately, the ladder is symptomatic of a far more serious problem that dates back at least a thousand years."

"And what is that?"

"The seventh-century Islamic conquerors let their new non-Muslim subjects carry on their own religious traditions as long as they paid the *jizya* and made no effort to convert Muslims to other religions. During the Byzantine Period, successive emperors had commissioned numerous churches, monasteries, and shrines throughout Palestine, but especially in and about Jerusalem. Eastern-Rite religious orders had cared for these properties previously, and their Islamic conquerors saw no reason to change that arrangement, which worked well enough until the Crusaders from the West arrived in 1099. The latter viewed themselves as the liberators of their Eastern-Christian brethren. Members of the Eastern Church suspected that the Crusaders had a more self-serving agenda."

"Why?"

"East-West tensions within the Christian Church surfaced as early as in the first century and intensified after Christianity became the official religion of the Roman Empire. The Eastern branch regarded themselves as the 'original' Christians. As they never tired of pointing out, the Apostles wrote the Gospels in Greek, not Latin. Leaders of the Western Church countered that argument by insisting that St. Peter, whom Christ himself appointed as the head of his church [Matthew 16:13-20] became the first Bishop of Rome, not of some Eastern city.

"The East-West rift widened as the Western Roman Empire crumbled from infighting and the barbarian invasions. The Eastern-Rite leadership began to wonder why a prelate in Rome who couldn't even guarantee his own safety insisted on dictating to the followers of Christ in the part of the world where Christianity originated."

"That seems reasonable to me."

"It did to the Patriarch of Constantinople also. Meanwhile, later Popes found it progressively more difficult to exert their authority even where the Latin Rite was long established, let alone over the theology and practices of the Eastern Church. Some didn't even try.

The Eastern and Western wings of the 'universal' Church drifted further and further apart. They split definitively in 1054—only forty-five years before the First Crusade. If the Crusaders expected the clergy of the Eastern Church to greet them with open arms, they were in for a big surprise."

Reginald looked at his watch. "So what does all this have to do with a two-century-old ladder leaning against a wall of the Church of the Holy Sepulchre?"

"Remember the struggles about what can and cannot be done on the Temple Mount. A similar jurisdictional tug of war developed early on at the Church of the Holy Sepulchre. The turf battle at Christendom's holiest shrine would have been difficult enough to settle had the interested parties wanted to reach a compromise. But they didn't. When Saladin retook Jerusalem, the degree of animosity festering between the Eastern and Western branches of the Christian Church astounded him. Even rival Eastern-Rite groups were sniping at one another. Something as petty as who should be responsible for unlocking and locking the Church each day had become a major bone of contention.

"Saladin had enough to do to reorganize services in a city that had been under foreign occupation for eighty-eight years. He didn't plan to fritter away his time arbitrating intra-Christian feuds. If the Christians couldn't settle their differences among themselves, maybe responsible Muslims could do it for them. He appointed two prominent Muslim families hereditary keepers of the keys to the basilica. Members of these two families still carry out Saladin's orders today, seven hundred sixty-nine years later."

"Surely you exaggerate. The behavior you describe may have been common among rough fighting men centuries ago. Educated clerics wouldn't have behaved that way."

"Unfortunately, they did and continued to do so for hundreds of years. In the nineteenth century, the East-West jurisdictional struggle flared up again. An out-of-patience Ottoman official managed to broker an agreement among the contending parties that nothing should be done in or to the church without the unanimous consent of the six groups responsible for its care. These gentlemen have never agreed to remove the aesthetically distasteful ladder."

"How ridiculous!" Reginald, like Saladin and the nineteenth-century Ottoman bureaucrat, had had enough of that subject.

We entered the basilica. Even an imposing array of sanctuary lamps and votive candles failed to make appreciable inroads on the pervasive gloom of the interior.

"Elias," I remarked, "this structure reminds me of Romanesque churches and monasteries I saw in Europe, although there's a hint of the Hagia Sophia in it, too."

"That's not surprising. Like many Christian churches you've probably seen in Lebanon, today's Church of the Holy Sepulchre is essentially a twelfth-century Crusader construction with occasional Byzantine touches."

"Elias, as you just pointed out, this is the holiest shrine in Christendom. Surely the local Christian community didn't wait more than a thousand years to build a church on this spot. One of my catering clients gave me a brochure about the Church of the Holy Sepulchre that claims that the earliest Christians celebrated liturgies here even before the Roman destruction of Jerusalem in 70 AD."

"I'll wager that brochure doesn't say that Christians have held services here *continuously* since before 70 AD. Christianity was subject to recurrent persecutions for several decades both before and after the destruction of Jerusalem. The faithful were reduced to meeting in private homes or in out-of-the-way places for self-protection. Only when Christianity became the official religion of the Roman Empire almost three hundred years later were Christians in any position to embark on a church-building program. Any shrine here in the first century must have disappeared by 135 AD. That's when the Emperor Hadrian built a pagan temple on what he thought was a useless plot of abandoned land."

Reginald perked up at that; apparently his guidebook was silent on the origins of the Church of the Holy Sepulchre. "So when was the first permanent Christian church built on this site?"

"The Emperor Constantine built a church in almost exactly the same place as today's Church of the Holy Sepulchre, but a Persian army leveled it in the seventh century. The Patriarch of Constantinople subsequently had the church rebuilt according to the original plans. The Muslim conquerors respected the church for three centuries thereafter, but a mentally unbalanced Caliph razed it to its foundations in 1009. Incidents like that inspired the chivalry of the West to undertake the First Crusade, which restored Jerusalem to Christian rule."

"Did the Crusader church also follow the Byzantine architectural plans?" *Amazing. He must be genuinely interested in the answer to that question.* I waited for him to crank up his lecture mode as soon as Elias stopped for breath, but nothing happened. He just looked thoughtful.

"No. The twelfth-century church is smaller because the Crusaders used part of the site for a monastery."

The partitioning of the interior of the church into an almost endless succession of chapels, each of which "belonged" to one or the other of the custodial religious orders, made the church appear even smaller than it did from the outside. According to Elias, only the traditional burial site of Jesus and the Stone of Unction on which his body was prepared for burial were common "property." Two separate Calvary chapels, one for the Eastern orders and the other for the Roman Catholics, were so close together that they almost touched, but the two factions continued to argue about which chapel, if either, stood on the exact site of the crucifixion.

When we exited the church, we headed for what was then heralded as the Upper Room, where Jesus and his Apostles ate the Passover on the night of his arrest. The building we saw could well have been there for two thousand years, and the "Upper Room" looked adequate for thirteen people, so it never occurred to me that this location might someday become controversial. However, when I visited Jerusalem some fifty years later, our guide showed our group an entirely different and more architecturally ornate room that somehow seemed less plausible.

We left the Old City by the New Gate. Before he left us, Elias took me aside and told me he had called the Joneses, who said they would be home that evening. They would expect me between 7:30 and 8:00. The cathedral staff would call me a taxi when I was ready.

CHAPTER FORTY-ONE

REUNION WITH FAMILY FRIENDS

MY PARENTS MET the Joneses in 1941 through the fortunes of war—at least on the Joneses' side. Willard and Christina were packed to return to Ramallah from a stateside leave early in December. The US entry into the war put their plans on indefinite hold. To support his family until transportation to Palestine again became available, Willard found temporary employment at the Chilocco (OK) Indian School, where my father was on the staff.

Ever since the outbreak of war in Europe in 1939, travel to the Eastern Mediterranean had been perilous enough, even for citizens of neutral nations traveling on neutral-registry ships. After Germany declared war on the US to fulfill its treaty obligations to Japan, Americans became fair game for attack by the European Axis powers.

Mediterranean travel was particularly hazardous because major maritime routes lay within range of German air bases in France, Italy, Yugoslavia, and Greece. The risk that the Axis might win the battle for the Mediterranean intensified early in 1942. The arrival of crack German troops in Libya to shore up the faltering Italian desert campaign aroused widespread fear that Field Marshall Rommel's army might overwhelm British defenses in the Nile Delta. If that happened, Palestine would lie open to invasion.

I was ten when the Joneses came to Chilocco and already a confirmed travel buff—destination irrelevant. Two years earlier, my parents had sent me with my maternal grandparents and two aunts on a five-week trip through Eastern Canada and New England to the New York World's Fair. By the time we returned to Chilocco, I'd added thirteen states to the six I'd already visited—and Ontario and Quebec to boot. Not bad for an eight-year-old born in the worst year of the Great Depression.

I doubt that the typical eight-year-old had a bucket list in 1939, but heedless of economic reality or potential international complications—the German invasion of Poland was only weeks away—I was busily compiling mine. My travel horizons had expanded to include European destinations almost at once after the 1939 trip, thanks to the impressive national pavilions at the World's Fair and Madeline Brandeis's *Children of the World* series, which I had read in its entirety.

Even my eight-year-old brain could understand that satisfying my newly discovered yen for foreign travel had to be a long-term goal, although I thought that grossly unfair. Worse was yet to come.

After the US entered the war, opportunities for domestic travel by civilians dried up virtually overnight. Congress banned speeds greater than 35 mph on US highways. The gasoline ration was only three gallons per week for everyone except those who could prove a defense-related need for a more generous allocation. We had to make it through the war with whatever tires we had on hand when rationing began.

How about buying a new car to get four new tires? Forget it. Tanks and military vehicles were rolling off the assembly lines of companies that previously produced cars for the civilian market. Even walking tours became impractical; the shoe ration was only two pairs per year, and my feet were still growing.

I turned my attention to travel substitutes in lieu of the real thing. For hours on end, I studied maps and crafted itineraries to follow as soon as the war was over.

The arrival of the Joneses at Chilocco delivered a hefty jolt of oxygen to my beleaguered travel fantasies. I had only a vague notion where Palestine was or who lived there, but Christina soon remedied that. Using a relief map of the country we made from unrationed flour, salt, and water, she pointed out where events described in familiar Bible stories took place.

She also left me a wealth of photographs and souvenirs from Palestine when she finally secured passage on a convoy to rejoin her husband in Ramallah in 1944. (Willard had departed for Palestine in 1943 via Brazil, Senegal, and Kenya, but the shortage of civilian transport kept him in Kenya for nearly a year before he was able to proceed to Ramallah.)

CHAPTER FORTY-TWO

CATCHING UP WITH THE JONESES

WILLARD AND CHRISTINA greeted me like a long-lost daughter. Christina reminded me that she'd baked an angel food cake for my eleventh birthday. Mother sent me to the Joneses' with sugar—which was rationed—and a dozen eggs from our wartime hencoop. The cake was almost too beautiful to eat, but the prospect of a rare sugary treat quickly overcame our aesthetic scruples.

"Are your parents still at Chilocco?" Christina asked.

"No, my father was transferred to Tuba City, Arizona soon after you left. Later we were stationed at Fort Wingate, New Mexico; Fort Yates, North Dakota; and Ft. Sill, Oklahoma before my father retired. My parents are now living in Arizona again."

Willard's first question brought us back to Jerusalem. "How did you find us?"

"By sheer happenstance. Bertha Vester came to Arabia this fall to sell Palestinian needlework and her book. When I asked about you, she confirmed that you were now living in Jerusalem quite near the American Colony. Elias, our driver, was able to obtain your address."

"We remember Elias as a schoolboy. As an honors graduate of AUB, he is overqualified for his present position, but just having any job at all in these times is a victory of sorts."

"Elias did mention your help with his job hunt. He is very grateful."

"Where is Elias taking you tomorrow morning?"

"I'm not sure. Reginald, my travel companion, arranged our Jerusalem itinerary."

"It seems a shame for you to waste an entire morning when your visit to the Holy City is so brief. Why don't you ask Elias to take you somewhere of your choosing if your companion has other plans?"

"Elias is Reginald's driver; I'm just along for the ride. I hardly know Reginald. Before he turned up as my seatmate on the Dhahran-Beirut flight, I hadn't seen him since a three-day period soon after I arrived in Arabia. At the time, we were both patients at the Abqaiq Clinic. He absolutely insisted that we tour together. That solved a complicated transportation issue for me, so I agreed, but there's a tradeoff. My ability to get changes to our itinerary is strictly limited. I do know that the service at the Shepherds' Fields and the Vigil Mass at the Church of the Nativity in Bethlehem are both on tomorrow's schedule. Elias will drive us back to Jerusalem after Mass."

The usually unflappable Christina looked startled. "How are you going to get to the Shepherds' Fields? If Elias isn't available, we'd be happy to give the two of you a lift. Willard is participating in the service."

"That's very tempting, but Reginald is insisting that we walk the seven miles to Bethlehem. He read in his guidebook that that's the custom. I'm toying with not going at all. These are the only shoes I have with me. They're definitely not up to a seven-mile hike through slush and snow."

Now Willard looked alarmed. "Who told you it's only seven miles to Bethlehem?"

"Reginald, of course. It's that infamous guidebook again."

"That book must have been published a number of years ago. It's double that distance by the road you'd have to take these days to avoid crossing the armistice line. You shouldn't even consider it. Even if you could keep up a pace of two and half miles per hour, it would take you nearly six hours to reach Bethlehem, and that doesn't count the time needed to detour to the Shepherds' Fields and back to Bethlehem. Just tell Reginald no."

"Consider it done. If he doesn't give up the idea of walking, I'll gladly accept a ride with you. And if you're not staying for the Mass, I'll take a taxi back to Jerusalem."

"Don't worry. We'll work this out somehow," Christina assured me.

Willard returned to the previous topic. "But if it were up to you, where would you go tomorrow morning?"

"Either to the Aqabat Jabr camp to get an idea of the scope of the refugee problem or to Ramallah to visit the Friends' Schools."

Willard nodded. "Both are excellent choices, but how did you hear about Aqabat Jabr?"

"Credit Bertha Vester's talk for that. She mentioned several refugee camps, but I remembered Aqabat Jabr because it's near Jericho—one of the few Palestinian locations I recognized."

"I'd especially like for you to see Aqabat Jabr. I'll have a word with Elias to see if that could be worked into tomorrow morning's schedule."

"Please do, because I have a sneaking suspicion that visiting refugee camps is not high on Reginald's list of priorities."

CHAPTER FORTY-THREE

RAMALLAH, 1922-1939

I ASKED WILLARD AND Christina to describe their experiences in Palestine from the time their ship docked in Jaffa in 1922 to the outbreak of WW2.

"Our first reactions were personal. When we started up the Jerusalem road to Ramallah, we pledged the rest of our lives to the welfare of the people of Palestine—regardless of faith or economic status. We had no idea then all that our commitment would demand of us over the years, but that was probably just as well. We had more immediate concerns to sort out.

"It suddenly hit home to us that we would be expected to begin our work at the Friends mission that very day. Nervousness overpowered our youthful enthusiasm. We hadn't been married very long; the Ramallah assignment was our first real job. We spoke no Arabic, and we had only the foggiest notion what our duties would be at the mission. We decided our best strategy would be to stay out of the way of our more experienced colleagues until we could figure out what we could do to help.

"Meanwhile, we continued to marvel that we were really in the Holy Land—the backdrop for Bible stories we'd heard over and over again in Sunday school as children. That realization filled us with awe then and still does today."

"Once you became more comfortable in your role at the Friends Schools, what were your impressions of the social and political environment in Palestine?"

"At first, we viewed the League of Nations' award of the Palestine Mandate to Great Britain as a net benefit for the Palestinian people. Most of the local people with whom we came in contact in those early days seemed to agree. They had read the documents that appeared to promise them full independence as soon as they were prepared to assume the responsibilities that status entailed. Since the ostensible purpose of the mandatory system was to prepare formerly subject peoples for self-government, they were eager to cooperate with the transitional process. They were confident that Palestine's apprenticeship would be brief."

"When did you first suspect that the road to independence might take longer than your Palestinian informants believed and be bumpier than you—and they— thought?"

"Very soon. Street demonstrations, general strikes, riots, and other breakdowns in the public order were facts of life from our earliest days in the Holy Land. We weren't too worried, though. With few exceptions, the demonstrations of the 1920s targeted the Mandatory Authority, which had ample resources to keep public protests under control."

"So disorders at that time didn't have a specific Arab-versus-Jewish character?"

"No. Arabs and Jews had lived together amicably in Palestine for centuries. With some few exceptions, they continued to do so throughout the 1920s. It didn't occur to the Arab majority that the tiny Jewish minority then living in the Mandate might multiply many times over within a very short period of time and become a serious threat to achievement of the Palestinians' goal of an independent Arab state."

"Did the Jewish population of the 1920s side with the Mandatory Authority, or did they have grievances of their own about what was happening in the country?"

"Neither group had received what they thought the British had promised them in exchange for their contributions to the Allied victory in WW1. Palestinian Arabs—who were not yet skilled in the art of deciphering diplomatic mumbo jumbo—believed that their reward for staging the Arab Revolt was to be full independence in a state of their own. At the same time, the Balfour Declaration promised the Jews 'a national home' in Palestine. The fact that the Declaration failed to define what 'a national home' meant or spell out when and under what conditions it would come into being left Mandatory officials ample wiggle room to reinterpret the Declaration any way they thought expedient."

"So the British reneged on the spirit of their wartime commitments, if not the letter?"

"Yes, but in defense of the British, they did try to honor both promises—albeit with a London-crafted compromise that was never going to be acceptable to either side. They tasked the first High Commissioner for Palestine, Sir Hubert Samuel—a highly respected civil servant and a Jew—with the responsibility of resolving the impasse created by conflicting wartime promises. But irreparable damage had been done long before Sir Hubert first set foot on Palestinian soil. The British government had promised the same territory to two peoples with quite different—and irreconcilable—postwar expectations."

"When did the Palestinian situation turn into a head-on collision between Arab and Jewish interests?"

"In the 1930s. Masses of Jewish refugees began to pour out of Europe in a frantic search for the safety denied them in their countries of origin. With their citizenship revoked and most of their assets forfeit to the states they were so desperate to escape, the list of countries willing to grant asylum to even a few Jewish refugees dwindled almost to the vanishing point. Taking in foreigners who might become public charges that the Great Depression-battered economies of potential host countries might not be able to support was almost universally viewed as an unacceptable political risk.

"A few imperial powers did remain open to limited increases in population diversity in their colonies. Among other reasons, they were counting on the new immigrants to serve as a counterweight to fractious local groups already clamoring for full independence. The British were willing to give this strategy a try—to a point.

"They upped the number of visas available to Palestine-bound Jewish applicants, although not nearly enough to accommodate all those in desperate need of a safe place to go. The result was an unmanageable rise in illegal immigration."

"How did the Arabs react to this change in the Arab-Jewish composition of Palestine's population?"

"That varied by socioeconomic status. Middle-class Palestinians were still counting on the formation of an independent Arab state once the Mandate ended. The increased percentage of Jews already in Palestine—with many more to come—put that goal in jeopardy. Leaders of Palestinian groups who favored working within the system put political pressure on the Mandatory Authority to return to the previous less generous Jewish-immigration quotas. That strategy failed for mathematical reasons. Middle-class Palestinians made up so small a proportion of the total population of the Mandate during the interwar period that British officials didn't take their protests too seriously.

"In 1936, the socioeconomic status and detailed grievances of Palestinian protesters shifted, and so did their methods of demanding a rollback of increases in Jewish immigration. Palestine was still very much an agricultural country then, despite its limited supply of arable land. The *fellahin* (peasants) who made up the overwhelming majority of the Palestinian population weren't interested in the niceties of political methods of protest. Their grievances—and fears—were economic. Many had become destitute as a result of Jewish purchases of land they had previously worked as tenant formers; others feared a similar fate might befall them at any time.

"Instead of sending letters of remonstrance to Mandatory officials, they took to the streets, much as protesters had done when Christina and I first arrived in Palestine. General strikes, street demonstrations, riots, and random acts of violence against soft targets erupted with increasing frequency but little practical effect from 1936 until the outbreak of war in 1939. The *fellahin* were no match for British troops stationed in Palestine, so the Mandatory Authority had little difficulty restoring order after each disturbance, at least for the time being."

CHAPTER FORTY-FOUR

WW2 AND UN RESOLUTION 181

I'D EXPECTED TO hear that the wartime transfer of British troops from Palestine to protect the Suez Canal resulted in an uptick in the anti-Jewish demonstrations of the latter half of the 1930s.

"You may find this surprising—I know Christina and I did—but the outbreak of WW2 had exactly the opposite effect. Wartime conditions achieved what no level of popular protest had succeeded in bringing about.

"Jewish Immigration to Palestine declined precipitously, even though European Jews were in greater danger than ever. Would-be Jewish refugees without proper documentation—*i.e.,* those fleeing Axis countries—who did manage to board buses, trams, or trains were subject to summary arrest. Although neutral countries sheltered some refugees who managed to reach their borders, their capacity to do so was increasingly limited by the wartime pinch on the food supply.

"Refugees headed for Palestine faced additional barriers to safe completion of their journeys. Without visas for their destinations, they were suspect as enemy aliens and subject to internment as they passed through Allied countries. If their escape from Europe required crossing the Mediterranean or the Black Sea—and it usually did—they had no choice but to risk their lives aboard seriously overcrowded and, often, barely seaworthy ships."

"Under wartime conditions, land transfer from Arab to Jewish ownership must have declined sharply. Did the *fellahin* protesters of the thirties think they had achieved their goal? If so, they must have decided that it was no longer worthwhile to take to the streets to make their point."

"That was part of it. Another key factor in the relatively peaceful relations between Palestinian Arabs and Jews during WW2 was that neither side wanted the Axis Powers to win. That was the last outcome the Jews wanted. For their part, the Arabs could see that Axis nations were imposing forced labor on defeated populations. Exchanging one colonial regime for another was not what they had in mind."

"You returned to Palestine in 1944. Did you believe then that improved Arab-Jewish relations would carry over into peacetime?"

"We hoped they would, but, as you know, they didn't. Survivors of the Holocaust were understandably traumatized by their experiences. They were determined to put as much distance between themselves and Europe as possible. Immigration to Palestine—legal and illegal—rose to hitherto unprecedented levels."

"When did major postwar Arab-Jewish violence first break out? I had thought that happened only after the UN vote to partition Palestine. My boyfriend in Venezuela disagreed. He served with the British military here from 1946 until the end of the Mandate. He insisted that serious disorders began at least a year before the partition vote."

"Your friend was right, although neither the Jewish Agency nor the surrounding Arab states resorted to open warfare then. The early disruptions that destabilized the entire country and caused the Mandatory Authority to lose all semblance of control were mostly the work of paramilitary formations.

"Isolated as we were in our West Bank backwater, we didn't take the increasing frequency of violent incidents as seriously as we should have. We mistook them for an extension of the 1936-39 riots. We never expected them to affect us directly."

"What caused you to change your minds about that?"

"Ambushes by one side or the other turned the main roads into lethal obstacle courses. Jerusalem is less than ten miles from Ramallah, but it didn't take many near misses for us to decide not to risk going there except in the direst of emergencies.

"Wasn't the public safety on the roads a basic responsibility of the Mandatory Authority?"

"Technically yes, but the Palestinian situation was deteriorating rapidly, and the war-weary British public had no stomach for military adventures anywhere for any reason. The London government notified the UN that it intended to withdraw from Palestine as soon as possible. In response, the General Assembly passed Resolution 181, which provided for the partition of Palestine. The British could hardly wait to exit the country. They were packed and ready to go by the pre-dawn hours of May 15, 1948, when Israel declared its independence as an officially Jewish state."

"Wasn't the Mandatory administration supposed to remain in Palestine until the following October to facilitate orderly transfer of power to Palestinian and Israeli officials in their respective zones? If the British had complied with that provision of the Resolution 181 implementation plan, would that have averted the worst of what happened next?"

"Many neutral observers we talked with thought it would have. Others offered equally compelling arguments that the timing of the British departure made little difference. The Mandatory Authority had struggled to regain control of the country since 1946 and failed. More of the same would only have made the situation worse.

"Many Palestinians thought the UN would intervene, but that was never a realistic expectation. The Security Council had no power of its own to deal with the violence already tearing Palestine apart."

CHAPTER FORTY-FIVE

GUERILLA TACTICS TO FULL-SCALE WAR

I ASKED IF THE sudden end of the Mandate affected the Palestinian and Israeli zones in similar ways.

"My knowledge of what happened in the Israeli sector is mostly hearsay, but missionaries working in the coastal areas told me that the transfer of power to the Jewish Agency was virtually seamless. Public services operated normally throughout the transitional period.

"As for what happened on the Palestinian side, I can tell you of my own knowledge that public services broke down here almost at once. The Palestinians—and Christina and I—awoke on May 15, 1948 to discover that the legal government of the country had slipped away under cover of darkness. Restoring public services in the Palestinian zone was an insurmountable challenge for the skeleton force of government employees still in place. But that wasn't the worst of it. A full-blown civil war was upon us, and internationalization of the conflict seemed imminent."

"Let me put my question another way. If the British had stayed on until October, would that have made it easier to evacuate and provide relief services to Palestinians living in or near the newly created Israeli sector?"

"If the British military had concentrated troops along the Proposition 181 Israeli-Palestinian border, both Israelis and Palestinians slated for displacement could have reached areas assigned to their respective groups with less risk. Delivery of food and water to refugees on the move would have been feasible and medical evacuations safer and timelier."

"Had the British troops remained in Palestine until October, would that have kept the lights on and the water running on the Palestinian side?"

"Not necessarily. The same electrical plants and water purification facilities had served residents on both sides of the battle lines in peacetime. That was unlikely to continue in an all-out civil war. It didn't help that many of the Palestinian officials still in place had worked in unrelated departments like accounting and personnel in peacetime. They were in over their heads when they attempted to operate electrical plants or keep water flowing to the towns and villages.

"On a lesser scale, our challenges were similar. We were trained as teachers, not administrators of relief services. Yet, by August 1948—two months before the British were originally scheduled to withdraw—we were already caring for thousands of refugees every day. The scale of population displacement was unimaginable. Had the British remained to secure routes along which supply trucks had to travel, obtaining food, water, and fuel to provide our refugees with basic services would have been easier—and more affordable."

"It seems to me that the fallout from conflicting WW1 promises to the Arabs and Jews and the disaster that befell European Jewry in the thirties and early forties would have doomed efforts to reach any sort of peaceful settlement in Palestine. But did the partition plan have to miscarry as badly as it did?"

"It never had a chance to succeed. The plan was based on several seriously flawed assumptions."

"What were they, and why did they doom the partition plan from the outset?"

"Once the details of Resolution 181 became public, no one we knew here thought that the land allocations stipulated in the implementation map would be acceptable to either side."

Willard cited post-WW1 experience in Eastern Europe to explain why he didn't think Resolution 181 or any other partition plan would have worked very well or for very long. The victors of WW1 set about redrawing the map of Eastern Europe so as to give formerly subject peoples "countries of their own"—a noble goal, perhaps, but a logistical nightmare. Even world powers can't just will a country into existence; they have to create it out of territory taken from others. As Willard saw it, displacing more than a million people involuntarily was not only unjust and inhumane, but ill-advised. It was bound to create a large population yearning to avenge what they saw as their undeserved misfortune.

I asked Willard what he thought of the plan to make Jaffa a Palestinian enclave, even though the city would have been surrounded by Israeli territory and the sea.

"That was a prime example of failing to take practicalities and the likelihood of negative outcomes into account when drawing national boundaries for ideological reasons. Remember the post-WW1 map that separated East Prussia from the rest of Germany in order to give the reconstituted Polish nation an outlet to the sea. The Germans weren't going to accept the loss of German territory inhabited mostly by ethnic Germans any longer than they had to. Unfortunately, the invasion of Poland in 1939 didn't just return the erstwhile Polish Corridor to German sovereignty. It also served as the opening shot of WW2, which cost an estimated 45,000,000 people their lives in the Atlantic-European Theater of Operations alone."

"What about the implementation plan's provision for the internationalization of Jerusalem? Would that have been helpful, or even feasible?"

"Internationalization of disputed territory didn't work in interwar Europe either. The WW1 peace treaties created three 'free' cities: Danzig, Memel, and Trieste. Military action by the stronger of each pair of bordering countries ended all three of those cities' internationalized status within two decades. Durable internationalization of Jerusalem would have been even more difficult to achieve."

"Why?"

"According to the partition map, the boundary between the Israeli and Palestinian zones was to have been about 20 miles from Jerusalem at the nearest point. If the baseless assumption of the mapmakers that Israel and Palestine would be friendly enough to form an economic union had been grounded in reality, internationalization of Jerusalem might have worked. By mid-1947, though, relations between the two sides were anything but friendly and deteriorating at worrisome speed.

"The Israelis were never going to settle for any arrangement that didn't guarantee them free access to Jerusalem, its religious sites and institutions, and its sizable Jewish population. Sure enough, once full-scale war broke out, one of the first major thrusts of the Israeli Army was to clear a corridor from their assigned sector to the Holy City."

"Speaking of warfare motivated by a desire to rescue persons of similar ethnic/religious backgrounds from foreign rule, did you expect the Palestinian crisis to explode into a full-fledged international conflagration?"

"We hoped it wouldn't, but we feared for the worst. Eight Middle Eastern countries (Egypt, Iran, Iraq, Lebanon, Saudi Arabia, Syria, Turkey, and Yemen) had voted against the partition of Palestine, so we suspected that at least some of the six Arab states that had cast nay votes would intervene on behalf of their Arabic-speaking brethren."

"Were you able to keep track of what was going on in the country after the British withdrawal?"

"We had very few sources of information about what was going on even a few miles beyond Ramallah. Repeated electrical outages ruled out the radio as a source of news most of the time. The breakdown of the postal system and the hazards on the roads meant that days-

or weeks-old newspapers were available only occasionally. It was mostly when the distraught parents of boarding students—especially those living in parts of the country in the new Israeli sector—started descending on the schools to collect their children that we learned what was happening in other areas of the country.

"Some of the parents told us horrific tales of narrow escapes along the road to Ramallah. We tried to convince ourselves that these tales were exaggerated, but we could scarcely ignore the random bullet holes in some of their automobiles.

"We asked whether they planned to return to their homes, but most of the men just shrugged. The women began to cry, and their children joined in, although the youngest ones had no idea what they were crying about.

"We were at a loss about what to do. Those first-wave refugees were desperate for reassurance about what would happen next, but we had no idea what to tell them. They had a more realistic sense of the dangers they faced than we did."

"What were you able to offer early-arriving refugees?

"Not much. We fed everyone who came to our door, but how long we could continue to do even that was an open question. Food prices were rising by the day and depleting our limited financial resources at an alarming rate."

"How did you house your 'unexpected' guests?"

"All but a handful of our boarders had left with their families prior to May 15, so we had a limited number of beds to offer the neediest of the first wave of refugees."

"How did the formal outbreak of war affect the flow of refugees to Ramallah?"

"A second wave of refugees mobbed the mission immediately. Most of them had climbed up to Ramallah overland from the coastal plain. Although it was not as hot then as it would be a month or two later, the May refugees, like those who came later in the summer, suffered grievously from lack of water and food during their trek to the highlands. Many simply collapsed on mission property. For them, continuing eastward on foot was out of the question. Yet all we had to offer them was warm meals and space to camp out.

"We were facing an even worse crisis than we realized at first. Even camping space would soon be at a premium unless the volume of arriving refugees declined. The search for additional reliable sources of food was a fulltime job, but that wasn't the hardest part. We had to scrape together enough money to pay for it. Most of the time, we had no idea how we were going to manage that."

"Did your refugees feel safe in Ramallah?"

Willard considered that question briefly before he replied. "Most of our refugees seemed to feel safer at the mission than at any time since the partition vote. They expressed no desire at all to leave Ramallah, which was defended by a unit of the Arab Legion. The refugees seemed to realize that they could never travel fast enough on foot to outrun mechanized army units.

"Another reason many refugees resisted the very idea of moving on beyond Ramallah was that they, like us at that point, still believed the war would be over soon. Then they could return to their homes. Ramallah would be closer to their towns and villages than destinations farther east, and the home-bound walk would be downhill all the way."

"It's hard for me to understand how you were able to accommodate your earliest arrivals, let alone the crush of refugees who poured into Ramallah in July and August. In normal times, the schools must have had fewer than two or three hundred boarders."

"Thanks to our decision to hold graduation ceremonies early, all our students were on summer vacation by late May. We were able to convert our dormitories, classrooms, study hall, and recreation center into space to deliver rudimentary healthcare and housing for refugees with the most serious health issues. It was a tight squeeze, but if the number of arriving refugees tapered off and the war wound down within a month or two, we thought we could manage. Surely the fighting wouldn't continue any longer than that. The Israeli advance had already reached, and in some areas, overrun, the boundaries allotted to them by Resolution 181."

* * *

The two sides agreed to a truce in June that rekindled the Joneses' hope for a peaceful settlement. They were to be sadly disappointed almost before the ink was dry on the agreement. The truce broke down irretrievably on July 8, and the siege of Jerusalem began. The war was not winding down. It might soon be ringing the mission doorbell.

The Joneses searched for ways to expand their capacity to deliver relief services to the refugees if the flow of new arrivals remained at current levels or increased during the worst of the hot season, as now seemed likely. It didn't help that the Joneses had no idea how many additional refugees they should be planning *for*.

Mobilizing their staff to come up with ideas to deal with a possible substantial increase in the refugee population was another challenge. Most mission employees still clung to their belief that the war would be over soon.

"Did you agree with your staff about that?"

"Not after the collapse of the June truce. By then, we were almost certain that hostilities would drag on much longer than we'd expected and leave drastically altered conditions in their wake. The war had already displaced too many people and accounted for too much suffering just to peter out for lack of interest."

"Did you share your conclusions about that with your staff?"

"No. We tried our best to discourage speculation about when the fighting would end. All of us needed to concentrate on finding better solutions to our immediate problems: housing, feeding, and healthcare arrangements for our rapidly expanding refugee population."

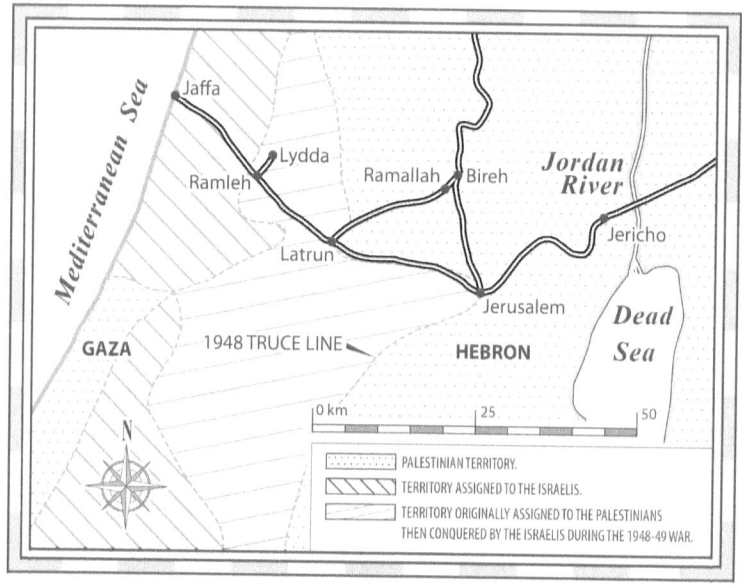

Route of the Refugees, July, 1948

"Were you successful in doing that?"

"No. Events overtook us."

Within a very few days, hundreds, and sometimes thousands, of refugees, many of them on the verge of collapse, crowded into Ramallah *every day*. Ramleh and Lydda, the largest cities in the Palestinian sector, had fallen to the Israelis. The only housing option for this third, and most numerous, wave of refugees was to camp out, despite their seriously compromised physical condition.

The end-stage fighting in Jerusalem had severed the mission's previous links with reliable suppliers of food, first-aid supplies, infant formula, and acute-care medical services. The price of kerosene for cooking and lighting shot up twentyfold within days. Finding gasoline for risky runs to Jerusalem for supplies available nowhere else was a matter of blind luck.

Even black-market food was scarcer and more costly than before. Fortunately, Willard had withdrawn the money from the school accounts before the Jerusalem banks closed. His foresight had enabled the mission staff to take in all comers in July, but those funds were nearing exhaustion by August 1.

I asked Christina how the challenge of caring for so many physically and mentally drained refugees had affected their personal lives.

"We were dead tired all the time and way too preoccupied with immediate problems to give much thought to that. Even now, I can't give you a good answer. A few things stand out though. Our son was in college in the US, so we knew he was safe, but postal service soon became so undependable here that we heard from him only now and again. That's hard for parents, and especially for a mother. We had converted our Meeting House to refugee housing, so we missed the tranquility of our customary place of worship. Because the roads were more dangerous than ever, and we couldn't afford to leave the Ramallah operation any more short-handed than it already was, we had to give up going to Bethlehem for Christmas Eve. We wondered if we would ever feel that special sense of spiritual renewal again."

"Did you give any thought to leaving the country while there was still time?"

Willard shook his head. "No. We were determined to honor our lifelong commitment of service to the Palestinians. We couldn't just leave them to an unknown fate now that they had nowhere else to turn."

"But weren't you at least tempted to seek refuge in a safer place temporarily?"

"No. Working for peace and reconciliation are key Friends' values. If there was ever a time and place when both were urgently needed, it was Palestine in the summer of 1948. Each time in Meeting, we sought guidance as to how we might best respond to that call."

"What did you do first when you finally had to accept that you were facing a long-term crisis?"

"Our first step was to reassure the residents of Ramallah and nearby villages that we planned to remain at the mission regardless of what happened in the future. To reinforce that message, we announced a date for the opening of the fall term for returning students, even though we weren't at all sure whom we could spare to teach them. Still, we hoped that at least a few students would be able to report for classes, although the odds seemed stacked against that."

* * *

"How many people did you have on staff over the summer? Weren't many of your workers on vacation during the most difficult months of the refugee crisis?"

"Staff shortages were an almost insurmountable problem. The entire teaching faculty was on summer vacation in July when the sudden arrival of the Ramleh and Lydda refugees almost swamped us. The few elderly Western missionaries at the mission pitched in by taking responsibility for some of the less physically demanding chores. We needed their help, but all of them were over 75. The risk was just too great that one or more of them would develop a life-threatening medical condition requiring treatment that might soon become unavailable on the Palestinian side. We urged all of them to retire and leave the country while the Allenby Bridge across the Jordan was still in the hands of the Arab Legion."

"So, how did you compensate for the gaps in your staff?"

"We hired a few qualified Palestinians. Many more were desperate for work, and we could certainly have used them, but we couldn't afford any more drain on our finances than was absolutely necessary. After the fall of Ramleh and Lydda, we were serving three meals a day to thousands of people."

"With so few people to carry such a heavy load, how did you cope?"

Christina spoke up. "I assumed responsibility for streamlining food-service procedures. With just two of us in the kitchen, we were serving one meal and cooking the next one simultaneously. That had to stop."

"What were your other most urgent needs?"

"Hundreds of refugees needed professional medical care, but all we had to offer was basic first aid. We'd always taken more complicated medical cases to Jerusalem. Now, that was too risky to consider except for surgical patients, women suffering serious complications in childbirth, and those with gunshot wounds or compound fractures."

"As crowded as your facilities were, how did you find space to dispense any healthcare services at all?"

"We designated our recreation hall as the mission infirmary. As a healthcare facility, it was hardly suitable. The only plumbing in the building was in the restrooms. The hall was also much too small to accommodate all those in need of in-patient care."

CHAPTER FORTY-SIX

MUCH NEEDED HELP— AT LAST

A TOTAL COLLAPSE OF basic public services was all the Joneses needed to make a barely manageable situation impossible. Where was Lady Luck when they needed her?

"In a way, she did drop by for what turned out to be an extended, life-sustaining visit."

"What happened?"

"By the end of July, the battle for Jerusalem had reached its most dangerous stage. We no longer took critical-care patients to the city at all unless death seemed imminent in the absence of immediate professional intervention. Fear that we medical amateurs might make ill-informed life-or-death decisions in such cases haunted us, but what else could we do? We were on our own.

"Then, one day, a representative of the International Red Cross rang our doorbell. He asked whether we could make space available for the organization to establish its Palestinian headquarters at the mission. We explained that we had no vacant facilities, but that we were eager to join forces with the IRC any way we could. Perhaps we could squeeze them into the makeshift infirmary in our recreation center. The IRC readily agreed to the arrangement and volunteered to pay us a generous sum of rent each month."

"How did you manage to feed the IRC in addition to the thousands of hungry refugees in your care?"

"It wasn't easy. The Jordanians sent bread when they could. We served meals heavy with rice, lentils, and hummus—unimaginative, but nutritious. Still, after the July influx of refugees, we could never have made ends meet without the IRC. With their rent money, we were able to supplement our menus with food items available only on the black market."

"Did the IRC bring in sufficient staff to care for all of your refugees in need of skilled medical attention?"

"We could always have used more trained medical workers, but the IRC did boundless good by providing competent care for refugees with the most serious physical issues. What we still lacked was healthcare solutions for those who weren't candidates for hospitalization, but who needed more specialized treatment than our amateur first-aid services could provide.

"We were about to admit defeat on that front, when we got another unexpected break. Medical personnel from the Egyptian Red Crescent Society hospital in Ramleh were forced to join the throng of refugees struggling to reach the Judean Highlands after the city fell to the Israelis. The ERCS chose to establish its headquarters at the Friends' mission for the same reason the IRC had. Until the April 1949 truce, they operated an outpatient clinic for our refugees in some of our converted classroom space."

* * *

I asked the Joneses if their summertime management headaches eased in late September, when the heat began to moderate.

"Unfortunately, no. By that time we had proof that most of our refugees wouldn't be able to return to their homes for a very long time, if ever.

"We had recently hired a refugee named Ibrahim to help newly arrived families set up their campsites. One day, Ibrahim rode to Jerusalem with an experienced employee to pick up supplies. Although he didn't really expect it to go through, he put in a call to his house in Lydda, which he had locked to safeguard his property when he fled the final Israeli assault. Much to his consternation, a voice came on the line immediately."

"And what did the voice say?"

"Shalom. Then the voice announced the name of the current occupants. Ibrahim sank into a deep depression that lasted for weeks, but he did honor our request not to tell other refugees about the call. Only the hope of returning to their homes kept many of them going. It would have served no good purpose to destroy their will to survive, even in the deplorable conditions in which they were living."

"How did this incident affect your relief operations?"

"We knew we had to reduce the number of refugees camping out around the mission, but we dreaded having to do it. Setting off again on foot toward uncertain destinations was bound to bring back the campers' worst nightmares of their flight from their homes only a few months before."

"Did you have to begin your camper-reduction program immediately?"

"Any delay would have been disastrous. During the summer months, bedding down on the grassy stubble in the fields around the mission had been feasible—if not very comfortable. That was about to change. Within a couple of months, the first rains of winter would turn those same fields into a sea of mud.

"The campers' situation wouldn't improve much when the sun came up. The vast majority of them had trudged uphill to Ramallah in June and July. The lightweight clothing they were still wearing in September would offer no protection at all from the winter wind and rain.

"Worse yet, we wouldn't have any way to alleviate their discomfort. Alternative accommodation wasn't available in any of the neighboring villages. Warm clothing, tarpaulins, blankets, and tents would have been godsends, but we had no access to any such items, nor the means to pay for them if we did."

* * *

While Willard and Christina were struggling to accept that moving on, however traumatic, was in the best interest of the campers, "expert" guests began to drop by to observe their relief operations. When Willard and Christina called attention to the emotional dimensions of the camper crisis, they were astounded by the responses of some visitors who had spent only an hour or so at Ramallah—most of it drinking tea in the Joneses' quarters. According to them, the solution to the housing problem was simple. The surplus refugees could go to other Arab countries.

The Joneses knew better. Neighboring Arab countries were already struggling to care for large numbers of refugees fortunate enough to have reached their borders. As just one example, by the fall of 1948, more Palestinian refugees were living in East Bank Jordan, a poor country, than indigenous Jordanians.

Lest I think their camper-reduction strategy hardhearted, Christina described how they handled it. "If campers had friends or family living beyond the Jordan, we urged them to ask their connections to help them resettle on the East Bank, even if they still had to camp out. The winters wouldn't be as cold or damp there. Furthermore, as Palestinian refugees, they'd be eligible for Jordanian citizenship. That documentation would allow them to work and access East Bank social services when needed."

"Did your strategy work?"

"It helped, but not enough. Some refugees simply couldn't face the need to start out for destinations that might turn out to be just as dangerous as the homes they'd been forced to flee during the summer months. For those who refused to consider the East Bank solution, we suggested communities still ably defended by the Arab Legion along the West Bank. At least it would be a downhill walk to the Jordan rather than an arduous uphill climb like the one they'd experienced enroute from the coastal plain to Ramallah."

"Were the UNRWA refugee camps in operation by this time? They would seem to have been a better choice, if available."

"The first UNRWA camps on Palestinian territory didn't open for another year. Adjacent Arab states were operating some camps in

1948, but, from what we'd heard, most of these were already severely overcrowded. We had no way of knowing whether they could accept any newcomers at all.

"At best, camps in the early years were just tent cities stretching as far as the eye could see. Still, if refugees could get into one of them, they would at least have food, water, and basic medical services. However, if we'd known then what we know now, I don't think we could have brought ourselves to suggest the camps at all. For far too many, they have become permanent living arrangements."

"I can see how difficult it must have been for you to follow through with your camper-reduction campaign. However, I have a question for you on another topic. How did you come to live in Jerusalem? I take it you've been here for several years."

"After I accepted my present position with the Near East Christian Council Committee for Refugee Work, it was impractical to commute from Ramallah to Jerusalem everyday, even though active hostilities had ceased. The most sensible thing to do was to relocate."

CHAPTER FORTY-SEVEN

JERICHO

THE NEXT DAY was sunny, but too chilly to banish the slush that made the Old City's cobblestones serious fall hazards. At breakfast, I relayed what Willard had told me about the distance to Bethlehem. Before Reginald could launch into a rebuttal, who should appear but Elias? Willard must have coached him carefully.

"Good morning, sir, lady. Since we don't have any specific plans for this morning, I gave some thought to destinations that might interest you. I remembered that you, sir, had shared the news that you have accepted a position with your government's foreign-aid program." *Reginald had mentioned nothing of the sort, but he looked like the cat that swallowed the canary, so he must have decided to ignore that "irrelevant" detail.*

"Perhaps we could take a spin down to the Aqabat Jabr Refugee Camp near Jericho. Given your professional interests, you might like to see how we handle distribution of relief goods and services on the West Bank." *That was laying it on with a trowel, but Reginald didn't seem to notice.*

"I suppose that might be useful for me professionally, but Nancy might find it boring." *When had my reaction ever mattered? Besides, I had just spent three and a half hours with the Joneses the evening before learning about that very subject. Our conversation was so absorbing that my hosts probably didn't get to bed before midnight.*

"Please don't bother about me. I could watch the women doing needlework." I had to bite my tongue not to add, *"while you're watching the staff unpack crates of used clothing."*

"Well, sir. It's up to you. Would you like to visit Aqabat Jabr?" If I'd had a transcript of our conversations, it would have been fascinating to analyze when Elias addressed Reginald as "sir" versus times when he didn't.

"Let's do it, then."

* * *

As we approached Jericho, Elias explained that the city had been a major oasis throughout much of its 10,000-year history. "Elias," I exclaimed, "this landscape reminds me of Death Valley. Where does the water come from that could ever have made Jericho any kind of garden spot?"

"This area gets some winter rains, but not enough to have much effect on the water table. The main source of the water that has irrigated Jericho's crops for millennia is a network of springs that riddle the highlands northwest of us. In their time, the Romans also diverted the Jordan for irrigation purposes."

"But how can we be sure that Jericho residents were ever able to make a living by farming?"

"A Biblical account provides a 'snapshot' of Jericho's agriculture in the second millennium BC. Remember that Moses sent twelve scouts to spy out the land west of the Jordan and assess the Israelites' chances of wresting it from the Canaanites. *[Numbers 13:17-20]*. The spies traveled north northeast to Hebron from the oasis of Kadesh Barnea (Biblical *Meribah*), where they established their base after they completed their trek across the Sinai.

"The spies' agricultural report was encouraging. The Canaanites had access to plentiful water and fertile land. To prove their point, they brought back samples of grapes, pomegranates, and figs. They counseled caution, however, as to the Canaanites' military capabilities: the Canaanites were powerful." *[Numbers 13:29]*

"But that passage doesn't even mention Jericho."

"Jericho came into play because a less-well-defended invasion point was imperative. If an attack from the south wasn't feasible, perhaps one from the east might be. Otherwise, the Israelites' only choice was to remain where they were, but they were heartily sick of desert living by that time. *[Numbers 20:2-5]* Another factor in their decision to resume their wandering may have been pressure from other tribes challenging their control of the Kadesh Barnea Oasis, on which the Israelites depended for their livelihood. For either or both of those reasons, they set out on a new migration, very likely in search of a more secure water supply to support the style of agriculture their ancestors had experienced during their centuries in Egypt."

Reginald looked skeptical. "This all seems farfetched. How did they know which way to go?"

"The Biblical account credits divine guidance, but the process of elimination would have worked just as well. They had ruled out an attack to the north on the basis of their Hebron reconnaissance. Their ancestors had struggled across the Sinai, so they knew they wouldn't find what they were seeking by traveling west (unless they were willing to return to Egypt, as some suggested). That left an approach from the east as their only viable option."

"Maybe so, but can you prove that's what they did?"

"Very easily, sir. The Israelites tangled with the Edomites on their way to a suitable crossing of the Jordan. Edomite lands stretched northward along the east shore of the Dead Sea. *[Numbers 20:18-20]*. Assuming the Biblical account of the Israelites' route is correct, they crossed the Arabah Depression and then traveled due north until they reached a point opposite Jericho. There they set up camp."

"What made the Israelites conclude that the lands across the Jordan would meet their physical needs any better than those on the East Bank? I don't see much evidence to support that conclusion." *Interesting. Reginald was at least listening to what Elias was saying, but he apparently didn't want to believe anything his guidebook failed to spell out in so many words.*

"Remember, sir. Moses looked across to the other bank of the river and saw 'the good land beyond the Jordan, that fine hill country, and the Lebanon (Mountains).' *[Deuteronomy 3:25]* If Moses could see that, so could the rest of the Israelites.

"That left military feasibility as the sole remaining caveat. Therefore, after the death of Moses, Joshua sent two spies to reconnoiter Jericho. *[Joshua 2:1]* Jericho was a satisfactory military target. The Jericho militia was away, and the civilian population feared the Israelites. The invasion could go forward *[Joshua 2:24]*."

"Elias, was the Israelites' assessment of the advantages of the lands on the West Bank justified?" I asked.

"Yes. After the Israelites crossed the Jordan, we are told that they ate of the produce of Jericho, which was sufficient to feed a very large invading population. As proof of that, the Scriptures tell us that the manna that had sustained them during their long years in the desert was no longer needed, so it ceased to descend upon them." *[Joshua 5:11-12]*

"So, why am I not seeing evidence of an agricultural bounty today, although I realize that this is the winter season?"

"Jericho doesn't seem to have changed much for more than a thousand years after the Israelite conquest. In the fourth century BC, Alexander the Great made Jericho his private estate. Herod the Great built his winter palace here during the first century BC, so Jericho must still have been a resort-like property then."

"What do Jericho farmers grow today?"

"Mostly dates and some oranges, but twentieth-century Jericho in no way resembles the lush paradise that it must have been centuries ago. Perhaps the climate has changed; wind or salinity may have impoverished the soil; or the needs of an increased population may have depleted the water table."

* * *

When we arrived at Aqabat Jabr, I was shocked to see so many people crowded into a relatively small space, although shanty-like housing had replaced the 1948 tents. The teeming mass of humanity in the camp gave new meaning to the phrase "man in the street." Fewer women and teenaged girls were in evidence; childcare and basic household tasks doubtless occupied much of their time. The men and older boys sat around on the walkways and went through the motions of making conversation, but their body language communicated only pervasive apathy.

Younger children appeared well cared for. Their diet must have been sufficient to fuel enough energy for them to chase one another up and down the walkways in what looked like a group version of tag. They alone appeared unaffected by the lethargy epidemic among their elders.

Elias told us that 30,000 registered Palestinian refugees lived in the camp right after UNRWA established it slightly more than a decade earlier. Shockingly few of them seemed to have found places to resettle elsewhere in the interim.

Reginald bestirred himself sufficiently to ask about the services other than housing the camp provided to residents.

"They receive regular allocations of basic foodstuffs. Infant formula is also available if mothers are unable to nurse their babies. Water is piped in, although water shortages and salinity are persistent problems. An onsite clinic provides healthcare services. Boys' and girls' primary schools are available. The camp also sponsors a limited sports program for teenaged boys."

"The men and boys aren't doing much at the moment. Why doesn't UNRWA put them to work doing something useful?"

"Sir, UNRWA has only a limited budget, out of which it must pay staff salaries, utilities, supplies for the schools and clinic, and foodstuffs. Would you like to talk with staff in charge of the budget and/or distribution of relief?"

"No. I understand the procedures. Besides, it's high time we started back to Jerusalem. We must be at the Shepherds' Fields in time to find seats for the service." *So much for Reginald's "professional interests."*

"As you wish, sir."

As we walked to the car, Elias stopped to talk briefly with a member of the UNRWA staff. I seized the opportunity to give Reginald a piece of my mind. "How could you suggest putting the men and teen boys of Aqabat Jabr to work, presumably without paying them anything?

Reginald, this is not a concentration camp. These people have lost everything through no fault of their own. They stay here because they have nowhere else to go."

"Work would teach those youngsters to make their own opportunities and stop depending on the charity of others for life's necessities."

"You must be brighter than that sounds. Where could they put that work ethic into action? They're sitting smack in the middle of a group of Arab states that cannot possibly absorb one more refugee into their economies, which suffer from astronomical unemployment rates as it is. Meanwhile, the rest of the world isn't exactly operating on 'come one, come all' immigration policies."

"Nancy, you're letting your emotions run away with you. Elias came from a similar background, and he has managed to make a success of himself and support his family. Why can't the Aqabat Jabr refugees do the same? What they need is a little American can-do spirit."

You pompous oaf. The sooner this conversation ends, the better. "Reginald, surely you must see the difference between Elias's situation and that of the teenaged boys of Aqabat Jabr. Elias came from a family wealthy enough to relocate in Lebanon, where, I would guess, they had the foresight to transfer some or all of their liquid assets before the end of the Mandate. His parents spared no expense to ensure that Elias had the finest education and vocational preparation available. He is an honors graduate of the renowned Ramallah Boys' School and AUB. In addition to his native Arabic, he speaks flawless English and probably French, since he spent his university days in Beirut. When the worst happened, he was already an adult with 'connections' who helped him to find work when almost everyone else in his situation ended up in refugee camps. How many long-term residents of Aqabat Jabr do you think had similar advantages? My guess is zero."

Before Reginald could work up enough steam to launch into a mind-numbing tirade, Elias returned. He apologized for keeping us waiting. He had been discussing a time-sensitive issue with a staff member on behalf of the Archbishop. That even silenced Reginald.

CHAPTER FORTY-EIGHT

CHRISTMAS EVE IN BETHLEHEM

WHEN I SHARED what Willard had told me about the distance to Bethlehem with Reginald, I sensed that he didn't believe me, but he had apparently checked with cathedral staff. He announced that he wouldn't be walking to Bethlehem after all.

After a quick bite of lunch in Jerusalem and a change to clothes more suitable for the December cold for me, we were on our way once more. Elias merged the cathedral car into the slow-moving traffic headed toward Bethlehem.

We arrived at the Shepherd's Fields a few minutes after three. Reginald's impatience had paid off this time. We latched onto the last two unoccupied places at an outdoor amphitheater that seated about 200 people. Later arrivals were going to have to stand—no telling for how long.

I looked about for something to do during the hour before the service began. Conversation? Unlikely. Reginald had counterattacked with an immediate, and so far wholly effective, campaign of silence in response to my criticism of his behavior at Aqabat Jabr.

I picked up the bilingual worship aid. Arabic class had taught me the sounds that go with the various characters in Arabic script, so I whiled away about half an hour sounding out words to see if I recognized any of them. This was more difficult than it sounds. Arabic script shows only the consonants; I had to try all the vowels in every syllable of every word. Sometimes I came across a word I recognized, but not very often.

When my interest in Arabic phonetics waned, I turned to the English words of the carols we were to sing. "Reginald, do you see any changes in the lyrics?" Still no response.

I plunged into my carol-reading detective work with gusto. Most of the lyrics were as I remembered them, but then I spied a clear-cut case of text tampering. The closing hymn was "The First Noel." The English version ended the refrain with "Born is our king, Emmanuel," in lieu of the traditional "Born is the King of Israel." That close to the armistice line, political correctness was probably a wise precaution.

Promptly at four o'clock, the dignitaries who were to lead the service filed in and seated themselves on the platform. Willard caught my eye and made a walking motion with his fingers. I shook my head no. He grinned.

The simplicity of the service moved me more deeply than I'd expected. Perhaps the authenticity of the setting lent immediacy to the familiar readings even after two thousand years. I asked Elias, who was standing next to us, where tradition held that the angel had appeared to announce the Holy Birth to the shepherds.

"Scholars are divided about that—mostly along faith-tradition lines. Since the most likely spots are practically on top of one another, arguing about which group's version—if either—is correct doesn't seem worthwhile."

Scholarly disputes of that sort probably didn't matter to any of us at the Shepherds' Fields that day anyway. We who had come from far away and those who lived nearby were gathered shoulder to shoulder to honor the birth of the Prince of Peace in a land in which peace seemed more elusive than ever. I thought of the families at Aqabat Jabr. When they were on the run and desperate to outdistance the danger pursuing them so relentlessly, they would probably have welcomed a chance to bed down on straw in a stable with a sturdy manger to accommodate their baby.

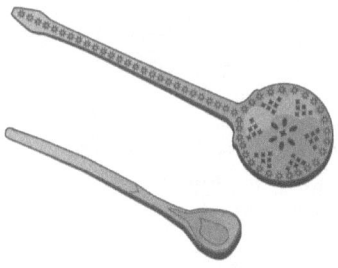

Hand-Wrought Serving Utensils, Rural Palestinian Territories

After the service, we made our way to a large cave where shepherds still sheltered their flocks in inclement weather, just as their ancestors had done for centuries. Our Palestinian hosts greeted us with overflowing warmth and served us the traditional mutton stew and Arab bread.

We drove into Bethlehem at about six-thirty. The Vigil Mass was scheduled to begin at ten-thirty, so I was apprehensive as to where we could spend the next four hours. Surely, in Christian Bethlehem, any commercial facilities appropriate for that purpose would be closed for the holiday.

I needn't have worried. Elias took us to his home. His wife and daughters welcomed us and served us mortadella sandwiches, cucumber salad, homemade pastries, and piping hot tea. The house was plainly furnished but absolutely immaculate. Some kind of heating device blunted the chill of the December evening.

About nine-thirty, Elias advised us that we would be wise to go to the church right away. Even though we had tickets, seating would be exceedingly limited. Many local people—who didn't need tickets—would be attending the Mass, because the Latin Patriarch was to be the principal celebrant.

Even our early arrival was too late for us to lay claim to any of the relatively few seats. I steeled myself for a long evening, but looked forward to an unforgettable experience. Elias had mentioned that both Eastern and Western congregations used the church. That explained the numerous icons on display throughout the basilica. I was sorry the building was so crowded. I suspected—quite correctly, but for reasons I never anticipated—that I would have no opportunity to examine that intriguing artwork up close.

The liturgy was essentially the pre-Vatican II Latin Mass, but local, or perhaps generic Eastern, influence made itself felt at miscellaneous times during the service. For example, a figurine of the Infant Jesus was processed through the church following the reading of the gospel. That would have been highly unusual in a Western Church of the time.

My impressions of this special Mass came to an end soon thereafter. Just before the consecration of the bread and wine, I fainted. We had been standing near a side door, so someone had moved me out onto a small landing just large enough for me to lie down on. A Singhalese priest was attending me. Reginald was nowhere in sight.

I explained to the priest that I was worried about locating our driver. He said he would try to find him at the end of Mass. Until then we would have no chance to make our way through the densely packed crowd.

* * *

Outside, sure enough, Elias was peering anxiously about, trying to catch sight of me among the throng pouring out of the church. Reginald had gone to introduce himself to the Latin Patriarch. Elias took me to the car, and then went back to wait for Reginald, who finally showed up about a half an hour later.

CHAPTER FORTY-NINE

BACK TO ARABIA

I HAD TO RETURN to Arabia on Christmas Day; the 26th was a regular workday for Aramco employees. At breakfast, Reginald asked me when my flight was scheduled to depart. "Two thirty," I told him. He said he'd asked Elias to stand by to drive me to Amman when I was ready. *Maybe there was hope for Reginald after all.* I assured him that as soon as I finished my coffee, I'd collect my belongings and be on my way.

I asked Reginald when he was returning to Arabia. He replied that he had nine more days of leave due him, so he planned to spend three more days in Jerusalem before proceeding to Petra. Then he would return to Arabia until January 30, his last work day. I thanked him for making arrangements for our transportation and housing and wished him well in his new assignment.

* * *

Elias met me in the lobby and carried my suitcase out to the car. "Elias, I'm keeping you from your family on Christmas Day. Why don't I just take a taxi?"

"Don't mention it. I'd be working today anyway."

On the way to the airport, he reminisced about his student years in Beirut. "They were the best years of my life. My family had many friends and business associates there, so my social life took off right away."

"Did you speak French before you went to Beirut?"

"I knew a little, but I became really fluent in Lebanon. Students preparing for business careers had to demonstrate high levels of proficiency in both English and French to graduate, because both were widely used as second languages throughout the region and in much of Europe.

"I took classes in French each term, but my secret weapon for improving my French as quickly as possible was to go to the cinema two or three times a week. Of course, no new films arrived from France after the spring of 1940, so theater owners offered patrons a steady diet of classics."

"You were at AUB during the last years of the Mandate, weren't you? How did the declaration of Lebanese independence affect you?"

"We scarcely noticed it, except that Lebanon had a new flag. Gone was the *Tricouleur;* on Independence Day, the new flag with the cedar tree on it fluttered atop all public buildings. No violence erupted at all. A British campaign to unseat Vichy French officials was over almost before it started."

"What else did you do with your free time during your student years?"

"One of my friends—a Kuwaiti from a wealthy family—had a car. We explored the countryside so thoroughly we could've had successful careers as tour guides. I even learned to ski in the Lebanon Mountains. There weren't any ski lifts then, so we had to climb up to the top each time we wanted to ski back down. Talk about a real workout. The ski season only lasted about two and a half months, so we rushed to the mountains at the first hint of snowfall."

"Do you ski now occasionally?"

"No. I wonder if I still know how. That's just another happy memory I'll never have a chance to repeat. Getting from Palestine to Beirut these days is not as easy as it was when we could drive up the coast road or take the train. Now, about the only practical way to go to Lebanon is to fly from Amman, but that gets expensive for a family of four."

"What did you enjoy most about the city itself?"

"That's hard to say. Great museums, art galleries, and concerts abounded, and it would be hard to beat Beirut's scenery. We had the sea to look at in Jaffa, but the Judean Highlands are no match for the Lebanon Mountains."

"Anything else?"

"How could I forget the food? The Lebanese had a great culinary tradition; they probably still do. French cuisine, done to a turn, was a specialty of deluxe restaurants in central Beirut. Tiny ethnic bistros all over the city served delicious meals at reasonable prices. My friends and I would go out for dinner and stuff ourselves like I used to do with Jaffa oranges."

"Did you get to know any of the owners well enough to ask them what life was like in the countries they came from?"

"Sometimes. An Armenian couple in their sixties owned our favorite bistro. Lia, the wife, did the cooking, while Aram greeted guests, took their orders, and waited on tables. Parnak, their son, manned the balalaika, while the Armenian customers sang along. The restaurant offered the perfect combination of great food, low prices, friendly service, ethnic art on the walls, and live music. Neighborhood Armenians always mobbed the place, so we took care to arrive early enough to have any chance at all of snagging a table. Once during a slack period, I asked Aram about Armenia. He explained that Armenia isn't a country—at least not anymore. Now, historical Armenia is partly in the Soviet Union and partly in Turkey."

"Did you ask Aram how he and Lia ended up in Beirut, and how long they'd been there?"

"He volunteered that information. Both of them were born and brought up in Van, an Ottoman city near the borders of Iran and Russia. Their families had lived in Van for countless generations.

"Relationships between local Christians and Muslims were cordial in Van; they looked forward to each other's folk festivals. Events at the Sultan's court in Istanbul never bothered the Van people very much. Even the Ottoman entry into WW1 just two months after Aram's and Lia's wedding wasn't a source of grave concern. Van was no strategic prize. Besides, the Germans were the greatest threat to the Russian army, with the Austrians a distant second. No one expected much action on the Ottoman front, at least not in the immediate future."

"So the war took a turn the Van people didn't expect?"

"They were right that the first Russian thrust would be against German armies defending East Prussia, but that campaign turned into a disaster for the invaders. After that defeat, the Van people expected the Russians to steer clear of further confrontations with the Germans if they could. The Ottoman Empire would be an easier target, although an invasion from the east would be ill-advised; surely the Russian military knew that. Hampered by mountainous terrain, primitive roads, and lack of an efficient rail system to move personnel and equipment, any Russian offensive would grind to a halt by sunset the first day. Besides, what the Russians really wanted was free passage through the Bosphorus and the Dardanelles—over a thousand miles to the west. 'Yes,' one elderly Armenian renowned for his wisdom declared for the umpteenth time to anyone willing to listen, 'the Ottoman Army can just lounge in their barracks and let geography do their work for them.' Everyone laughed every time they heard that."

"I take it the Ottoman military thought it prudent not to take any chances."

"Probably so. They had a point. Fighting off a joint attack by the Russians via the Black Sea and the British from their bases in Egypt would have been very difficult if the Empire had had to deal with domestic unrest at the same time."

"I suppose it was only realistic for the Ottoman leadership to be uneasy. Immediately before the war, they'd lost huge chunks of their Empire—especially territories with majorities of non-Muslims—to homegrown independence movements and/or European powers intent on gobbling up the remnants of the so-called 'Sick Man of Europe.'"

"Exactly. Fear that the Christian minority within the Empire might take advantage of Ottoman vulnerability while the imperial army was struggling against the Allied invasion at Gallipoli was almost certainly the motive for the expulsion of whole communities of Armenians and other Christians in 1915, including Lia and Aram."

"Why did the Armenians become the main target for Ottoman fears?"

"I asked Aram about that. His explanation was that nationalism was rampant throughout the region at the beginning of the twentieth century. Paranoid officials in Istanbul probably whispered in the Sultan's ear that Ottoman Armenians would cooperate with a Russian occupation in order to be reunited with their ethnic kin across the border."

"You certainly know a lot about Middle Eastern history. Did you study it at Ramallah?"

"Yes. It was a prominent topic on the entrance exam for AUB."

"Did you continue your study of Middle Eastern history at the university?"

"Yes, but not as a major part of my academic program. I've learned more about it since *Yom an-Nakba* (the Day of Catastrophe). I'd like to go back to tell Aram and Lia that I finally understand what it means to be a refugee now that I have become one in my own country."

"You mentioned that you had two brothers. Did they get away from Jaffa safely?"

"Yes, but they went south toward the Egyptian border with our uncle. They live in Gaza now, so we haven't seen them since 1948."

"Did you have any sisters?"

"I had three sisters, but only two are still living. My older sister was pregnant when we fled Jaffa; she died in premature childbirth on the road. One of my remaining sisters married in Gaza; she has a large family now. The other managed to reach Cairo, where she married a Coptic Christian. She and her husband are very poor, so she has never been able to visit us, even though it's easy to fly directly from Cairo to Amman now."

At that, we made the turn into the airport. Elias carried my suitcase to the door and handed it to a porter.

"Elias, I can't thank you enough for making our visit to Jerusalem so informative and enjoyable." I gave him the address of my parents, since I didn't have a US address yet. "If you ever come to America, let me know."

We shook hands. I stood rooted to the spot until the car disappeared into the distance.

CHAPTER FIFTY

THE GREAT DECISION

MY MAIL INCLUDED an uncharacteristically thick letter from my mother; she usually limited herself to aerogrammes. Just before the Christmas break, I'd written my parents to say that I was giving *some* thought to returning to the US when my contract expired in June. However, I would need a firm job offer before I did anything irreversible—like give notice.

I told Mother she could facilitate my job search by going to the placement office at Northern Arizona University to find out which California school districts had high-school French or Spanish positions open. She must have been overjoyed to hear that I was ruling out elementary teaching. She'd been urging me to "promote" myself to high school for years.

The California bit was a stickier wicket. I reminded her that a whopping pay cut and loss of my lucrative catering income were in the offing if I took a stateside teaching job. California teachers' salaries were significantly higher than those in Arizona at that time, so I planned to focus on job opportunities in the Golden State, at least for the time being. With my fingers crossed, I told her I knew she'd see the logic of minimizing the financial hit of returning to the US as much as possible.

I also reminded her that I was not exactly a shoo-in for a high-school teaching job in California or anywhere else. While my paper qualifications verified my proficiency in oral and written French and

Spanish, my teaching experience was limited to grades K-4. I'd never completed a single course in high-school pedagogy. To complicate matters still further, my graduate-level preparation in French and Spanish had taken place abroad. (In the early 1960s, attempting to get equivalent credit for foreign study for licensure purposes was hardly worth the aggravation, red tape, and all-too-frequent unsatisfactory results.) Whether I could qualify for a high-school teaching credential valid for either subject was a gigantic question mark.

For job-hunting purposes, it didn't help that I was 12,000 miles from California. The customary pre-selection interview was out of the question. Bottom line: a potential employer would have to hire me sight unseen. All I could do was to apply for suitable positions with several school districts and hope for the best.

Mother must have been ecstatic to receive my letter. She sent me a detailed report of her reconnaissance mission with commendable promptness, despite the inconvenience of a winter trip to NAU. The elevation at Flagstaff, where the university is located, is just shy of 7,000 feet, which means a foot or two of snow on the ground—and in the streets—by January. Mother absolutely abhorred snow in any quantity, but because of the urgency of her errand, she braved slipping and sliding on the horseshoe turns in Oak Creek Canyon with nary a murmur.

Even though I could probably have obtained most of the information I was seeking from other sources, Mother contributed the skills of a world-class networker to my job hunt. Her report demonstrated just how artfully she'd chatted up the placement staff and teased out hard-to-access information about employers and teaching conditions that would have been impossible for me to obtain if, in so doing, I had left a paper trail. She and a placement technician had gone over the list of vacancies carefully to eliminate districts in isolated areas and those reputed to have dreadful climates and/or working conditions. Ten districts had survived their rigorous screening process. Mother admonished me to get right on this, because the placement technician had warned her that some of the most desirable districts started sending out job offers as early as February 1.

The next day I brought home an atlas from school to locate the ten districts. The only places on the list I'd ever been—and then only briefly—were Laguna Beach and Long Beach. My map work culled the list down to five candidates (including those two), so I decided to cast a wide net. I would apply to all five and hope for at least one firm job offer.

* * *

I went to school early the next morning to catch Andy before anyone else arrived. The last thing I wanted was for the company to know what I was up to before I was sure about that myself. Upon seeing me in the office when he opened the door, Andy ventured a guess that this must be serious.

"Possibly. Will you treat what I have to say in confidence?"

"Absolutely. Are you preparing a lawsuit or something?"

"No. It's just that I'd rather this scrap of news didn't become general knowledge quite yet."

"Shoot."

"I've decided to return to the US at the end of my contract if I can find a professionally appealing job in a suitable location."

"Would you mind telling me why? Is it something I said or did? What am I going to do for a French teacher for the primary grades? Who's going to cater the back-to-school open house? How am I going to explain this to the parents of students who expect to be in your classes next year? You should at least have brought me a complimentary bottle of your best 'bourbon' if you were planning to drop this one on me." At least he was smiling.

"Let me take those questions one at a time. You've done absolutely nothing to upset me. Quite the contrary. Moving right along, from what I hear from camp gossip, you're not likely to need a French teacher for the primary grades next year. Wagging tongues insist that all K-3 children will have to take Arabic. That will leave no room in their schedules for French."

"You're half right about the Arabic. However, that's not certain yet. The company is looking for qualified Arabic-speaking teachers to staff the three camp schools, but they're not having spectacular luck with their search. Most Saudi teachers aren't comfortable with the prospect of coeducational classes, and many of them lack sufficient proficiency in English to work effectively with the parents. Also, the company hasn't decided whether to phase in Arabic over time or to implement it in all grades at once. If the former, your present assignment should be safe for another two-year contract."

"I wouldn't care to place a bet as to which way they'll jump. I suspect their decision will be more political than educational. Besides, I have the equivalent of a graduate degree in French, so I'd like to give more advanced classes a try. That's why I'm looking at high-school openings only. If all I can find are elementary positions, I'll consider staying here."

"No comment on your snide remark about the Dhahran Office. However, let me give you a counteroffer on the rest of what you said. Suppose a junior-high-school French position were to open up here? Would that interest you?"

"Wait a minute. Is Harriet leaving?"

"Not that I know of, but she's due home leave in September, and you never know how those things will turn out."

"That's too risky for me. By that time, I'll have already indentured myself to some stateside school district. As for the catering, the dining hall would be happy to receive your order."

"Dining-hall output doesn't have your food's pizzazz—or flavor."

"Thanks, but flattery will get you nowhere this time. As for the parents, they've been extraordinarily supportive of my work. However, I have no doubt that they'll do the same for whoever takes my place. Their separation anxiety should be only a temporary headache for you. Just in case, though, I'll send Jomo over with a bottle of three-month-old 'bourbon' later this afternoon. Will Tina be home to receive your 'medication?'"

"As far as I know. I'll check with her at lunch. I don't want 'bourbon' traceable to me ending up at an illicit soirée in the labor camp."

"By the way, may I give your name to prospective employers as a reference?"

"Sure, but you do so at your own risk."

Sun, Sand and Single

* * *

About three weeks later, I made my daily pilgrimage to the post office with my usual rock-bottom expectations about hearing any response at all to my stateside teaching applications. In my box lay two fat manila envelopes. Maybe the company had sent us something to read, or worse yet, do something about? Then I saw the US postage. Someone had spent serious money to send those envelopes. I scrutinized the return addresses. One envelope was from Laguna Beach; the other, from Long Beach. The thickness of the mailings was reassuring; it only takes a single sheet of paper for a rejection slip.

At my apartment, I opened my prizes. The Laguna Beach position was for high-school Spanish; the Long Beach offer, for advanced high-school French classes. At least I'd have a choice.

For the sheer beauty of the setting, I leaned toward Laguna Beach initially. Of course, on the one day I'd spent in Long Beach, a November haze shrouded the city. Comparing that with Laguna Beach in full sunshine hardly seemed fair. The salaries were comparable—and about a third of what I was making in Abqaiq, even without my catering and piano-teaching income. I could only hope that a much lower cost of living would compensate for such a drastic reduction in pay.

Visions of living at the beach, where the sun shone year round, and breezes smelled of salt rather than hydrogen sulfide, flooded my imagination. I dragged myself back to reality. Regardless of which job I accepted, I was choosing between two places *to work*. I scrutinized the job descriptions.

I spotted a problem with the Laguna Beach offer that couldn't easily be fixed. It didn't specify the level of Spanish I'd be teaching. When I applied, I said that I spoke fluent Spanish and had taught in Spanish in Venezuela; both statements were true. However, my students in Venezuela were five to seven years old. I had absolutely no difficulty teaching them to sing "*Patito, patito, color de café*" and guiding them through the numerous adventures of *Dani y Elena*. Suppose I had to communicate the intricacies of the Mexican novel to high-school seniors? Talk about setting myself up for failure.

With the French classes, I'd be on solid ground, whatever the specifics of my teaching assignment. I had a strong academic background in French literature, history, and culture, so designing curricula for fifth- and sixth-year French classes shouldn't be much of a challenge. With a twinge of regret, I expunged my highly romanticized image of life in Laguna Beach from my thoughts. Long Beach it would be.

One unusual requirement for responding to the Long Beach offer leaped off the page at me. I was to send a cable stating that I would accept the position before the district would issue a contract for me to sign. Sending a cable was easier said than done. We didn't have secure cable service in the Aramco camps or, for that matter, international telephone service available to garden-variety employees like me. Then I realized that my upcoming *Id al-Fitr* jaunt to Beirut couldn't have come at a more auspicious time. The holiday was only a week away. With any luck, the good people in Long Beach hadn't the slightest notion how long it would take for a bulky manila envelope to wend its way to Saudi Arabia. At least I hoped not.

CHAPTER FIFTY-ONE

FAREWELL TO BEIRUT

GEORGES VOLUNTEERED TO send the cable for me. My preferred vendor assured me that the flavoring agents I needed for the bakery would be available for pickup in Dhahran the following Thursday. That left me with plenty of time for personal shopping—a high priority, since I was almost certain now that my time in the Middle East was fast drawing to a close.

After breakfast, I strolled along the Avenue des Français, admired the view for what might be the last time, did a little window shopping, and went into one of the more promising-looking establishments. I bought a pair of Bedouin chairs and two camel saddles reinforced to serve as backless seats or ottomans for direct shipment to my parents in Arizona. For myself, I couldn't resist a stunning 5' X 8' rug from Balochistan (southeastern Iran). The merchant made a bundle of it to make it borderline manageable on the plane and promised that it would be delivered to the Normandie within the hour.

* * *

My shopping complete, I wandered over to the Phoenicia Hotel to see if anyone wanted a guide to the gold *suq*. A very nice Canadian couple—Ian and Elspeth—did. "Do you speak French?" I asked.

"No. We're from Manitoba. We learn French in school, but we don't get much chance to practice it. Most French Canadians live in the eastern provinces."

"In that case, I'll interpret for you in each of the shops you choose, although at some point, I want to go by a shop owned by an Armenian friend of mine."

As we squeezed through the narrow entrance to the *suq*, I suggested that they visit at least two or three shops before making any purchases. That way, they'd have a better idea of the range of merchandise available.

Elspeth was as overawed by the glitter as I had been on my first visit. "Who buys all these things?"

"They do a booming business. Both local people and tourists shop here, although foot traffic is rather light today. That's probably because of the *Id al-Fitr* holiday. Muslim gold purchasers must be home feasting with their friends and relatives."

"What's *Id al-Fitr*?"

"The holiday celebrates the end of the month of Ramadan, when Muslims fast from sunrise to sunset. Ramadan's a little like Christian Lent. *Id al-Fitr* is the first day of the next month, so the highlight of the day's activities is the breaking of the month-long fast. Families also visit the graves of loved ones at this time of the year."

Just then we went by a shop run by an Iraqi named Salah. The house specialty was enamel-on-gold jewelry. Elspeth immediately spotted a bracelet in the shop window that appealed to her, but she couldn't find one small enough to fit her wrist, so Ian consoled her with a ring of similar design.

We continued down the walkway that went by Boghos's shop. Before I could say anything, Elspeth stopped to view the jewelry in his display window. "Let's go into this one."

"What a coincidence. This is my Armenian friend's shop." Boghos greeted me with arms outstretched. I introduced Elspeth and Ian. He said something in what must have been Armenian to a teenager who was polishing some small golden bowls. The boy put down what he was doing and left the shop with the air of a man on a mission.

Boghos chided me in French. "It's about time you came back. I have something for you." He reached under the counter and handed me a small package. I looked at it dubiously.

"Boghos, thank you, but they'll think something not quite legit's going on here."

"Just tell them you're making a delivery for me. You're delivering it to you. This is for bringing that woman to the shop the last time you were in Beirut. That necklace was my biggest sale of the month. Keep up the good work."

I turned to Ian and Elspeth. "Is there anything in particular you'd like to see?"

Elspeth looked at Ian. He smiled indulgently as if to say "Go ahead. We're on vacation."

Elspeth squeezed his hand and said she'd like to look at some conservatively styled earrings. I relayed that to Boghos, who immediately produced a tray of items that fit that description reasonably well. Elspeth selected a pair of studs with a delicate floral design that seemed almost custom-made for her. Ian took out his wallet to pay for them just as Boghos gave me a surreptitious wink. In French he said, "I've already factored in the discount this time. No need to discuss that further."

Just then, his helper arrived with tea and pastries. "Please," Boghos said in French to Ian and Elspeth, "here's a little something to tide you over until lunch." They looked puzzled, so I translated, glad to know they really didn't speak French.

To make conversation, I asked Boghos to tell us where he came from and how he had ended up in Beirut. He had been born in 1908 at Kars, he said, near the border with Russian Armenia. When he was seven, the Armenians and other Christians in the town were expelled into Syria and Iraq. Both his parents died during the march, but his mother's youngest sister took him with her to Aleppo, where they lived for several years. Then his aunt heard from other Armenian refugees that work was more plentiful and better paid in Beirut, so they came south.

They didn't have passports, but Lebanon was still part of Syria then, so they didn't need them. Boghos went to work as a jeweler's helper, just like the lad who had fetched the tea and pastries. The year before, the French had received the Syrian mandate from the League of Nations, so Boghos studied French at night to make himself more valuable to his employer. In return, his boss taught him all he knew about the jewelry business. The shop owner was a kindly man, but lonely. His wife was long dead, and they had had no children. He died in 1934. Boghos paused for a minute. "Imagine my surprise when I learned that he had willed his business to me. I've been here ever since."

I translated what he said for Ian and Elspeth. "What a touching story," they agreed.

Elspeth could scarcely tear herself away from the jewelry counters, so while she and Ian looked at necklaces, I told Boghos that this was probably my last trip to Beirut; I was planning to return to the US after several years abroad. Boghos wished me well. "I sometimes think I'd like to visit Kars again, but then I realize it wouldn't be at all like I remember it from my childhood, so I haven't gone, even though that would be possible now. You're right to go back to your own country while you still have friends and family there, although it too has probably changed. That doesn't take long. I only hope that your return will be happier than mine would be if I visited Kars and didn't meet a single soul who even knew that there had once been a thriving Armenian community there."

We said goodbye to Boghos and started back to the Phoenicia. As I turned to go, Ian spoke up. "Please have lunch with us. I'd really like to hear more about the expulsion of Christians from the Ottoman Empire and how you met Boghos."

CHAPTER FIFTY-TWO

NATALYA (3)

I RACED BACK TO the Normandie after lunch. I thought of Elias, Aram and Lia, Gilda, Ibrahim, the Palestinian refugees cooped up in Gaza, the residents of Aqabat Jabr, and the unknown number of survivors of the horrors of the WW2 camps on the Israeli side. Would they agree with Boghos that returning to their pre-refugee homelands in the hope of recapturing the happiness of their long-ago lives would be a futile and disheartening experience? Or were they still clinging to the by now forlorn hope that they could return "home" someday to resume their lives as they had once been? That line of thinking reminded me that I had another refugee to visit that afternoon.

Three o'clock was fast approaching, so I grabbed the first taxi I could find and gave the driver Natalya's address. As I walked up the steps to her doorway, everything looked normal, but I was still uneasy. Natalya answered the doorbell, but I could tell immediately that her health had declined rapidly in the two and a half months since my Christmas visit. She was paler, thinner, and definitely less energetic. Natalya threw her arms around me and hugged me. "Thank God, you've come. I worried that something might interfere with your *Id al-Fitr* trip. I'm afraid we can only have tea today; I don't have any pastries on hand." The piano was missing.

"Natalya, you must know by now that I don't come to see you just to gorge myself on your excellent pastries. But tell me, how have you been, really?"

"Well, when you're old, it's just one thing after another."

"Yes, but how have you been since I last saw you?"

"About a month ago, I had to go to the hospital. I'd been having dreadful pains in my stomach. I could hardly keep anything down."

"How did you get to the hospital?"

"My next-door neighbor, Galina—she's Russian, too, from Vitebsk—took me in a taxi."

"And what did the doctors say was the matter with you?"

"I have a couple of bleeding ulcers."

"What are they doing for you?"

"They gave me some pills and a diet to follow. That's why I don't have any pastries. I wouldn't be able to eat them anyway."

"Are the pills helping?"

"They seem to be, but eating's a chore now instead of a pleasure."

"What about tea? Is that on your diet?"

"No, but I cheat sometimes."

"Tell you what. Let's just skip the tea for today. I don't want to get you into trouble with your doctors. Anyway, I just finished a late lunch. I definitely don't need anything to eat or drink."

Just to change the subject, I told her about the things that I'd bought for my parents and the Canadian couple I'd taken to the gold *suq*. She told me her life story again. I plied her with questions to keep her going.

Finally, I asked her if she still had music to sell. I explained that I was planning my pupils' spring recital and needed some new pieces worthy of the occasion.

"Yes, I saved what I have for you. As you may have noticed, I sold the piano. I haven't played very often these past few years. The arthritis in my hands wouldn't let my fingers go where they were supposed to, so I couldn't stand the sound I was making." That might or might not be part of the reason, but what about the doctors' and pharmacists' bills?

"Let me see what you have."

Natalya went to a chest beneath one of the windows that looked out onto the street and took a stack of music out of a drawer. I looked through it and thought again that I really should take up Russian. That way, I'd at least know what the compositions were called.

"These are museum pieces. How much do you want for all of them?"

"They're a gift. I won't be able to use them anyway."

"Thank you, but I couldn't possibly accept them that way. They're far too valuable. Besides, you've entertained me royally each time I've visited."

"Well, just give me what you think they're worth." I took out my wallet and transferred three hundred Lebanese pounds (about a hundred dollars) to a hotel envelope I found in my purse. To distract her so she wouldn't open the envelope until I was safely out the door or, worse yet, press me as to when I planned to return to Beirut, I asked her for her address so I could write to her. (I just hoped she wouldn't remember that I already had it.) The last thing I wanted to do was to break the news to her that I wasn't planning to return to Beirut . . . ever. She rummaged through another drawer for a pen and paper.

"Natalya, I'm so glad that we've had this chance to visit. Obey your doctors, and get your strength back." She walked me to the door. We embraced, and I walked down the steps to the street. She watched me until I made the turn toward the bus stop, and then closed the door.

* * *

Once she was safely inside I doubled back to see if I could find Galina. I hoped she spoke French. Otherwise, communication was going to be very difficult. The house on the left side was dark, so if Galina lived there, I was out of luck. The lights were on in the house on the other side, so I made my way carefully in that direction, sticking to the shadows in case Natalya was watching from a window. Much to my relief, a cheerful-looking, middle-aged woman answered the door immediately. "Galina?" I asked.

"Yes, my name is Galina," she replied in passable French.

"My name is Nancy, and I have a favor to ask of you."

"Oh, you're the Nancy Natalya talks about so much. Please come in. She looks forward to your visits so eagerly. I'm glad you've come at this time. She's not well."

"Yes, I can see that. I was just here at Western Christmas. She has clearly lost ground since then. I live in Saudi Arabia. That's why I can't come very often. I'd like to leave my address with you so you can let me know if she takes a turn for the worse. I'll try to come if that happens, but every time I leave Arabia, I have to apply for an exit permit. It takes about two weeks to get one." Even as I said that, I wondered how I could possibly deliver on that promise. The exit permit was the least of the obstacles I'd have to overcome. I'd have to take time off work, and it would be next to impossible to convince the company that I needed to go to the bedside of someone I'd seen only three times in my life.

"Yes, certainly."

I handed her my address, thanked her, and headed for the bus stop.

CHAPTER FIFTY-THREE

RIYADH AFTER ALL

IN EXPAT ARABIA, "Going anywhere for the holiday?" meant "Are you planning an international trip?" When we had a yen to get out of town for a few days, we couldn't just gas up the car (if we were among the few expats who had one), stick some AAA maps in the glove compartment, and strike out in any direction the spirit moved us. Foreigners needed numerous permissions to travel outside the areas of their companies' operations and legitimate business to transact at their destinations. That let most of us out.

Then, without fanfare or explanation, the government notified the company that employees could now visit Riyadh without having to dream up plausible excuses for our trips. We speculated endlessly—and inconclusively—about the reasons behind this sudden change of bureaucratic heart.

There *were* strings attached. We could travel only in groups on Saudi-owned buses. We had to remain together at all times, follow a prescribed route, and visit a preapproved program of sites *only*. A qualified guide would accompany us every step of the way. Despite those annoying constraints, I was determined to take advantage of this previously unheard-of opportunity to visit the Saudi capital. I phoned Nedra in Ras Tanura to share the news. She was as eager as I was to sign up while two places were still available on one of the buses.

Even considering that Riyadh jaunt was rash on my part; I had a large catering order to deliver the day after our scheduled return. With questionable logic, I sold myself on the notion that I could fulfill my catering obligations *and* visit Riyadh within a seventy-two-hour timeframe. Just to make that marginally possible, I stayed up until midnight the night before our departure to deal with last-minute catering minutia.

My anxiety-generated stamina the night before did me no favors the next morning. Our departure was scheduled for five, so I had to get up by four, *at the latest.* Had I fudged on the time even slightly, I would have arrived at the bus stop just in time to wave goodbye as the bus sped toward the Dammam-Riyadh junction.

* * *

Our first stop on our mandatory itinerary was at the ruins of Dir'iyah. *Ruins* was the operant word. Whoever had done the ruining had made a thorough job of it. Nedra asked how Dir'iyah fit into Saudi history, but I couldn't help her with that. I had a vague notion that I'd heard the name somewhere before, but I couldn't remember in what context.

The guide correctly assumed a similar level of ignorance throughout the bus. He immediately launched into a detailed and difficult-to-follow lecture, all the while pointing repeatedly at collapsed huts and piles of mud bricks. The soundtrack of his lecture became marginally more comprehensible once he moved beyond the details of fifteenth-century Arabian-Desert construction/destruction.

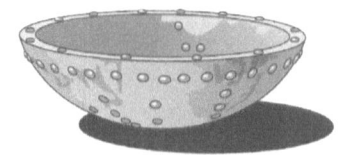

Wooden Collection Bowl for Camel's Milk

His next topic was a series of decisions made by an eighteenth-century Dir'iyah chieftain that were to have long-term implications for religious practices and cultural norms in the Kingdom of Saudi Arabia. That chieftain, Muhammad ibn Saud, granted asylum to a dissident, on-the-run religious scholar named Muhammad ibn 'Abd al-Wahhab. The latter advocated a return to a fundamentalist reading of the Koran and the form of Islam 18th-century Muslims believed to have been practiced during the lifetime of the Prophet.

His guest's core message resonated with his host. The chieftain's and his guest's shared vision of a less violent Arabian interior became the basis of a close collaboration between the Al-Saud and the ultraconservative form of Islam still practiced in all its rigor in Saudi Arabia in the 1960s.

After the guide completed his Dir'iyah lecture, we traveled another dozen miles to our final destination, Riyadh. Our first stop was at the zoo. No one else was in sight. Was that a coincidence, or did the zoo close early that day because a mixed-gender bunch of *kuffur* (unbelievers) was due to arrive any minute? Probably the latter. Normally, men and boys were allowed at the zoo on Monday, Wednesday, and Friday only; women's and girls' visits were limited to Sunday, Tuesday, and Thursday. What a shame. A zoo outing would have been a wonderful opportunity for family bonding.

The zoo displayed desert- and savannah-dwelling animals in settings that simulated their habitats in the wild. All that kept most of the animals from joining us on our walk through the park or annoying their four-footed neighbors was a patchwork system of waist-high berms.

I hoped the animals—at least those with jumping capability—had been fed recently. Saudis didn't seem to share our feelings about getting up close and personal with wildlife that outweighed us.

Things went from bad to worse when the guide virtually ordered us to "pet the rhinoceros." Somewhere I'd heard that rhinos charge when threatened, but this one probably took one look at us and decided we were too puny to be much of a threat. Still, I wondered about that vicious-looking horn.

For me, the most terrifying episode of the zoo visit was the sight of a handler headed straight toward me with a young African lion *on a leash*. Looking for dinner, perhaps? I was a bundle of nerves by the time the call came to return to the bus. We still had our city tour to do, but surely no feral animals over a certain weight were allowed on city streets? Driving around town looking at new buildings might be boring, but it should be safe.

* * *

It didn't take long to complete the government circuit. More than a dozen imposing buildings—the ministries of this and that—were crowded together on a stretch of bare ground with recently paved streets. The absence of more than a few cars in the parking lots around the new ministry buildings led us to suspect that most of them were still unoccupied, but we weren't interested enough to verify that assumption with the guide.

The next stop on our pre-approved program was our hotel, where we were to have dinner before our night tour. Night tour? I remembered with regret that we had to remain together at all times. "Nedra, he's got to be kidding. Speaking for myself, I'm on the verge of collapse." I looked longingly at my bed. The color drained from Nedra's face.

The dinner was tasty, but the servers were the main attraction. They were very tall, very powerfully built black men, perhaps from the Sudan. Their white uniforms and turbans made a dramatic contrast with their skin coloring. Scimitars hung at their sides. I wondered why. It's unsettling when hotel managements feel the need to arm their restaurant staffs.

After dinner, Nedra and I hung back, looking for an opportunity to slink away to those bewitching beds we could almost hear calling our names. No such luck. The guide escorted us personally to the bus. I asked him where we were going. (A "Riyadh by Night" performance seemed unlikely.) "To the *suq*." Didn't he realize that we were veterans of *suq* shopping? Maybe so, but the *suq* was on the "program." He was going to take us there, by force if necessary.

Sun, Sand and Single

We saw nothing remarkable about the Riyadh *suq* from the entrance except that it was larger than the ones we were used to. I told Nedra I didn't think I could last long enough to walk through a *suq* of any size until I got some rest... in one of the hotel's singularly inviting beds. She felt the same way; she'd had to get up at three in Ras Tanura to avoid missing the 4:15 departure of the tour bus from Dhahran.

In desperation, I asked the guide if we could remain on the bus. No, he said. We must visit the *suq*.

The guide started the tour by explaining the contribution of *suqs* to the local economy, while Nedra and I made our escape by inching around the back of the bus to the other side. I wondered what the penalty was for not "staying together at all times." Meanwhile, we loitered in the parking lot and shared our impressions of the trip so far.

* * *

The next thing I knew, I was being assisted onto the bus by two Aramcon men and taken to the bench seat in the back to lie down. One of the overseas-Arab employees was engaged in a knockdown, drag-out verbal battle with the guide. All I caught from their conversation was "*la, la, la*" (no, no, no) from the Aramcon in a voice that threatened to wake the dead, or worse yet, attract the attention of the Saudi police. The potential consequences of the latter seemed to jolt the guide off message, so silence was suddenly restored.

At the hotel, a very solicitous manager met me at the door. He asked two Aramcon women to see me upstairs and told Nedra to call the desk and ask for him personally if any problem arose.

When Nedra opened the door to our room, she laughed so hard tears streamed down her cheeks. Hotel staff had placed a gigantic spray of flowers in an urn in front of the dresser and a small basket of fresh fruit (a rare luxury in Saudi Arabia) on the cabinet where we'd stowed our suitcases. I looked at the flowers in puzzlement. "Do you suppose death is imminent?"

"Hardly, but it seems they think you're pregnant."

"What gave them that idea?"

"That's probably the only women's condition that attracts the attention of Saudi men."

"Okay. What brought all this on? My memory seems to have sprung a leak."

"Do you remember standing behind that wretched locked bus?"

"Yes. I was slipping in and out of consciousness from lack of sleep and, as I recall, you weren't far behind me."

"Well, your body overruled your determination to stay awake. You must have been asleep on your feet. All the sudden, you marched over to a parked car, draped yourself over the hood, got comfortable, and were out like a light. The car hadn't been there very long; the hood was still warm. You woke up when the others came back. The guide was beside himself when he saw your sleeping arrangements. The others were concerned, too, until you looked around, slid off the car, and rejoined the group. Meanwhile I explained that you'd had less than four hours of sleep the night before, and that hadn't been enough."

* * *

The next morning we ate our fill of fresh fruit before going downstairs for our continental breakfast. While I was eating, I spotted the Arabic-speaking fellow who had defended me so ably the night before. I went over to his table to thank him, but I wasn't sure exactly what for. "What were the two of you arguing about?"

"The imbecile wanted to take you to a hospital. He was sure you were pregnant and about to give birth, even though you're very thin and your stomach is flat as a board. I told him that he absolutely could not take you to a hospital or anywhere else without a representative of the American Embassy in attendance. With that, he gave up the hospital idea without protest. He must have realized that an international incident would hardly ingratiate him with his boss."

CHAPTER FIFTY-FOUR

ROUGHING IT BEDOUIN STYLE

*I*D AL-ADHA BEGAN on May 10 in 1962. Our chartered plane arrived in Amman just after 5:00 pm. We spent the night in five-star luxury at a hotel with a superb kitchen, comfortable beds, and an unlimited supply of hot water. That kind of gracious living wasn't going to last. We were headed for Petra. For the next three nights, we'd be camping in caves deep in Bedouin territory for want of more modern accommodations.

The next morning, we made a flying visit to the ruins of Jerash in the mountains of Biblical Gilead. Ruins seemed like a misnomer: Jerash is such a well-preserved provincial Roman city that I half expected men in togas to come walking down the street. We hated to tear ourselves away, but after a couple of hours we had no choice. Jerash is a hundred and forty-five miles north of Ma'an, the jumping-off spot for Petra.

From Ma'an, a short but bumpy ride brought us to the head of *Wadi Musa* (Moses's Valley) and our rendezvous with our local guide. No road went down to Petra in 1962, so our guide broke the unwelcome news that we would be riding down a dry streambed on horseback. Arab handlers would assist us to control our mounts and prevent them and us from falling onto the rocks below. Mules would carry our packs, camping gear, cans of drinking water, and food for a three-day stay. The Bedouins at Petra had kerosene lanterns for lighting in the caves.

I missed most of that spiel after the bit about riding down a rock-strewn streambed on horseback. When I was just six and on a full-sized horse for the first time, the beast dragged me some thirty yards—with one foot still in the stirrup—before a stable employee managed to stop him. Since then, I'd limited my horseback riding to situations of extreme urgency, none of which had ever included slipping and sliding downhill over a nearly endless procession of boulders.

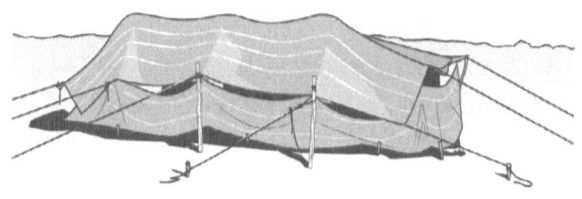

Bedouin Tent, Ma'an-Wadi Musa Road

Still, I could hardly languish at the top of the *wadi* for three days without food, water, or a bedroll. I sized up my assigned mount—an old nag who seemed to have given up fighting anything or anybody. That was as good as it was going to get, so I climbed on. No reaction from the horse; she continued snacking on the sparse vegetation.

We all arrived at the bottom of the *wadi* with everyone's bones intact. The horses had tripped regularly, but no one had fallen. Still, I thought we should have ridden the mules and let the freight take its chances on the horses.

We were the sole visitors to Petra when we arrived, so we had our pick of caves, not that that mattered much. For reasons we preferred not to think about, the entrances to the caves were accessible only by ladders. We immediately agreed to a no-food-in-the-caves policy without a single dissenting vote. The last thing we needed was hand-to-hand nocturnal combat with Jordanian rats, or worse.

We were tired and hungry, and it was almost dark, so we set about opening cans for the evening meal in a designated area at least fifty yards from the entrances to our caves. The bill of fare featured the unappetizing contents of the cans with bread we had bought in Ma'an. We burned our trash in a soot-marked rocky area and buried our wet garbage. Warned that our water supply was sufficient only for limited drinking, making tea or coffee, and brushing our teeth, we opened some cans of orange juice to quench our by now nagging thirst.

* * *

After breakfast the next morning, we set out to explore our immediate surroundings, one of the undisputed wonders of the ancient world and a future UNESCO World Heritage Site. Most of the evidence of human presence in Petra through the ages is concentrated in what looked like a partially filled-in *wadi* between two roughly parallel rows of cliffs. The cliffs' color—a variegated mixture of rose, gold, and cream—is so unusual I wondered if that formation exists anywhere else in the world.

The guide told us that Petra receives only about six inches of rainfall per year. I hoped the entire 1962 allotment wouldn't fall on us while we were there. Six inches of rain can turn a desert streambed into a raging torrent within minutes. Besides, water on those boulders could make them perilously slick about the time we had to ride up *Wadi Musa* at the end of our stay.

Thousands of years before, the guide told us, an unknown tribe based in Petra had hewn the caves out of solid rock. Protection from predators, human and animal, must have been the workmen's motive.

Thanks to its location just off the ancient inland trade route from Egypt to Damascus, the succession of tribes that settled in and about Petra waxed rich by selling supplies to passing caravans. *Wadi Musa* gave some protection from impromptu raiding, although not from frontal assault. Petra had changed hands several times over the centuries.

"Who sculpted those extraordinary Greco-Roman façades at the entrances of the caves?" someone asked. "They look like the work of experts."

"We know approximately when they were done, but not by whom. A powerful tribe called the Nabataeans was established at Petra by the third century BC. Thanks to their profits from the caravan-supply business, they were certainly financially able to bring in skilled craftsmen to do the work. Alternatively, Pompey the Great, who conquered this area in the latter part of the first century BC, may have commissioned the sculptures then. Still later, the Emperor Trajan annexed Petra and its environs in 106 AD. Trajan, like most Romans, was an enthusiastic devotee of the style of architecture you see before you, so he may have been responsible for Petra's 'beautification project.'"

"I read somewhere that the Israelites who wanted to pass through this area on their way to the Promised Land ran into objections from local tribes," someone commented. "Is that true?"

"According to the Biblical account, yes *[Numbers 20:18-20]*. Petra was on the edge of Edom. The Israelites asked the Edomites for safe conduct, which the Edomites refused. The Hebrew Scriptures tell us that the Israelites carried a long-lasting grudge against them as a result of this incident, but the Edomite response was understandable. The tribes on this side of the Dead Sea were nomadic. They lived by hunting, selling water from oases they controlled, and grazing animals where environmental conditions permitted. Imagine what went through Edomite heads when the Israelites asked them to allow a large number of able-bodied men to traverse their land. The Israelites promised to pay for water, but that assurance must have fallen on deaf ears. How could the Edomites hope to collect any debt from the Israelites with the latter swarming all over their territory? The ancient world was a dog-eat-dog environment. Being too trusting of outsiders was unwise and could lead to subjugation, if not annihilation.

"According to *Numbers 20:20-23*, the Israelites turned away and went somewhere 'on the border of Edom.' Local tradition holds that their destination, Mt. Hor, was one of the peaks near Petra. That would make sense. If the Edomites followed the Israelites and attacked, the *Wadi Musa* was defensible. The mountains behind the Israelites would have secured their rear.

"Tradition further holds that Aaron, the brother of Moses, died in Petra. No one is sure today which of the peaks is the Mt. Hor of the Exodus, but that one over there has long been known as *Jebel Nebi Harun* (mount of the prophet Aaron). Many believe that is his burial place."

One of our tour members remarked that he was surprised the names of Moses and Aaron were still attached to topographical features at Petra even if the Israelites passed this way during the Exodus. "Surely the population of this area has been almost 100% Muslim ever since the Islamic conquest?"

"The population here is entirely Muslim, but the existence of land forms with names associated with personages in the Hebrew Scriptures is not at all strange. Both Islam and Christianity accept several Hebrew prophets in addition to Moses and Aaron. Examples are David (*Daoud*), Solomon (*Sulaiman*), Elijah (*Illias*), Elisha (*Al-Yasa*), and Ezekiel (*Dhu'l-Kifl*)."

We spent the remainder of that day and all of next going into the caves with the most elaborate façades, climbing peaks, and hiking trails said to date to ancient times. We managed to collect a handful of Israeli coins, which could only have been issued after the end of the Mandate, so they shouldn't have been on the Petra side of the armistice line at all. The border was evidently more porous than either the Israelis or the Jordanians might have wished.

* * *

Our last night in Petra, just after dark, we were in our caves packing our gear and cleansing our grimy, smelly selves with minute quantities of our rapidly diminishing supply of water. We had noticed earlier that day that new arrivals had set up camp farther down the *wadi*, but we had paid them scant attention. Their caves were well beyond our cooking area, so we didn't expect to run into any of them near our own camp.

Suddenly, we heard singing and what sounded like the clash of metal on metal—all to the skirling of bagpipes. We thought our neighbors must be Scots, but we were wrong.

Our guide hastened down his ladder to find out what was going on. The rest of us weren't far behind. The music played on, and we could make out dancing in the distance. A couple of the men had brought binoculars, so we could see that the dance looked like a ritualized representation of a battle between warriors armed with swords.

When the guide came back, he was still shaking his head in disbelief. One of the newcomers was English, a former general in the Arab Legion who had served in Transjordan even before the beginning of the Mandate. He was terminally ill, and he had come back to die surrounded by his former comrades in the place where he had spent so much of his life. The ex-legionnaires were performing this traditional dance to celebrate their dying general's life.

How strange, I thought, that a man so ill should have made a lengthy and uncomfortable journey to die in a place where he had once found fulfillment, but which had changed almost beyond recognition in the intervening years. On the other hand, had he not returned to Petra, would he have had to die alone—or in the company of impersonal strangers?

* * *

Back in Abqaiq, I found a letter from Galina in my mailbox. I had written to Natalya just before the Riyadh trip. According to Galina, Natalya had died in her sleep shortly afterward, seemingly without warning. Galina found my letter while she was clearing out Natalya's things. Perhaps it was better that way, Galina said. Now she wouldn't suffer anymore—either from physical pain or from the memories of all she had lost and could never recover.

I agreed. "Rest in peace, Natalya. I hope that you are now reunited with your loved ones in a place where you'll never be lonely again."

CHAPTER FIFTY-FIVE

INTO THE FUTURE

MY CONTRACT WITH Long Beach finally arrived. I signed it and sent it back. So, where was that surge of relief I was expecting now that I had finally settled on a definite plan for my immediate future? All I felt was acute uneasiness. In lieu of the champagne we expats had never managed to make successfully, I should have been breaking out bottles of grape juice and sharing my news with my longsuffering friends, who would have thought it high time. I did nothing of the sort.

I asked myself over and over again whether I really believed that returning to the US to live was the most sensible choice for a supposedly ready-to-settle-down thirty-one-year-old. Maybe it was, but my rationale didn't sound quite as convincing as it had half an hour earlier. What, exactly, did "settle down" mean? A good question, and one to which I had no good answer.

Much had changed for me since those first bewildering months in Arabia. Now, an overabundance of social activities jockeyed with one another for space on my calendar. I had parlayed breaks in the company work calendar to enable me to visit eight of Saudi Arabia's nearest neighbors plus the Palestinian territories, some of them multiple times. My Aramco salary, augmented by the profits from my side businesses, had spared me the slightest financial worry about hopping on a plane for a long weekend at a destination hundreds of miles away. So why was I turning my back on everything I'd professed to want long before I climbed the ramp of that company plane at Idlewild?

All I knew was that for several months something had been nagging me to cut the nonsense and get on a departing plane. Ginette's decision to remain in the US at the end of her home leave and Karen's resignation immediately following our return from Cairo had hit me hard. Even though Jane, Karen's replacement, had rapidly become one of my closest friends, the realization that my travel companions from the Egyptian trip were now pursuing other interests in other places reminded me that Abqaiq wouldn't be forever for me either. So why not?

Teaching in Abqaiq was a dream assignment that kept whispering "stay, stay, stay." The children were talented, highly motivated, and mostly well behaved. They were interested in everything, perhaps because they had traveled so extensively at such early ages. Their parents were exceptionally supportive of the school. Andy was the kind of principal teachers always hope to work for and, if they are very lucky, sometimes do.

Still, all that could and would change, to be replaced with what? If I stayed, my third-graders would be in another teacher's class next year. My first-year French students would be third-graders, but would they be marching off to Arabic class instead of staying with me? Most disquieting of all, if the camp rumor mill had it right, Andy planned to leave when his contract was up at the end of the next school year. Would I be as happy in Abqaiq then?

I reminded myself just how cyclical the oil business is. Knowing when to leave is an essential career skill in the oilfields—especially overseas assignments. Sudden shifts in host-countries' power structures and/or economic conditions can transform expat paradises into beds of nails overnight. Wasn't it my spot-on recognition of red flags in Venezuela that brought me to Arabia in the first place?

I gave myself a mental pat on the back for that logical, if not particularly convincing, pep talk. I swore to resolve all lingering go-stay issues before my scheduled departure, although I still had no idea how I was going to manage that.

"Forget about the go-stay dilemma. All that is irrelevant now," I admonished myself. "You've signed a contract to work in California in what promises to be a professionally rewarding assignment. Your gender will no longer bar you from promotion. You've accumulated sufficient funds to buy a car—which you'll be able to drive whenever and wherever you please—and a house, if you want one. Financing that graduate degree you've been pining for should pose no problems. Concentrate on the pluses of returning to the US."

Good advice, but no cinch to follow, even though I'd begun to realize that compulsive roving has its downside. My aunt and uncle, who spent a total of thirteen years as expats in Arabia, Afghanistan, Iran, and Mexico, struggled to readjust to stateside living for much longer than they expected. In some ways, they never quite succeeded. Their advice: no matter how long you live as an expat, you never stop being a foreigner. When you begin to feel like a foreigner in your own country—and that happens sooner than you might think—it's time to call a halt to the expat life. After only a few years, the country you return to will no longer be the country you left. Being at home nowhere is a miserable way to live. The Armenian jeweler Boghos, a refugee—that is, an "involuntary" expat—had said as much.

Fine. Then out came my threadbare security blanket. Nothing I'd done so far about the next school year was absolutely irreversible. "Really? How about that contract you just signed? Let's get the chronology of this transition straight. Despite your misgivings, when exactly did you begin to lean toward returning to the US?"

At some level, it must have been soon after my Christmas trip to the Holy Land. I'd been silently saying goodbye to Arabia and all it had come to mean to me ever since. "So, get cracking on your travel arrangements," I warned myself. "Moving from one continent to another isn't a spur-of-the-moment proposition." My home leave was scheduled to begin on June 23. I'd need an airline ticket and the required documentation for the countries I planned to visit on my way back to the US. I started to add "even if I later decide to return to Arabia . . ." But I was just kidding myself if I still thought of that as a workable plan.

I'd packed the clothes I wasn't taking with me in lockable trunks in a probably futile attempt to shield them from the depredations of the packers and exit Customs. Jane was set to take over my piano pupils. She was a truly gifted musician, so the students were getting the better end of that deal. Camp Service had already moved my disreputable-looking but still tuneful piano to her quarters, leaving me with a jarringly empty spot in my living room.

Having checked that I had sufficient glassware in inventory to receive the output, I ran the still for the last time on May 1. That would see me through until the first week in June, when I planned to discontinue all catering operations. I asked Jane to find a suitable owner for the still once I exited the country. I didn't want to go down in history as the Aramco employee who abandoned a still that later ended up in the hands of a Saudi packer, even though I would have been safely out of the country by the time anyone noticed. I could almost smell the smoke of burning bridges.

Signs abounded that my irrational insistence on keeping my return option open was fooling no one, but I tried to ignore them. Andy had passed on a warning from his boss that I was absolutely not to come back on another contract and then resign within a month or two. My friends didn't have any trouble seeing through the "top secret" label I'd plastered all over my plans either. Several of them gave me "ungoodbye" parties, but I just couldn't bring myself to confirm their quite justifiable suspicions that I was going, going, and would soon be gone.

Still, what if I couldn't qualify to teach at the high-school level in California? What if enrollment in the advanced French classes I was expecting to teach failed to materialize? What if a tenured staff member asked for the assignment for which I had been hired? As a newcomer, I could be shunted into an entirely unacceptable teaching situation. If I hadn't resigned, I could still return to Arabia as long as I reported for work on the day after my home leave expired. That was true in theory, but then I remembered yet again that I had signed a teaching contract for the upcoming academic year—in California, not in Abqaiq. My clothes were packed; my piano was now comfortably ensconced in Jane's living room; and Jane knew exactly what I was planning to do, because I'd commissioned her to dispose of the still. Whom was I kidding about my intentions? Myself, that's who.

* * *

My failure to make my impending resignation public made it difficult to know what to do about Jomo, although he probably knew exactly what I was planning to do anyway. (He would have had to be blind not to notice all those trunks packed and ready to go cluttering my apartment.) Still, fairness demanded that I tell him officially that I intended to stay in the US at the end of my leave so that he could look for another job while I was still around to give him a reference. I finally decided to pay him for the two months of my leave plus an additional month to give him a cash cushion during his job search. Then, as soon as I was absolutely certain about my own plans, I would write to Leila to ask her to help Jomo to find new employment. Maybe she, or one of her friends, would hire him.

CHAPTER FIFTY-SIX

DEPARTURE

MY TAXI ARRIVED promptly at 1:00 to take me to the airport to catch the 4:30 shuttle to Manama (Bahrain), where I planned to overnight. I was booked on one of the new jet flights to Karachi the next day—my first stop on a six-week grand tour back to the US via the Indian Ocean-Pacific route. After two and a half days in Pakistan, I would continue on to India, Nepal, Burma, Thailand, Cambodia, Vietnam, the Philippines, Hong Kong, Macao, Japan, and Hawaii—in that order. The company was picking up the tab for the air. Hotels, meals, and out-of-pocket expenses were my responsibility.

Had the details of my top-secret itinerary become common knowledge, I would been an object of envy among well-traveled Aramcons. For my last hurrah as a cost-is-no-object expat *en voyage*, I'd booked stays at a series of five-star hotels renowned for their country-specific elegance and vertigo-inducing room rates. World-class writers like Somerset Maugham, George Orwell, Graham Greene, and André Malraux could have given me street directions to any one of them.

Instead of updating the Gertrude Bell fantasy of my arrival, I'd fashioned a new, more realistic script for my departure. I would be playing myself this time: a self-made jetsetter ready to kick my luxury-travel-to-exotic-destinations habit, although not for the next six weeks. Once I became dependent on a barebones stateside salary to finance my touristic wanderings, reality would make it a lot easier to do the kicking. Ultra-first-class travel halfway around the world with stops at storied locations would be out of the question for me for years—perhaps forever. That thought tempered my excitement about my upcoming pan-Asian itinerary, but only briefly. I clung tenaciously to the Persian poet Omar Khayyam's famous dictum: "Make the most of what ye yet may spend, before ye too unto dust descend." At least I had that one right; I was spending a bundle.

Musician Playing the Oudh, a Traditional Arab Instrument

The driver loaded my luggage into the taxi and headed for the Dhahran road. Taxis still lacked air conditioning. Arab music wailed incessantly—the perfect audio accompaniment for my final exodus from the Arabian Peninsula. The temperature was a "moderate" 118° versus the 122° of my arrival. June was normally the height of the *shamal* season, but not that day. The wind restrained itself admirably. My last view of Arabia was unmarred by pits made by ballistic sand striking the lenses of my sunglasses.

As the taxi gathered speed, I watched the landscape glide by and melt into the past. Two years before, that same stretch of sand and stone had struck me as a perfect illustration for a work of science fiction: an uninhabitable hunk of a defunct planet that had somehow attached itself to earth. Now, I could make out a Bedouin camp in the

Sun, Sand and Single

distance and the silhouette of a camel and its rider on the horizon. Reluctant to let those images of the triumph of life over desolation go, but powerless to retain them, I gazed at the desert's subtle palette and contours as they, too, faded from my life.

We arrived at the airport about 2:00. Gone was the weather-beaten Customs and Immigration shed of my arrival. Before us stood the glittering new Dhahran International Airport, opened just three months before. The facility spoke volumes about Arabia in transition. Its soaring arches, marble floors and brass fittings throughout evoked the splendor of the Umayyad Caliphate. Its austere setting bespoke the timeless functionality of Bedouin Arabia.

My boarding pass and baggage checks in hand, I cleared Customs and Immigration and staked out a comfortable seat next to my departure gate. I had hoped for at least one expat with whom to chat until boarding, but no such luck. My Manama-bound companions were all decked out in white *thobes* and red-checked *gutras*.

The shopworn topic of the wisdom or lack of it in my decision to leave Arabia moved in to fill the conversational void. Another inconclusive rehash of the "will I or won't I" scenario seemed inevitable, but I was determined to head it off at all costs. I struggled to shift my attention to something—anything—else. Legally, I had left Arabia the moment I took a single step beyond passport control. Allowing myself to bog down in the ruts of a past I'd closed the door on when I signed my stateside teaching contract was pointless now. But had I closed that door as securely as I'd thought?

I scarcely had time to remind myself that I had just completed my final ride across the Arabian Desert when memories of the day I first set foot on those same sands swept over me anew. I had wondered then if the Aramco plane had deposited me at the ends of the earth in error. But what triggered a replay of my angst of two years ago now that my last day in Arabia was nearing its end? I looked at my watch; I could almost see the minute hand racing by. In less than thirty minutes, the Manama shuttle, with me aboard, would exit Saudi airspace.

"Buck up," I told myself. "You've committed yourself to repatriation; now make it work."

I tried. I really tried to think of all the advantages of the Long Beach job I had obligated myself to assume in September, but I kept forgetting what they were. To distract myself from nonproductive lines of thought, I tried to visualize the action-packed experiences awaiting me on my gilt-edged oriental odyssey. That ploy didn't work either.

I knew even less about the countries I planned to visit in the next six weeks than I'd known about Arabia when the company plane touched down on the Dhahran runway in 1960. My sole sources of information about my stops on this trip were vague memories of *Fox Movietone News* coverage of the WW2 Pacific campaign and the noncommittal blurbs about each country I was scheduled to visit supplied by my slightly out-of-date *Pan Am Travel Guide*. With only a hazy idea of what to expect in places like Rangoon or Siem Reap, my effort to concoct an engaging fantasy about my homeward-bound travels broke down almost immediately.

"Never mind. Just let Rangoon and Siem Reap surprise you. Unexpected experiences often become treasured travel memories," I told myself firmly. "Spend any time you can spare figuring out why it took you so long to decide that a decade of expat living was enough. Do that before the Manama shuttle takes off. Otherwise, that question will preoccupy you all the way to Phoenix. Need I point out that that would spoil your lavishly financed trip of a lifetime?

"Let's begin with the facts. Have you figured out yet exactly what kept you awake so many nights over the past few months? No? All right. Let's begin with the Arabian side of the equation. Do you seriously want to return to Abqaiq at the end of your leave? It certainly doesn't look like it. Granted, you shilly-shallied for months before reaching a decision, but you finally signed a contract to teach in California and did everything short of giving Aramco notice of your intentions. Yet you're still looking back over your shoulder. Whatever happened to that woman who used to buy a dozen dresses and six pairs of shoes in a single morning while shopping for the next overseas contract? Anyone who knows you at all well would be amazed at your sudden transformation into a chronic ditherer."

I was surprised myself. Was I still obsessing about what leaving Arabia would do to my finances? Surely that concern was overblown, even for someone like me who grew up during the Great Depression. With my savings from my Aramco salary and catering income, and barring an unlikely worldwide economic collapse, I should be financially secure for years to come. So why couldn't I give that worry a rest?

I thought I knew. Rewind to a decade earlier. My college diploma in hand, but handicapped by negligible vocational preparation of any kind, the only job I could find was as a teacher of a second-, third-, and fourth-grade classroom in a three-teacher school in the mountains of New Mexico. The building lacked indoor plumbing. Our one kerosene heater fought a valiant, but mostly losing, battle against the bone-chilling cold of long winters at an elevation of 7,000 feet. My pay for that gig was $2,800 *for the entire year*, which included a small stipend for janitorial work I was expected to do—and to which I devoted as little attention as possible. Another teacher and I had to share a 10' x 12' rented room just to make ends meet. A public restroom with a tacked-on shower was our bathroom.

Could I possibly be worried that accepting the Long Beach job—and the significant salary cut that came with it—would subject me to living and working conditions like those I suffered through as a recent college graduate? I hoped not. Anyway, if I couldn't make a decent living as a teacher, I could always do something else that paid better and didn't entail a worksite 60 miles from the nearest town. The success of my catering business had taught me that.

Besides, I wouldn't be starting from financial scratch this time. I'd stashed most of my oil-company earnings in reputable American banks. If necessary, I could subsidize my standard of living long enough to avoid lodging in a miniscule room with a fellow teacher—who chain-smoked—while the two of us worked our way up the salary scale. Foreign travel would have to be on hold until I got myself on my financial feet, but I'd figure that part out when the time came.

Having faced up to the financial implications of relocating in

California for what I hoped was the last time—at least on this trip—I shifted my thoughts to why I had opted for repatriation over returning to Abqaiq. Maybe I'd simply outgrown my yen for expat living.

Still, living abroad had been my preferred lifestyle throughout my adult years. Like most twenty-somethings, I was still trying to figure out what I wanted to do with my life. I'd thrived in the "betwixt and between" environment of expat status, which allowed me to experiment with a variety of options without triggering a barrage of criticism from self-appointed nags who had different ideas about how I should be spending my twenties.

No one expected us expats to understand all the customs or abide by all the social constraints of our host countries. Most locals were delighted if we occasionally managed to communicate comprehensibly in the host-country's language. Better yet, no busybodies from home followed us around to see whether we were complying with the often petty dos and don'ts of US society in the stuffy 1950s.

Maybe what was worrying me most was that I wasn't sure how well the adult I'd become as a result of prolonged expat living would fit into a once familiar environment that must have changed in countless ways in my absence. I had left the US to study in France in the waning days of the McCarthy era, and I was returning to it in the Age of Aquarius. That prospect was even more unsettling than boarding a plane to a destination I couldn't locate in an atlas.

I must have been asking myself the wrong questions over the past few months, but which were the right ones? How about this one? Was I ready, or even eager, to give up the expat lifestyle? If so, this had to be a very recent development.

If I could have gotten a labor permit, I would probably have looked for a job and stayed on in France as my cousin Ruth had done. I'd still be in Venezuela if my job prospects had looked more secure there. I'd never given serious thought to returning to live permanently in the US up to that point and didn't consider that option then. I picked Arabia over two other foreign job offers, because the Abqaiq position offered travel opportunities of special interest to me.

Then, I'd shifted my position in re oil-company globe-trotting by the time I had to decide whether to sign a contract with Aramco for 1962-64. Almost a year before, I'd categorically nixed another foreign-oil-company job anywhere in the world and narrowed my choices to staying on in Arabia or returning to the US. After months of vacillation, I'd finally decided on the latter.

Key question number two: at least subconsciously, had I begun to wonder whether money and travel were all I wanted out of life? Arabia had provided plenty of both, just as I had expected. I was able to save enough money to finance travel throughout the Middle East, but, neither travel nor money alone had proved enough to keep me in Abqaiq.

That led to another question I should have been asking myself all along: would a life built on the shaky foundation of serial tourism punctuated by just enough work to pay the bills for my expat-on-the-road lifestyle make me happy? I was no longer so sure.

I recalled that the sages of old went out into the desert in search of wisdom and direction in life. I wondered why that hadn't worked for me. Then, I realized that in a way it had—through some of the people I'd met during my time in the Middle East. Voluntarily or involuntarily, they'd left their previous lives behind—and achieved astonishing personal growth and inward peace in infinitely more difficult circumstances than I was ever likely to face.

Take the Joneses. They'd lived in Palestine forty years by the time I visited them at Christmas, 1961. Even twenty years in one place would have given me a severe case of itchy feet. Not so, the Joneses. Willard and Christina had invested their entire adult lives in their ministry to the Palestinians. In the end, they had shared the privations, danger, and mental anguish of the refugees who straggled into Ramallah during the 1948-49 War. They had rejected any suggestion that leaving Palestine would make them "happier."

That didn't sound like me at all. The commitment of the two years my Aramco contract demanded had been a stretch. In the end, I had signed on the dotted line in exchange for specific material benefits and travel opportunities. It was a business deal. Now, I had fulfilled the terms of my contract, and the company had made good on its promises. Without a new contract, I had no further obligation to Aramco, and the company had no further obligation to me.

I had no legitimate complaint. I had profited handsomely from my time in Arabia. After a rough start, I'd enjoyed my time in Abqaiq, but I now suspected that enjoyment and happiness weren't exactly the same thing. I was still looking for the latter. As a *voluntary* expat, I had the luxury of searching for a meaningful life somewhere else. That's what I planned to do, with what results only time would tell.

Involuntary expats in the Middle East—*i.e.,* refugees—who outnumbered us voluntary expats many thousands to one faced obstacles to getting their lives back together that made ours seem trivial—as, in fact, they were. Natalya, Boghos, Elias, Lia and Aram, Gilda, and Ibrahim had suffered the loss of family, homes, and almost everything else they cherished, but they accepted that they could never return to the past, so they worked fearlessly and tirelessly to come to terms with the present—and the future.

The time had come for me to take a leaf from their book. Wandering about the world until I was half blind, hard of hearing, and lame would never add up to a worthwhile—or satisfying—life. If I had learned nothing else in Arabia, I had learned that . . . at last.

The loudspeaker announced boarding for my flight. With only about a dozen passengers on board, the sole flight attendant closed the aircraft door almost at once. As the plane lifted off for the short hop to Manama, I whispered, "*Fiy amaan illah, Arabiya. Fiy amaan illah.*" (Goodbye, Arabia, goodbye. Go in the care of Allah.)

ACKNOWLEDGEMENTS

MANY PERSONS ASSISTED me along the multiyear road that led to completion of *Sun, Sand, and Single, An American Woman in Saudi Arabia, 1960-62*. Special thanks are due to the following for their insightful suggestions, technical assistance, and constant encouragement:

My students from Long Beach, California—too numerous to cite individually—who prodded me mercilessly for decades to "put my Arabian story down on paper."

June Maki, who chaired the eightieth-birthday party that set me on the road to authorship.

M.G. Lord, former *Newsday* political cartoonist and award-winning author, who persuaded me to attend the Yale Writers Conference five years ago, when I was just beginning to write *Sun, Sand and Single* and wasn't at all sure how to go about it.

My instructors at the Yale Writers' Conference—M.G. Lord, Colleen Kinder, Eileen Pollack, Jonathan Levi, and Louis Bayard—who guided me as I transitioned from academic to memoir writing.

My fellow participants at the Yale Writers' Conference, whose responses to early drafts of the manuscript helped me to fine tune my handling of pivotal story elements.

Professional editors/published authors Molly Lyons, Nicole Brokat, David Landau, Carla King, and Cali Gilbert, who reviewed the *Sun, Sand and Single* manuscript at various stages in its development and offered me invaluable technical tips.

John Zwaans, my indispensable computer consultant, who rescued me from numerous electronic crises perpetrated by my slightly dated operating system.

Anita Anderson, my line editor, who checked and rechecked the manuscript in search of errors and inconsistencies that had somehow escaped my attention, and who helped me to find solutions to a potpourri of problems I encountered during the development of the *Sun, Sand and Single* manuscript.

Walter Gray, my copy editor, who reviewed the manuscript multiple times to identify and suggest rewrites of awkward and/or ambiguous sentences.

My beta readers: Patrick McGovern; B.J. Weigand; Norma Grady; the late Alan Coe; Michael Quinlan; Father Dan Lackie, OFM; Rosann Monaghan; Barbara Ellis; and the late Robert Ellis.

Danya Ata and Soroya Elzeilak, descendents of 1948 refugees from coastal Palestine, who shared poignant details of their families' experiences during and after the Arab-Israeli War.

Tarik Ata, who answered my questions about Islamic beliefs and practices.

Lamis Hashem, a native of Damascus, who reviewed the two chapters that described my 1961 visit to that city, and contributed intriguing bits of local color to my description of Damascus as it was then.

ABOUT THE AUTHOR

WHEN NANCY GRAY arrived in France as a Fulbright Scholar in 1954, the pros and cons of independence for predominantly Muslim Algeria, Morocco, and Tunisia dominated almost every front page and café conversation.

Intrigued by the heat generated by the decolonization debate, she devoted her winter break to a fact-finding tour of French North Africa. Upon her return to Paris, she added a systematic reading program focusing on literary and political works by North African writers to her research agenda. Little did she imagine then that within six short years, she would be living and working in Saudi Arabia, the cradle of Islamic culture.

A five-year participant in the Yale Writers' Conference memoir group and a member of the Independent Book Publishers Association, the author is a Fellow of the Royal Geographical Society (London) in recognition of her many exploratory journeys in the Middle East and other parts of the developing world.

www.ingramcontent.com/pod-product-compliance
Lightning Source LLC
Chambersburg PA
CBHW021118300426
44113CB00006B/194